SPORTS QUOTES

The Insiders' View
of the Sports World

SPORTS QUOTES

The Insiders' View
of the Sports World

Bob Abel and Michael Valenti

Facts On File Publications
460 Park Avenue South
New York, N.Y. 10016

SPORTS QUOTES

Library of Congress Cataloging in Publication Data
Main entry under title:

Sports quotes

Includes index.
1. Sports—Quotations, maxims, etc. I. Abel, Bob. II. Valenti, Michael.
GV706.8.S665   1983   796   82-15558
ISBN 0-87196-776-6
ISBN 0-87196-269-1 (pbk)

Printed in the United States of America

10 9 8 7 6 5 4 3 2 1

Dedicated to the memory of Bob Abel, who originally had the idea for the book, but who did not survive to see it in print.

MV
July 1983

Contents

PREFACE

Dealing with quotes is like working with fluid history. Thousands of words are written and spoken daily about sports and most of them are, to be charitable, discardable. But then there is the occasional good one that illuminates this somewhat parochial area of our national life. Some of these quotes are flat out and go straight to the heart of the matter; others are crude and blustery; the most interesting ones reveal more than the speaker thinks he's saying; a few verge on the poetic and (forgive us) the divine. Linked together, they sometimes speak with an eloquence not usually associated with the playing fields.

What we have tried to do in this long-overdue Thinking Man's Guide to the Significant Sports Quote (a discarded title) is to bring together quotes on every aspect of sports. We found precisely 50 aspects, and so the book is divided into 50 categories. This wasn't an organizational gimmick—it just came out to a neat 50. Of course, ultimately the individual quote must stand on its own; but we found, to our consummate delight, that in juxtaposition with other quotes around it, a relatively straight-forward quote can take on nuances of meaning it does not seem to carry alone. Additionally, the interplay between quotes—whether reinforcing or contradictory—is often as significant as the quotes themselves.

In the process of selection, we have gone to great pains to leave out the predictable, the commonplace, the ephemeral, and the obvious hype. For the most part, the quotes appear in chronological order, which provides a kind of historical framework. Chronology was sometimes given overriding value, but wherever we felt that it was more meaningful to pursue a series of connected events or shifts in an individual's or organization's actions, we jettisoned chronology for connectedness.

Each of the 50 categories has an introduction, the purpose of which is to provide some sketched-in background or lay out the parameters of the quotes that follow. Within every category the quote appears first, followed by notes on who said it and under what circumstances.

Finally, since the book is a kind of informal oral history of sports in America, the great majority of selections are things people actually said. But there are some exceptions. We have included some letters to the editor, signs, advertisements, stadium chants—any evocation of fan enthusiasm or disenchantment that we felt deserved recognition as part of the tumultuous history of sports in our time. Form itself was never our first criteria. History, we both felt strongly, is not confined to "official" happenings.

Bob Abel
Michael Valenti

SPORTS QUOTES

The Insiders' View
of the Sports World

1. THE BASIC GAME

Playing the Game

When Casey Stengel, looking gloomily up and down the New York Mets bench, asked rhetorically, "Can't anyone here play this game?" he meant play it adequately. That meant just enough to get by without embarrassing him or themselves. The quotes below are about players who play the game more than adequately; they play it with inspired excellence. They play it in a manner that brings the fans out to the stadiums to see the game as it should be played. Other motives, some of them ignoble, bring the fans out, but at their generous best the fans' loudest applause is for excellent play.

But with the sports explosion of the last two decades the players have found they are more than just players—they are also celebrities. Like TV stars, actors, and rock singers. This has subtly transformed both the style and level of play in many sports. It has affected the interaction between players on the same team as well as the quality of play on the field. What has suffered most is the concept of the player as a total athlete; someone, in short, who does everything well. What has been encouraged is the notion of limited talent; perhaps it was inevitable after football teams first broke down into offensive and defensive units, and then even further, into third and fourth special teams. So today we have the hitter who only DH's, the basket shooter who seldom passes the ball, the penalty killers and enforcers in hockey, the taxi squads and the like.

Stengel, master pragmatist, might have accepted all this— but he wouldn't have liked it.

1 I can't run from 1st to 2nd in 3.5 seconds. I don't think I could when I was younger, and I'm slower now. So the key is that instant when the shift of the pitcher's anatomy tells me that he can't come to 1st. He has to go to the plate. I go on that shift. That extra instant is all I need to make it safely.

> **Lou Brock,** at 35, on the nuances of base-stealing. Brock stole a record 118 bases that year (1974).

2 We chase him and chase him and when we get him, we're too tired to enjoy it. He makes for a long afternoon. Guys our size, when we do that much running we're ready for a stretcher .... He gets great enjoyment out of running our tongues out.

> An unidentified member of the **"Fearsome Foursome"** (Brown, Jones, Lundy, Olsen) of the Los Angeles Rams, on the trials of trying to unscramble quarterback Fran Tarkenton.

3 The sixth man has to be so stable a player that he can instantly pick up a tempo or reverse it. He has to be able to go in and have an immediate impact .... The sixth man has to have the unique ability to be in a ball game while he is sitting on the bench.

> Former Boston Celtic coach **Tom Heinsohn** in 1975, when Paul Silas had taken over the "sixth man" role perfected by Frank Ramsey and John Havlicek.

4 Baseball is the only sport I know that when you're on the offense, the other team controls the ball.

> Former Boston Red Sox outfielder **Ken Harrelson,** during a TV sportscast in 1976.

5 I've seen [Ken] Stabler look left, look right, look left and come back right. That's what we call shopping around. Any time a quarterback can do that, he's in business.

> Freeway **Joe Namath** in May 1977, hopeful that the Rams' line would do the same for him.

6 People have this thing about scoring points. I was taught to play the game from a total concept, to be able to do everything reasonably well, some things extraordinarily well. If a guy is simply a great shooter, and he has a bad night, he's a liability. If I'm not shooting well, I'll try to be an asset in other ways.

> All-pro **Rick Barry,** who holds the NBA record for
> assists by a forward (19), set while he was with the
> Golden State Warriors.

So many players are limited in what they can do—and some of   **7**
them are called superstars. A lot of players don't know what it is
to make a pass. It's not that they don't know how; it's just that
they're not looking for anybody.

> **Ibid.**

Sudden death is better theater. It adds a dimension to golf that   **8**
does not otherwise exist. It's better to have a definitive ending on
Sunday than to drag it out to an anticlimactic thing on Monday.

> **Frank Chirkinian**, a CBS Sports producer and a
> golfer himself, on sudden-death playoffs.

The longer you play, the better chance the better player has of   **9**
winning.

> **Jack Nicklaus,** in 1977, with another view of the
> matter.

There are things kids do in the city that they don't do anywhere   **10**
else. We love court savvy. You don't teach it; you get it in the city.
New York kids have court savvy.

> North Carolina's basketball coach, **Dean Smith,** con-
> sidered one of the best, in 1978.

The way to run faster is with a four-fifths effort. Just take it nice   **11**
and easy . . . . Going all out is counterproductive. Our greatest
athletes have been the sleepy-looking guys. Joe Louis. Joe
DiMaggio. John Unitas. An athlete who wants to die for dear old
Rutgers or San Jose State misses the point. He's no good dead.

> **Bud Winters,** San Jose State track coach and men-
> tor of world-class athletes.

When the ball is over the middle of the plate, the batter is hitting   **12**
it with the sweet part of the bat. When it's inside, he's hitting it
with the part of the bat from the handle to the trademark; when
it's outside, he's hitting it with the end of the bat. You've got to
keep the ball away from the sweet part of the bat. To do that the
pitcher has to move the hitter off the plate.

> **Don Drysdale,** a feared and respected pitcher in his
> days with the Los Angeles Dodgers.

Relief pitching is the penthouse or the warehouse. Sometimes you   **13**
throw three average pitches and get three outs. Then you throw

10 good ones, but two or three are bad ones, and you end up like I did tonight.

> Twenty-year veteran **Jim Kaat,** pitching short relief with the New York Yankees in 1980.

14 A hitter sees the ball come off the bat maybe three, four times a year. Other times, it's a matter of practiced coordination.

> Former Los Angeles Dodger **Reggie Smith,** trying to regain his own eye-hand coordination in the midst of a season (1980) filled with injuries and long layoffs.

15 Sugar [Michael Ray Richardson] is making his assists going 90 miles an hour. It was much easier to get an assist in my days and before teams ran so much. We played a setup game and it was easy to find the scorers. There was never the pressure there is today.

> Former New York Knicks coach **Red Holzman,** praising Richardson after he established a new team season assist record in February 1980.

16 Everybody who pitches, pitches with some pain. You just learn to live with it. You don't remember pain, you just think about it when it hurts, then you forget it. I would throw a pitch and it would hurt, but then the pain would go away . . . until the next pitch.

> Hall of Famer **Bob Gibson,** who threw hard for the St. Louis Cardinals.

17 If I just hit the fastball hard, it tells me I can handle his velocity that night. It also gives the pitcher the same thought.

> **Mike Schmidt** of the Philadelphia Phillies, on the importance of that first time at bat.

18 The guy who can really hurt you is a linebacker or defensive back who finds he doesn't have any pass coverage responsibility because his man is loafing and obviously out of the picture. A guy like that can peel off [leave his man] and get over in time to give me a real jolt because he knows he isn't responsible for covering me. He can just think about hurting me instead of covering me— and that, man, can be trouble.

> Pittsburgh Steeler **Lynn Swann** in 1980, on one of the perils of pass-receiving.

19 I'm like a machine out there, just throwing pitch after pitch as quickly as I can. My mind's in neutral. I've got only one pitch (a sinking, split-fingered fastball), so it doesn't matter who the hitter is, I'm only gonna throw my nasty s.o.b. And now that I have a rep

[1979 Cy Young Award winner], the batters help me out. They're the nervous ones. They get over-anxious and swing at bad pitches.
> St. Louis Cardinals relief pitcher **Bruce Sutter.**

Hitters always have one thing in mind—they have to protect themselves against the fastball. If they're not ready for the fastball, a pitcher will throw it right by them. If they're ready for the fastball and don't get it, they can adjust to the breaking ball. But with a screwball, it isn't the break that fools the hitter, it's the change of speed. They don't time it.   **20**
> Hall of Famer **Carl Hubbell,** who invented the screwball, commenting in 1981 on Fernando Valenzuela, who throws it.

I think the ideal size for a goalie is somewhere between 5-11 and 6-1. Any bigger, and your agility is cut down, and the big guys like Dryden and John Davidson seem to suffer back problems. Little guys like me have to come out of the crease to cut down the angles and jump around a lot to make saves. Being small, you have to be flashier to prove your courage.   **21**
> New Jersey Devils goalie **Chico Resch,** who is only 5-8 himself.

If you get someone who's good at the net and he's jumping and guessing well, then you have four places you can go: a passing shot down the line, a passing shot cross-court, a lob, and a shot straight down the middle. If someone is so good that he's getting all the lobs and all the passing shots, then you have to go down the middle . . . . Besides, I don't ask them to come to the net.   **22**
> Czech tennis star **Ivan Lendl,** explaining why he has no qualms about hitting directly at—and sometimes deliberately hitting—an opponent.

I know, speaking from a pitcher's viewpoint, the hardest team to beat is one that comes at you with a lot of speed. You get a guy who bunts for a base hit, steals second and third and comes home on an infield grounder and all of a sudden you're down a run and the ball ain't gone anywhere.   **23**
> New York Yankee **Ron Guidry** in 1982.

Roger [Craig] came to me and said, 'Don't you think you need another pitch?' I said, 'Yeah, I do. I can't get by on my fastball because it's not an overpowering fastball. But I do have good control.' He said, 'Let's get rid of your slider,' which wasn't a very good pitch of mine, and he taught me an overhand curve and a split-fingered fastball. I picked both pitches up real quickly.   **24**

They're the reason I cut a whole run off my ERA.

> Pitcher **Milt Wilcox** in spring training 1982, ac-
> knowledging his debt to Detroit pitching coach Roger
> Craig, who helped him become a winner in 1981.

25 The first thing we look for in a potential attackman is his level of
fear. Does he take that extra step to the goal before he shoots,
even though he knows he's going to get hit? We can't teach an
attackman this. An attackman has to be a good stick-handler and
have exceptional peripheral vision. If he has these three things, we
can teach him to be a dodger.

> Johns Hopkins lacrosse coach **Henry Ciccarone,** in
> 1982. The Blue Jays have a long winning tradition in
> lacrosse.

26 I *feel* the play before the ball comes. I know when a player is going
to make a long pass or a short pass by looking at him in his eyes.
To look at the ball, that is no good, the ball can't tell you where it
is going to go. I see from his eyes, that is why so often when the
pass is made, I put up my foot, and the ball comes to it.

> Former New York Cosmos sweeper **Carlos Alberto,**
> who was very adept at getting into a melee and
> emerging with the ball.

Coaching and Managing

There seem to be as many coaching philosophies as there are
coaches, but for those who require guidelines there are the polarities
of the hard line and the soft line. Both are supposed to lead to the
same results (according to the opposing practitioners): building
character and winning. The first used to get mentioned a lot and
seems to be fading in inverse ratio to the size of stadiums; the second
is considered, well, very desirable. So desirable that, when you are a
college coach and looking for what is called a "new challenge," they
don't ask you if you are a disciple of Lombardi or Paterno, of Bobby

Knight or Dean Smith, but what your win-loss record was at Succotash State. If it was lopsided enough you might even get a six-year contract at close to $287,000 per, as Jackie Sherrill did at Texas A&M. That's security. You could even stop teaching chemistry for that.

Of course you'd be expected to travel a lot around the state, visiting alumni groups, and outside the state, recruiting. A sort of good-will ambassador with a whistle, you might say. And you'll be expected to fill that big new stadium every Saturday. Nobody said it wasn't a pressure job. But then, in time, you might even get a crack at the pros. Now if you're looking for responsibility or a challenge or whatever you want to call it, that's really ulcer country.

Better by far to manage in the big leagues. Some of the same conditions prevail, of course. There are the hard-liners (Billy Martin, Frank Robinson, Earl Weaver) and the soft-liners (Lasorda, Bob Lemon, Joe Torre). Some managers don't quite conform to pattern; sometimes they're secretly kicking butts or springing for hot-fudge sundaes. Nothing much about building character, though. Ballplayers with long-term contracts aren't supposed to have character these days—even the ones with foundations.

But you don't exactly have job security. You've got maybe three years to produce, and then changes have to be made. They can't fire the whole team or dump all the starting pitchers (though the San Francisco Giants did just that in 1982 and almost snagged a pennant), so they fire the manager. Stengel was fired after winning 10 pennants—for not winning an eleventh. Now you know just what hard line means.

But there's a joker in the pack. If you don't say too many harsh things about management, you're now eligible for the Ex-Managers Round-Robin Club. There are only about 50 members and there are 26 franchises. At the rate of five and a half firings a season, that's close to 100 percent turnover every leap year. Outsiders—even minor-league managers who speak Spanish fluently—rarely crack the circle. You wait it out doing color, coaching, or putting in a new patio for Ruth and the kids. It's only a question of time. Everyone knows you've managed (was it Texas or Minnesota?) and therefore have proven managerial credentials.

But, as Stengel cautioned, try to stay under 70.

If you can accept losing, you can't win.   **1**
If you can walk, you can run.
No one is ever hurt. Hurt is in your mind.
       Vince Lombardi's philosophy of the game, as
       frequently expounded by the Green Bay Packer
       coach.

2   Seriously, coach Lombardi is very fair. He treats us all like dogs.
> Former Packer lineman **Henry Jordan,** recalling his
> standard joke whenever he shared a post-season din-
> ner dais with Lombardi.

3   This has never happened to me before. It will never happen again.
If you don't have any pride, I do. I'll be here again next year, but
some of you may not. We'll win if I have to use three teams—one
coming, one going and one playing.
> Post-game locker room lecture delivered by the late
> **Buck Shaw** to his hapless Philadelphia Eagles in
> 1958, Shaw's first year with the team. Two years later
> the lackluster Eagles were NFL champions, beating
> Green Bay. Shaw then retired from football.

4   Simmons had a great arm; he could really fire. When I took over
the team he was strictly a thrower. His problem was that he had
received too much well-meaning advice. He had been over-
coached more than any pitcher I ever saw . . . . The only thing I
ever did was to call him aside and say, 'Would you go back and
pitch just the way you did when you were on that Egypt,
Pennsylvania Legion team?'
> **Eddie Sawyer,** who managed the 1950 Philadelphia
> Phils "Whiz Kids," including two premier pitchers:
> Robin Roberts and Curt Simmons.

5   Quigg was in front of Chamberlain and someone else was behind. I
told the kids, 'If he gets the ball, wrestle him if you have to. If they
beat us I want him to do it on the foul line.'
> Former North Carolina coach **Frank McGuire,**
> recalling his blunt strategy for containing the seven-
> foot, one-inch Wilt Chamberlain in the 1957 NCAA
> title game. The Tar Heels, 20-point underdogs de-
> spite a 31-0 season, beat Kansas in triple overtime,
> 54-53.

6   The Pirates were a last-place club when I took over, but there was
some potential there. I tried to innovate when I was managing. For
instance, I had a theory that your best hitter should lead off, your
second best should bat second, and so on . . . . Based on the 154-
game schedule . . . the leadoff man would go to bat 17 times more
than the number two man. And the number two man would go 17
times more than the number three man. Same thing for numbers
three and four. So that's 51 more at-bats than if he's hitting
fourth. That can be four or five more home runs, which can mean
four or five ball games for you. I tried it out at Pittsburgh for

about 65 games. What happened? We continued to lose. It was a last-place club any way you wrote out the lineup.

Bobby Bragan, who got his first opportunity to apply his managerial wizardry in 1956, reminiscing.

My players can wear their hair as long as they want and dress any **7** way they want. That is, if they can pay their own tuition, meals and board.

Grambling football coach **Eddie Robinson** in 1971. Robinson builds men first and then pro prospects.

The wheeze about building character is a joke. Most boys we get **8** are 18. Their character has long since been built, usually in the home. About all we can teach a kid is how to play football.

John McKay, USC football coach in 1972.

I was a college coach for 33 years, and I never believed a boy was **9** too small. If he could play, I'd find a spot for him. You can't have too many good players. Good players win games for you, not big players.

Lynn "Pappy" Swann, former University of California football coach.

If you keep the opposition on their asses, they don't score goals. **10**

Fred Shero, coach of hockey's Philadelphia Flyers in 1974.

I think there should be bad blood between all clubs. **11**

Former Baltimore manager **Earl Weaver,** following an Orioles-Yankees beanball incident, in response to a reporter's question as to whether he expected antagonism between the rivals.

I don't know what other people feel like when their team loses. **12** But I've got a pain inside.

Former New York Jet coach **Charley Winner,** the morning after his team lost to Miami's Dolphins, 43-0.

'The book' is a refuge for dull, unimaginative, uncreative and **13** incompetent managers to hide behind, and it is never questioned. The book is dull and overused. The book is a part of lazy thinking and the enemy of intelligence . . . . I want to bring baseball fully into the 1970s, and the way to do that is to pinpoint the deficiencies of the traditional attitudes which add up to the book.

Premier base-stealer **Maury Wills,** in a 1976 book written with Don Freeman, called, appropriately, *How*

to Steal a Pennant. Wills finally got a managerial shot
with Seattle in 1980, but didn't get much of a chance to
substitute his book for the traditional one. He was fired
in April 1981.

14 Out of 25 guys there should be 15 who would run through a wall
for you, two or three who don't like you at all, five who are indif-
ferent and maybe three undecided. My job is to keep the last two
groups from going the wrong way.

New York Yankee manager **Billy Martin,** in mid-1976.
Next year's team had a different chemical composition—
millionaires don't run through walls. Billy has since
gotten fired, rehired, refired and rehired again.

15 I don't want any hot dogs on my team. If you're a hot dog you tend
to get careless in the clutch.

Penn State football coach **Joe Paterno.**

16 I don't communicate with players. I tell them what to do. I don't
understand the meaning of communication.

Chicago White Sox manager **Paul Richards** in 1976,
when asked if he planned to initiate a dialogue with
one of his players, Blue Moon Odom.

17 'Fellows,' he would say, 'here is a picture of my daughter. She is as
pretty as a picture and I love her very much. But she likes to eat
and if you guys keep losing, I am going to lose my job and I will
not have enough money to buy food for my daughter and she will
go hungry. So, for goodness sakes, win for my daughter.'

Former court star **Bob Pettit,** recalling Red
Holzman's hotel room bull sessions with his Milwaukee
Hawks. The story, from Pettit's autobiography,
merited retelling when Holzman retired temporarily
from the New York Knicks in spring of 1977.

18 All those miles . . . all those trips . . . . I guess that's what I'll remember most about college coaching, the trips, the nauseousness,
the highs and lows, going through a case of beer, trying to race
back from somewhere. You know what happiness is? Happiness in
sports is winning on the road.

Retiring Marquette basketball coach **Al McGuire,** in
1977.

19 A manager is like a fellow swimming in the ocean with a cut on his
arm. Sooner or later the sharks are going to get him. Do you think
I'm going to manage here for 20 years? Hell, no.

Eddie Stanky, after taking over the managerial reins of the Texas Rangers in mid-season, 1977. The following day, he resigned, saying he was "lonesome and homesick."

My horses get the best hay in the country. It is grown specially in Washington State and vanned across the country to my barn. My horses are bedded down in the best straw money can buy. If I have a stakes horse running anywhere but at Belmont, I take him to the track in a private van . . . . Why should I spend months working on a horse, then load him into a van with a lot of other horses and run the risk that he will be kicked? **20**

   Leading trainer **Frank "Pancho" Martin,** on why his horses have such an enviable winning percentage.

The emphasis will continue to be on hitting. The other team's got to realize we can hurt people. I don't coach to hurt people but I coach to hit people. And that's what we're going to keep doing— hitting people. **21**

   New York Jets coach **Walt Michaels,** after a 1977 game with the Baltimore Colts. The Colts won it, 20-12, and placed six players on the injury list in the process.

A dynasty can't happen any more. Competition is so close that a single injury or lapse can stop you. If you win and just one guy starts thinking he's bigger than the team, you're gonna slip. You can motivate today's player with pride and ego but it's not the same as the old days, when he was motivated by hunger or desperation. **22**

   Boston Celtics general manager **Red Auerbach** on basketball's new breed.

When you have a really good team, it takes away some of the ingenuity, the inventiveness and the coachability through which a coach can express himself. **23**

   San Francisco U. basketball coach **Bob Gaillard,** in tendering his resignation after the 1977-78 season. The previous year he'd been named Associated Press coach of the year for leading the Dons out of the doldrums to a 29-2 record.

I don't believe you can be emotional and concentrate the way you must to be effective. When I see a great play from the sideline, I can't cheer it . . . . The players don't want to see me rushing around and screaming. They want to believe I know what I'm doing. **24**

Dallas coach **Tom Landry,** explaining his deadpan
style. He was actually photographed grinning after the
1978 Super Bowl, despite the score: Steelers 35,
Cowboys 31.

25 But if we win the national championship, so what? It sounds corn-
ball, but that's the way I feel . . . . My best team will be the one
that produces the best doctors, lawyers, fathers and citizens, not
necessarily the one with the best record. Let's keep it in context.

Football coach **Joe Paterno** in 1978, after 28 years
at Penn State.

26 Coach Hayes has been relieved of his duties as head football
coach at Ohio State University. This decision has the full support
of the president of the university.

Ohio State athletic director **Hugh Hindman,** the
morning after the 1978 Gator Bowl. In the closing
minutes of the game, Woody Hayes punched a Clemson player after a key interception.

27 Soviet coaches are really coaches. They're trained to be coaches.
To be a coach in Russia, you have to be a top player, then go to
the university and learn to be a coach. Take courses in anatomy
and all sorts of things. Over here you see a lot of people coaching
who don't know anything or who are doing it for their own ego.
The trouble with a lot of our people is that they're afraid to learn.
But the Russians are always looking to learn.

Fred Shero, Philadelphia Flyers coach in 1978,
speaking about coaching hockey in the USSR in
general and Soviet coach Anatoly Tarasov in
particular.

28 Listen, I was the first black manager in baseball and there was
incredible pressure. I don't blame anyone else. I was too
tough . . . I lacked patience. But we had a rough situation, too. It
was my first job as a manager and I wanted to win—badly. I
probably got on guys a little too hard, with the wrong tone of
voice.

Frank Robinson, now piloting the San Francisco
Giants, looking back on his first managerial stint with
the Cleveland Indians in the late 70s.

29 I gave it everything I have and just don't have anything left . . . . I'm
retiring from football coaching, and I'm never going to coach again
in my life.

John Madden, after 10 very successful years with

the then Oakland Raiders, citing a deteriorating ulcer condition. Madden soon joined the ex-athletes' beer commercial fraternity.

I'm not into that business of being relevant to kids. I'm not playing **30** on their team: they're playing on mine. We have certain ways of acting here. My kids are not going to come in here and say, 'Hey baby.' It doesn't make you less of a man to have respect for people.

> Georgetown basketball coach **John Thompson,** who has been called a black version of the White Shadow. Thompson has guided the Hoyas regularly to the National Collegiate tournament. Only one of his players has failed to graduate.

This league got rid of all its players over 30. The kids don't think **31** they have to learn anything. It goes back to junior high and the playground. The kids coming along today have so much ability, they tell their first coach, 'Man, I want to dunk.' What's the coach going to do? He lets them dunk.

> **Butch Beard,** former New York Knicks assistant coach and former backcourt man with smarts, commenting on the NBA in 1981.

They get to high school and the first thing they ask a college coach **32** is, 'How much are you going to pay me?' And the second thing is, 'How much playing time will I get?' They don't care what style of ball the college plays because they figure if they get their playing time, they'll do it their way. Then these kids come into the league and they don't know what to do if their first move doesn't work.
> **Ibid.**

We don't want the athlete here who can't stand criticism. We only **33** practice two hours a day, and I can't waste time whispering in people's ears. I tell the players there are only two times when I'm going to stop criticizing them—when they become perfect or when I've given up on them.

> Oregon State's **Ralph Miller,** third in total victories among active coaches, before the 1981 NCAA tournament. Miller espouses nonstop pressure basketball.

I don't want to be a players' coach. Who's the last players' coach **34** to win a championship? Players' coaches and comedians always fall. I want to be a coaches' coach, a coach for the purists, and I think that's my reputation. Bobby Knight and I are the leading basketball clinicians in this country.

New York Knicks coach **Hubie Brown** in 1982, a tough
and controversial coach whose job will be to bring team
basketball back to New York.

35 I demand 100% effort from my players. I demand that they conform and become a part of a total team. In Kentucky, I started
with a whole new team and won the ABA title in the first season,
and the second year we lost in the seventh game. In Atlanta, we
got rid of all the no-cut underachievers who weren't playing to
their potential and replaced them with hungry people who were
subservient to team play, and we won.
Ibid.

36 Earl [Weaver] saw what happened with Bambi [George Bam-
berger]. He quit and sat out a year and then the Mets came to him
and made him a fabulous offer. Earl has to be thinking that the
same thing will happen to him. Next year there are going to be 26
managers looking over their shoulders, knowing Earl is out of a
job and by the middle of the season, he's going to have his pick of
about 10 or 12 jobs.

One **baseball man's** reaction to Weaver's announced
retirement as Baltimore's manager at the end of the
1982 season.

37 Neil, don't you know, young man, that I've had a bypass. You have
to take it easy on me.

New York Mets manager **George Bamberger** to his
ace reliever, Neil Allen, who seldom did things the
easy way.

38 Coaching has changed. Twenty years ago, the coach never left the
campus. Now, I balance the budget, market the product, do pro-
motions, handle personnel, sell the program, recruit and coach.
Like it or not, it's a different type of business now.

Jackie Sherrill, new head football coach and
athletic director at Texas A&M, whose $287,000
annual salary is probably the highest in college ranks.
In 1982 he made more than 40 trips throughout the
state to speak to alumni clubs.

39 My salary is coming out of ticket sales. And I work for the president of the university, not the president of the booster
club . . . . Besides, a good professor can make money, too. He can
earn $70,000 to $90,000 a year and then make money from writing books or articles and from giving lectures. And a professor
doesn't spend 40 days a summer raising money for his depart-

ment. Remember, I'm not selling Jackie Sherrill Enterprises, I'm
selling Texas A&M.
                    Ibid.

Officiating

They are virtually unnoticed—until there's controversy. When
there's trouble, opposing sides and irate fans descend on them like
locusts and demand justice—swift, complete, and irrevocable. They
must maintain their cool at the moment when others have fire in their
eyes and are ready to fight. They are the umpires and judges and refs,
the linesmen and stewards, the indispensable officials who run the
game and must interpret the rules by which it is played.

Except for baseball, they are greatly underpaid, considering
the responsibilities they bear and the strenuous and sometimes
dangerous nature of their job. Ballplayers half their age wave them
out of their line of vision as if they were inanimate objects. Skaters
and linebackers barrel into them. Tennis players spit at them. More
obscenities are hurled at them in five games than most of us hear in a
year. Like Rodney Dangerfield, they get no respect. If they blow a
call, there are immediate screams for the introduction of instant
replay on giant electronic screens "to show them up." They are
accused of tolerating violence, turning a blind eye to infractions,
favoring a champion or an odds-on favorite, stubbornly refusing to
reverse a bad call.

Occasionally the accusations are justified; more often, officials are simply being scapegoated—for exerting authority, for
being right, for being old, for being underpaid.

They stand for adherence to the rules, and as Bill White wryly
observed on a recent New York Yankee telecast, at least half the as-
semblage would like those rules to be suspended on any given play.

Kill him! He hasn't got any friends.   **1**
                    Traditional cry that greeted umpires in the early
                    days of baseball. After World War I, it was shortened
                    to "Kill the umpire!"

I'm willing to lay my knowledge and judgment on the line. If I   **2**
know I'm right, they can burn the stadium down around me and I

won't care. Part of the joy of officiating is walking off the field with that warm feeling that 'I was right.' Then you put controversy behind you and go about your business.

> Veteran NFL ref **Gordon McCarter,** known for his toughness and integrity.

3   Umpiring's tough . . . you're always half wrong.

> New York Yankee telecaster and ex-ballplayer **Bill White,** in a compassionate moment during a rhubarb-filled New York-Milwaukee game in June 1982.

4   I immediately got the feeling I was wrong on the call, when every Baltimore guy on the field charged at me with intent to maim. Actually, I never saw the ball, but I had to call something. I figured I had a 50-50 chance to be right.

> Former umpire **Ron Luciano,** looking back on a home run call he blew in a Baltimore-California game in 1975. Luciano, umpiring at third, raced down the line on a long fly, but lost sight of the ball as it curved away from the foul pole.

5   Refereeing is nothing more than angles. You're looking for the best angle to see a developing play. Once you've got the position, you don't change it. I've seen new referees hustle themselves out of a perfect angle, just to let other people think they're hustling. That's ridiculous. I don't move unless it's absolutely necessary.

> Veteran NBA referee **Darrell Garretson,** who keeps his per-game coverage under six miles.

6   Hockey is the fastest it's ever been, but 55 years ago it had one official and today it's still got one official. There isn't a man, dead or alive, who can skate with 30 players for a full 60 minutes.

> **Dick Irvin,** coach of the Montreal Canadiens in 1952.

7   All this violence, an awful lot of it goes back to the officials. Some officials have become complacent. Some are not physically capable of keeping up with the game, some look like bartenders. Some people think the game has become too fast for the officials. But what's happened is that the referees have become too slow for the game. I know this, if I was the supervisor of officials this year, six would have gone.

> Former NBA referee and supervisor of officials **Sid Borgia,** after widespread violence on the courts in 1977.

8   It [the use of electronic umpires] will never happen, because when you

do that you've taken away all the alibis. Who can the managers blame   **8**
losses on? Who can pitchers and hitters blame their troubles on?
Believe me, the umpire will always be with us.

> Former NL ump **Beans Reardon,** throwing the con-
> cept of electronic umpires right out of the game back
> in 1969. Despite instant replays, he called that one
> right.

Holding penalties—you could call one on every play, but the   **9**
officials don't. And they never call back-to-back holding penalties
against the same team. That's why, when your team is called for
holding, everyone holds again on the next play—because it won't
be called. Hell, we teach that on the sandlots down South.

> Former Michigan State quarterback **Al Dorow,**
> speaking as head coach of the Hamilton Tiger-Cats in
> 1971.

Officials should be organized, tested and controlled like a football   **10**
team. But we didn't even test their eyes extensively until a few
years ago, and we still don't test their judgment enough . . . . There's
no continuity in handling them. That's not organization, it's
embarrassment.

> **The owner of a 1975 NFL team,** bemoaning the
> haphazard nature of officiating in what is essentially a
> weekend sport.

If you're serious 90 percent of the time, you'll go crazy out there.   **11**

> American League umpire **Ron Luciano,** once one of
> baseball's flakier officials, now doing TV color.

You can say something to popes, kings and presidents, but you   **12**
can't talk to officials. In the next war, they ought to give
everybody a whistle.

> Former University of Texas basketball coach **Abe
> Lemons.**

I am cautioning you, sir. I am noting down your name because   **13**
what you have done is completely out of character with this game.
And if you continue, I shall be forced to eject you.

> A 1974 interpretation by Seattle Sounder coach **John
> Best** on what it actually means when a soccer referee
> holds a yellow card over his head as he whistles for a
> foul.

The officials blew this one. They're more powerful than the Pope.   **14**
Tomorrow they'll go back to their $12-a-day jobs and there's

nothing we can do about it.

> Tampa Bay coach **John McKay,** after a fourth-down
> sign was missed in the last 21 seconds of a Steelers-
> Buccaneers game in 1980. Pittsburgh took over, ran out
> the clock, and won, 24-21.

15   Most of the established stars in the NBA had quirks that the refs
let them get away with. For example, they tended to wink at my
goal tending and the 'Russell' elbow . . . . (My strategy, which
worked fairly well, was to get the referees to accept the flailing
elbows as my 'style' so that they wouldn't call fouls on me) . . . .
And the referees let Bob Pettit take a whole bunch of little steps
just before he shot the ball. (I always protested Pettit's steps, and
one night a referee just laughed and said, 'Well, maybe he was
walking, but he didn't go very far.')

> Former Boston Celtic star **Bill Russell,** in his 1979
> book, *Second Wind.*

16   Arguments are healthy. It's good for a manager to talk about an
issue. But kicking dirt and throwing his hat and nose-to-nose confrontations are verbal abuse bordering on physical abuse.

> **Dominic Infante,** professor of rhetoric and com-
> munication at Kent State, on abusing officials.

17   As long as they don't question the umpire's integrity or imply that
he was drunk, I take no action.

> American League president **Lee McPhail** in 1981, on
> the never-ending controversy over the umpires' calls.

18   I won't be afraid to come down hard on players involved in serious
stick incidents. I never used the stick [illegally] when I played. I'm
going to crack down on the thing I didn't do.

> Former NHL player **Dave Schultz,** named com-
> missioner of the Atlantic Coast Hockey League in 1982.
> In his turbulent nine-year career, Schultz piled up 2,294
> penalty minutes.

19   Officiating is the only occupation in the world where the highest
accolade is silence.

> NBA referee **Earl Strom,** without his whistle.

20   Decisions of the judges will be final unless shouted down by a really
overwhelming majority of the crowd present.

> **Addenda to the competition rules of the first open
> boomerang tournament** held in Washington, D.C. in
> July 1974, sponsored by the Smithsonian Resident
> Associates.

Injuries

Injuries, fans say complacently, are part of the game. They sure are. When Willis Reed appeared on the court with a ruptured thigh muscle and loaded with painkillers so that he could play in the final 1970 NBA playoff game against the Los Angeles Lakers, the partisan crowd went wild. All the hobbled Reed kept thinking was, "I've got to play Wilt Chamberlain on one leg." Reed managed to play for 28 inspired (and gruelling) minutes, and emerged as a hero.

In 1978, Bill Walton found himself in a remarkably similar playoff situation. The Portland Trail Blazers' physician injected his ailing left foot with an anti-inflammation drug. Walton played for 15 minutes, then left the game in pain. He was roundly accused of dogging it. X-rays the following day revealed that Walton had a broken foot, which sidelined him for the entire 1978-79 season. Numbing the area, Walton felt, masked—or induced—a major injury. Walton eventually asked to be traded because of this, and the injury seems to have decidedly muted a once-brilliant career.

Joe Namath was called gutsy for playing in game after game with badly battered knees—which led eventually to a crippling nerve injury in his leg. After bruising his big toe in an All-Star game, Dizzy Dean returned to the mound too soon and, because he was favoring the sore toe, brought on a chronic shoulder condition that abruptly ended his career in his prime.

The gung-ho advocates may wish to point to Tommy John at this point. His is the rare success story: he had a tendon transplant in his weary pitching arm in 1974, and now threatens to pitch longer than Luis Tiant. Or maybe even Satchel Paige.

Injuries, indeed, are part of the game. When the football season starts, you can find a list of them every Saturday, team by team. Sometimes they fill a whole page.

I taped a pad to my left ankle because it hurt; I taped the other **1** ankle as a decoy so they wouldn't know which one is injured.
> Michigan tailback **Glenn Doughty's** ploy against violence on the gridiron in 1969.

If I can change the score, I'm not going to worry about getting hurt. **2**
> **Pete Rose,** when he was diving into third base for Cincinnati.

3 I've come to terms with pain and the possibility of an injury . . . . I understand it now. When all the glory is gone and you've got that little crook in your walk—then you'll have to ask yourself, was it worth it?

> Former New York Jets fullback **John Riggins** in 1975, on the mental anguish he experienced when he suffered his first serious football injury two years earlier.

4 All his life, a football player always has people around him—teammates, coaches, front-office people in the pros, teachers and guidance people in college and high school. But when something like this [a serious injury] happens, all of a sudden, you're all alone. When they roll you into the operating room, you're all alone.

> Former New York Giant fullback **Larry Csonka,** who underwent surgery on his left knee in 1976.

5 It was during October, after I'd already won 22 games. I was very, very tired, and I even had second thoughts about pitching that day . . . . I threw a pitch and felt the pain. I felt something tear. When they opened me up, they told me the nerve was severed, and I remember how scared I was. My arm began to shrink. It just withered. There was no muscle, no bicep.

> **Randy Jones,** remembering his 1976 season with the San Diego Padres, the bittersweet year he won the Cy Young Award and sustained an injury that would plague him for the next five years.

6 They both [ankles] hurt all the time. Yards of tape before every game, buckets of ice after every game. I'll see how they heal this winter and, if they don't, then I'll worry. What's it done to me? It's humbled me.

> **Fred Lynn,** with the Boston Red Sox in 1977, sitting in the locker room with both feet immersed in tubs of ice, after a late-season game.

7 Coaches think they need to hear the sound of hard helmets hitting together to make it sound like football. If they want to arm the players, they might as well issue helmets like the Germans wore in World War I, with spikes on them.

> **Dr. Don Cooper,** Oklahoma State team physician, who believes soft outer-shell helmets (and shoulder pads) should be mandatory.

I've got a knee injury myself now, the first one I've ever had. The pain **8** with me is so intense you wouldn't believe it and yet I've got nothing like he's [Bobby Orr] got. I don't know how he stands it. He never complains, he never talks about it, yet I know he must be in awful pain . . . . It's strange, isn't it? It seems that the greats, if they're going to get a serious injury, it's the knee. Mantle, Namath, Sayers. And then you look at a guy like Gordie Howe, 49, and still playing. Here's Orr, only 28, this greatest of players—it's a goddam tragedy.

> **Stan Mikita,** on his Chicago Black Hawks 1977
> teammate, Bobby Orr.

I used to get a jolt from my foot up my body every five seconds or **9** so. It went on for about three weeks and almost drove me crazy. Medication wouldn't help it, morphine wouldn't help it. I lost 30 pounds . . . . Then I lost the feeling in my foot. The neurosurgeons all assured me that the feeling would come back, and it has. But it took three years.

> **Joe Namath** describing the nerve injury in his
> leg, which began when he had his first knee
> operation.

They [injuries] change attitudes of players today . . . . If he doesn't **10** have a no-cut [contract], he'll go the route. He plays in pain. There are guys today who stay out a month with injuries that our old guys used to play with.

> Boston Celtics' **Red Auerbach** on the new attitude
> about injuries.

The worst mental depression I suffered came when the cast was **11** removed and I looked at my arm. I have good muscle development in my arms, but by then my right arm had shrunk from atrophy. It scared me. It was the same thing that had happened to my foot the year before.

> **Pat Zachry,** following a 1979 elbow operation to
> reroute the ulnar nerve. The former New York Mets
> pitcher had missed nearly half a season in 1978
> with a broken foot.

I don't know if I should tell you this, but I was injected six times in **12** my front and five times in my back just prior to that game. Then, at halftime, I got shot up in the ribs and the cartilage again.

> New York Jets quarterback **Richard Todd,** after a
> 1981 game, on the ubiquitous use of painkillers.
> Playing with a broken rib and torn cartilage,
> Todd sprained an ankle as well.

13 My body has betrayed me. I had never been through anything like that [injuries]. It hurt my confidence. I couldn't be as cocky as I always was on the ice. I had a body that needed to be rebuilt and it was something I'd never thought of having to do.

> New York Islander **Denis Potvin,** as his team girded for a try at a third straight Stanley Cup in 1982. This great defenseman's woes included severe thumb injury, broken clavicle, and deep groin injury over the last three seasons.

14 Every time a man pitches, he is systematically injuring his arm. A pitcher's durability will depend on the genetic capacity of the arm to recover from the insult of pitching.

> New York Mets team physician **James C. Parkes II,** in 1980.

Violence

"Violence is as American as apple pie." H. Rap Brown said that in another context in the 1960s. It's just as true in the 1980s, but the focus has shifted. In sports it has become so commonplace that Jim McMillian of the Portland Trail Blazers calls it "part of the game." The game he's talking about is basketball, which not very long ago was considered a "gentleman's sport." No longer.

The vast postwar expansion in most sports (and especially contact sports) has doubled and then trebled the profit margin. Individual sports have become more uniform, more regulated—and more competitive. Aggressive play is encouraged, even when it spills over into abusive play. That pie Brown referred to is very real and has grown to mammoth size; cutting it up has honed the competitive edge while blunting the sense of fair play.

Hockey, the scapegoat sport, is usually signalled out as the worst offender, where violence is tolerated if not actually encouraged. But if this is so, the gap between hockey and other contact sports has been narrowed. In basketball and football players are using amphetamines to make themselves meaner, to unleash the Hyde side of their personalities. Even in horse racing, there have been several savage incidents; in the 1975 Kentucky Derby, someone from the

infield threw a full beer can at the front-running horse, hitting him
in the head.

Even a new sport like indoor soccer seems to be programming itself from the outset to capitalize on the contemporary lax
enforcement of interpretable rules. It tolerates a move called
"boarding," which is like body-checking in hockey, except that
here you slam your man into the arena's boards.

There's even a penalty box offenders go to if they're
caught doing it and the officials feel pushed enough to send them
there. Outdoor soccer, since it is not enclosed, cannot hope to
emulate this indoor innovation.

One final statistic to underscore the point that stricter
penalties and severe fines (as in basketball) are needed to
discourage violence in sports: In the mid-1970s the Canadian
Ophthalmological Society tested the eyesight of Canadian professional hockey players. It found that 37 of them were blind in one
eye as a result of playing injuries.

Any team that loses its aggressiveness is dead . . . . we'd be playing   **1**
with guys with broken wrists or ribs. You know a guy has a broken
wrist, you hammer him there a few times and you don't have much
trouble with him for the rest of the night. It's nothing personal. I'd
do it myself.

> **Punch Imlach,** coach and general manager of the
> Toronto Maple Leafs in the 60s, in his 1969 book,
> *Hockey Is a Battle.* In his stormy years in Toronto,
> Imlach won four Stanley Cups.

When a player enters an arena, he is consenting to a great number   **2**
of what otherwise might be regarded as assaults. The game of hockey could not possibly be played unless those engaged in it were
willing to accept these assaults.

> Canadian judge **M.J. Fitzpatrick,** commenting on
> the 1970 indictment of the Boston Bruins' Teddy
> Green for criminal assault, following a wild stick-
> swinging brawl on the ice.

It is both good law and good sense that the force and effect of the   **3**
criminal law should apply equally and evenly inside and outside
the sporting arena.

> Canadian judge **Aaron Brown,** in his 1976 ruling
> stating that the Detroit Red Wings' Dan Maloney had
> to stand trial for criminal assault. During a game with
> the Toronto Maple Leafs, Maloney allegedly
> repeatedly slammed Brian Glennie's head against the
> ice, resulting in a severe concussion.

4   When I get a chance, I like to knock a guy's head off. Then I look
into his eyes to see how he feels.

> **Ed Shubert,** 1972 linebacker for Drexel University.

5   The Flyers are the top draw in the [National Hockey] league. People pay money to see them. If the other teams were as successful,
I'd be pleased, regardless of how they achieve success.

> NHL president **John Ziegler,** speaking about the
> Philadelphia franchise back in the 70s, when they were
> known as the "Broad Street bullies."

6   I've been blessed with their abrasive natures. They make other
teams wary and cautious.

> Former Philadelphia Flyers coach **Fred Shero,**
> counting among his 1975 blessings his three "enfor-
> cers," including Dave Schultz, the most heavily penal-
> ized player of recent times.

7   Those guys think they can take the law into their own hands.

> **Dave Schultz,** traded to the Los Angeles Kings in
> 1976, about his rowdy former teammates.

8   We're seeing a new sort of violence. It's being used not as a means
to an end, but for recreational purposes, for pleasure.

> **Dr. Arthur Beisser,** Los Angeles psychiatrist and for-
> mer athlete.

9   The players ain't stopping fights like they used to. It's gotten like
hockey. Everyone stands around and lets the guys fight and they
shouldn't do that.

> **Jim Loscutoff,** former Boston Celtic once known as
> "Jungle Jim," commenting on the changing attitude
> toward violence on the basketball courts.

10   There is no place in our sport [basketball] for violence. We do not
need fights between players to maintain fan interest. Our sport
has all the elements of excitement inherent to it, and it has no
need for the dimension of violence.

> NBA commissioner **Larry O'Brien,** after some un-
> scheduled 1976-77 punchouts on NBA courts.

11   The spontaneous fight that breaks out as a result of frustration is
an outlet. To eliminate that outlet is to bring about retaliation in
more severe form.

> NHL president **John Ziegler** in 1979, arguing against
> ousting players for fighting, as is done in college hockey.

I went to a fight the other night and a hockey game broke out.   **12**
> Comedian **Rodney Dangerfield,** in 1978.

I have been lucky in the past not to have killed anyone in the ring   **13**
and I thank God that I never hurt anyone seriously while I was
boxing.
> Former heavyweight champion **George Foreman,**
> announcing his retirement after a 46-bout
> ring career.

It's not for the money, it's for the integrity of baseball . . . . If you   **14**
let Randle or any other player get away with this kind of violence,
then anyone could punch out his manager or coach, get traded and
then come out smelling like a rose.
> **Frank Lucchesi,** manager of the 1977 Texas
> Rangers, explaining why he filed a $200,000 suit
> against Lenny Randle for personal battery. Hos-
> pitalized for five days, Lucchesi dropped the suit
> when Randle entered a no-contest plea and was fined
> $1,000 by the Texas courts.

If the [runner] is close enough to hit you with a body block, you're   **15**
not going to make the double play anyway. I'm not excited about
getting knocked into left field. The flying body block is football,
not baseball.
> Former Minnesota Twin shortstop **Roy Smalley.**
> Smalley's comments were prompted by the 1978 rule
> change restricting offensive base-running.

If you automatically kick out a player for fighting, how are you   **16**
going to prevent teams from sending out a player at the beginning
of the game and goading the other team's best player into a fight?
> **Scotty Morrison,** NHL referee-in-chief, with a moral
> dilemma.

Who is this guy, Queensberry? I don't see anything wrong in stick-   **17**
ing your thumb into any guy's eye. Just a little.
> Two-ton **Tony Galento** to a New Jersey boxing
> commissioner, recalled by the latter when Galento
> died in July 1979.

When you come down to the lobby, I'm going to blow your brains   **18**
out.
> Phone call to Pittsburgh Pirates star **Dave Parker,**
> shortly after he signed a $1-million-a-year contract in
> 1979.

19 In most cases, the athlete who is chosen to receive the death threat symbolizes something to the sick person who is making the threat. It could be the unemployed auto worker looking at somebody who's just been written up as having a tremendous salary or someone who happens to be a very popular figure, a very articulate figure, a good-looking person. These are all things that somehow the other person is not.

> NFL security director **Warren Welsh,** in 1981.

20 To go to the match was to escape from the dark despondency into the light of combat. Here, by association with the home team, positive identity could be claimed in muscle and goals. To win was personal success; to lose, another clout from life. Football [soccer] was not so much an opiate of the masses as a flag run up against the gaffer bolting his gates and the landlord armed with his bailiffs.

> British author **Arthur Hopcraft,** in his 1980 book called *Football Man.* (The English "football" is what we call soccer.)

21 I just wanted to flip him [Mike Allison] because I was teed off. He got me near the eye. I figure anybody hits you, you should hit him back. Isn't that the way the game's supposed to be played?

> Philadelphia Flyer **Bobby Clarke** in 1980, after a collision with New York Ranger Mike Allison. Clarke, cut on the face, retaliated. Allison suffered severe jaw and neck bruises as a result of Clarke's high sticking.

22 When they let things go early, and they always do, that's why third periods [in hockey] get out of control. I'm not talking about taking a check; that is part of the game. I'm talking about all the cheap shots guys have to take in this league, especially guys who won't drop their gloves and fight. I don't care who knows I'm not going to fight; I'm not going to let this game turn me into being a person I'm not.

> New York Islander **Mike Bossy,** after a brawling 1980 game with the Rangers in which 68 of the match's 100 penalty minutes came in the third period.

23 From here on, any pitcher who throws at a Yankee batter will be served with a lawsuit within 24 hours or during his next visit to New York .... The Yankees will exhaust all legal remedies to protect their players as human beings and as valuable parts of the Yankee organization.

> Statement made by **George Steinbrenner** following the September 1981 beanball incident involving Reggie Jackson and Cleveland pitcher John Denny at Yankee Stadium.

That's my bread-and-butter play—over the middle. I'm not afraid **24**
of getting hurt, but I think about Stingley a lot. He ran about the
same pattern. When I heard about his injury, I was shocked. I
thought to myself: 'Why him and not me?' I say a prayer for him
every week before I step on the field.

> Dallas Cowboy receiver **Drew Pearson,** recalling the
> crippling injury suffered by [New England's] Darryl
> Stingley after a particularly hard hit by Oakland's
> Jack Tatum.

My idea of a good hit is when the victim wakes up on the sidelines **25**
with train whistles blowing in his head and wondering who he is
and what ran over him . . . . I never make a tackle just to bring
someone down. I want to punish the man I'm going after and I
want him to know that it's going to hurt every time he comes my
way . . . .

> Former Oakland free safety **Jack Tatum,** now with
> Houston, in his 1980 book, *They Call Me Assassin.*

An amateur footballer who plays in, of all things, the Edinburgh **26**
Churches Sunday League, has been banned until the year 2012.
The 30-year ban was imposed by league officials after the player
was found guilty of assaulting a referee during a Cup tie . . . . The
name of the player has not been revealed by the league, who hope
their action will be a warning to others.

> **Editorial comment** in the British soccer magazine
> *Shoot!,* pointing to the growing number of incidents of
> attacks against sports officials.

Rookies

It's difficult to believe they were all rookies once. But they were. They
all went through the rites of initiation, were the butt of jokes played on
them by older players who'd been through it. They had to establish
who they were; not only their playing skills but also what sort of
men—or boys—they were. And that final acceptance that came with
not being called "the kid" or "Omaha" anymore—the recognition
that they had a name, a number, and most important, a place on
the roster.

With the explosion of new sports franchises, there are many more of them; in some sports, they've got draft choice numbers. The lower the number the better their chances of sticking with the team—presumably. But it doesn't always work out that way. They still have to fit into the fabric of the team, become part of an entity that was there before they were.

In the quotes below, we tried to find reflections of the wonderment, the puzzlement, and sometimes the private agony of that unpredictable first year when an athlete is being tested at the professional level.

1 I'm a rookie. It says so on my bubble-gum card.

> Chicago White Sox catcher **Brian Downing** in 1974, defending his eligibility for Rookie of the Year honors.

2 If you play me, you'll never be able to farm me out.

> **Pete Rose,** in spring training with the Cincinnati Reds in 1963, to his manager, Fred Hutchinson. Rose hit .500 against big-league pitching, and won a slot at second base.

3 Yogi threw the mask up in the air. And I said, 'If it comes down, Yogi, you're out of the game.' Then Casey kept giving me all that crossword-puzzle stuff, and I told him, 'Hey, I just ran Yogi. You might as well go with him and wash his back.' The other umpires told me, 'You just lost your job.' But I was still around 20 years later.

> **Frank Umont,** after only a month as a big-league umpire, throwing both Yogi Berra and Casey Stengel out of a 1954 Baltimore-New York game.

4 I wasn't going to walk him. That wouldn't have been fair—to him or me. Hell, he's the greatest player I ever saw.

> St. Louis Browns rookie **Bob Muncrief,** about DiMaggio in 1941. Muncrief, the pitcher in the 36th game of DiMaggio's hitting streak, had retired Joe D. three times, and refused to walk him in his last at-bat. DiMag singled, and kept the streak intact for another 20 games.

5 If that starts to happen, I want somebody on the club to smack me down. I want somebody to say, 'You're too cocky. You're not that good. You're only a rookie.'

> Rookie of the Year **Mark Fidrych,** midway through the 1976 season, when asked if sudden fame was going to his head.

Going to the Canadian Football League is identity suicide.   **6**
>Cincinnati Bengals 1976 rookie linebacker **Reggie Williams,** explaining why he turned down a more lucrative offer from the Toronto Argonauts.

They [the New Jersey Giants] have a very spirited team, and their   **7**
defense is good, but you can't be a contender with a rookie
quarterback. There's no way.
>Dallas Cowboys coach **Tom Landry,** looking at the 1977 New Jersey Giants. The quarterback was Jerry Golsteyn; Landry was right.

Kid, just go down there and throw yourself on the fire.   **8**
>Seattle Seahawk coach **Andy McDonald,** instructing rookie Steve Raible on how to break the wedge on kickoff returns.

Getting Steve Cauthen to ride your horse with a five-pound   **9**
allowance is like having a license to steal, and trainers know it.
Cauthen looks like the best young rider to come onto the race
track since Willie Shoemaker in 1949.
>Former jockey **Sammy Renick,** on the 16-year-old apprentice jockey, winner of 29 races and $375,000 in purses in his first 21 days of racing in New York.

It's amazing how fast you grow old in this game. At first you're the   **10**
rookie righthander; next season you're that promising righthander;
then suddenly you're the 'Old Man.'
>Los Angeles Dodgers' veteran pitcher **Don Sutton** in 1977.

I just didn't want to be a quitter. My dad told me, 'Let them   **11**
release you.' So I didn't set any time schedule. Who wants to grow
up?
>Twenty-eight-year-old Cleveland Indians rookie **Tom Brennan,** on why he hung on for four years in Triple-A ball. Using tricky stop-action delivery in his major league debut, Brennan beat the Yanks 6-2 on six hits in September 1981.

Well, basically in pro ball everybody's pretty good.   **12**
>N.J. Giants rookie **Butch Woolfolk,** when asked what the difference was between college and pro football.

It's getting worse all the time. Our biggest problem is that kids are   **13**
playing organized baseball before they ever really practice and

learn the game . . . . Unfortunately, too many parents and coaches
think winning at an early age is more important than learning . . . I
have seven guys who work for me. As a group, we see an average
of 30,000 players a year. This year we saw four players who had
major league potential, only four.

> Philadelphia Phils scout **Tony Lucadello,** on the
> prowl for talent for 39 years, who thinks it's thinner
> than ever.

14   Give him an apple and a road map.

> **Baseball training camp saying** for a rookie heading
> back to the minors.

Sports Arenas

In the 1930s and 40s the hue and cry was that the stadiums should be
standardized; now it's that they should be covered. This gave birth to
the concept of the Dome: Astro, Metro, Super, King, Silver. The roof
blots out the sun, yes—but the rain and the snow as well.

Underfoot we now have Astroturf and other galactic syn-
thetics—or grass. The difference here is that one is mowed, the other
vacuumed or shampooed. Read the instructions before cleaning.

The 1970s and 80s have also seen the emergence of multi-
sports complexes like New Jersey's Meadowlands, with racing night
and day plus a pinwheel choice of football, basketball, soccer, etc. Its
tentacles extend to the problem-ridden metropolitan areas around it
to pry loose faltering franchises.

Even college basketball, once a parochial game played in on-
campus gyms, has moved to the nearest big-city arena, where it can
be played before 60,000 point-conscious fans.

All this has changed the nature of the game, made it diffuse
and remote for many, some of whom remember the intimacy and
magic of the more modest sports arenas of the past: Ebbets Field,
Wrigley Field, Shibe Park, Jamaica race track, Fenway, and perhaps
most of all, the old Madison Square Garden.

1   You know, those parks in those days—St. Louis was a rockpile.
Both the Browns and Cardinals played on it, and the sun pounded

it all summer. Ebbets Field in Brooklyn was built on a city dump.
In Baker Bowl in Philadelphia, poor Gerry Nugent couldn't afford
water. We always said that if we could play around-the-year in Cincinnati, down there in the river bottom where floods brought up
new silt every spring, we'd last 10 years longer.

> Brooklyn Dodger outfielder **Babe Herman,** recalling
> the playing fields of the 1930s.

Hitting fly balls off Vida Blue don't do you any good. My best bolt   **2**
don't go out of here. It's a bleeping fly ball.

> Former Detroit catcher **Bill Freehan,** lamenting in
> 1971 about the acreage between home plate and the
> outfield seats in the Oakland Coliseum.

It's nice pitching in an airport.   **3**

> **Vida Blue's** reaction on hearing Freehan's comment,
> above.

You look at that big wall and you feel like you're part of the game.   **4**
In the new parks, it's like looking out on a prairie. You've got to
make people think they're in a theater and the ball park's the
stage.

> A hosannah to Fenway Park's famous left field wall
> (dubbed the "Green Monster") by Boston Red Sox
> general manager **Richard O'Connell** in 1973. Visit-
> ing outfielders would swap theatrical effects for a lit-
> tle more outfield.

If a horse can't eat it, I don't want to play on it.   **5**

> Itinerant infielder-outfielder **Richie Allen,** comment-
> ing in 1974 on Astroturf.

Artificial turf has taken away the great plays but also the bad   **6**
hops. You used to see good fielders able to adjust, but on turf,
everything is more mechanical. Turf makes good fielders into
great ones, and turns poor fielders into good fielders, but it takes
away part of the game.

> Former Baltimore Orioles shortstop **Mark Belanger,**
> one of the best, in 1980.

It's the first time I ever played on an unnumbered interstate   **7**
highway.

> New York Yankee third baseman **Graig Nettles,** on
> the Dodger Stadium brick-and-mortar infield, during
> the 1978 Series.

8 I'd love to play in Madison Square Garden. I don't care if it was in
the Sahara Desert. Just the name is legend.

> All-Star forward **George McGinnis,** then with the
> Indianapolis Pacers. Traded to Philadelphia, he
> enjoyed the Garden magic as a 76er, until 1982.

9 I want one [a dome stadium] like this, only bigger.

> Former Louisiana Governor **John J. McKeithen,** at
> the Houston Astrodome opening in 1967. On April
> Fool's Day, 1975 his wish came true: New Orleans'
> Superdome officially opened.

10 Architects have tremendous egos, but no one man could have conceived and planned this building. We picked the best brains in the
country and then we used computers to build it.

> **Nathaniel "Buster" Curtis,** head of the architect-
> engineer-computer combo that produced the 97,365-
> seat Superdome.

11 The Superdome is an exercise in optimism. A statement of faith.
It is the very building of it that is important, not how much it is
used or its economics.

> New Orleans Mayor **Moon Landrieu,** in a 1975
> exercise-in-reelection thinking.

12 The first day [he'd gone to the Superdome], somebody led me
from the parking lot to the dressing room, and I've been using that
route since. I'd be afraid to try another way. I might not make it
until halftime.

> **"Pistol Pete" Maravich** of the New Orleans Jazz,
> the Superdome's basketball home team.

13 The Superdome is a compromise. They have to be able to convert
from football to basketball to baseball to concerts and trade
shows.
When you feed in all those factors, you can't come out with a seat-
ing arrangement that is perfect for any one sport. I don't think
they will ever build a place like this again. Separate stadia are the
answer for sports, and they're cheaper.

> **Dick Gordon,** executive vice-president of the New
> Orleans Saints and a former astronaut, with a more
> cosmic view.

14 This golf course [the Harbor Town links on Hilton Head Island,
S.C.] is so good that there is no way you can attack it. You just go
for the pars and putt from 20 feet and hope for the best. You can't

even chip well from these fringes because they are so inconsistent. Some are grassy, some are sand, and you get lies that make it hard to chip with an 8-iron, sand wedge or pitching wedge. Some of the fellows are using putters just to get the ball rolling.

> Pro golfer **Frank Conner,** during the 1982 Heritage Classic. Conner finished second to Tom Watson.

When one exits Shea with its aeronautical backdrop on a dark **15** night, he feels the saucer stadium is going to elevate and whoosh off, like the fans, to God knows where.

> Sportswriter **Joe Flaherty,** on the new home field of the N.Y. Mets, in 1976.

2. MORE THAN MUSCLE: THE INNER ATHLETE

Psychology of the Game

The one statistic you won't find in any evaluation of two athletic opponents is a measurement of either one's brain waves. And even if there were a detailed EKG reading, it would tell you very little about his desire to win, his mental toughness, depth of concentration, or game expectations.

It's become a sports cliche that players must "psych themselves up" for a big game. This is largely a misconception. In an athletic contest of any duration, a calm and confident mental attitude is far preferable to the stresses that accompany revving one's self up. The latter does get the adrenalin flowing, which can be extremely useful for one big play—such as a key tennis serve or trying to kick the football through the uprights at an awkward angle from 42 yards out. But it also triggers a cordon of tension across the back and neck, which might help a sprinter, say, but would cripple a miler.

Mental set, therefore, can be as crucial a factor as talent. It is one of the component factors that makes sports fascinating; it's why, in part, the best teams don't always win. Contests are played by athletes who think—all the time. A dollop of worry here, a lurking doubt there, indecisiveness at a critical moment—all these psychic elements can escalate into a stunning defeat.

34

What do athletes do to forestall this runaway phenomenon? Well, a runner or a pitcher will concentrate on pacing himself, to wall out any tinge of doubt or fear by adhering to a disciplined regimen; a fighter will concentrate on going the distance, cognizant that a second enemy—exhaustion—is as menacing as his flesh-and-blood rival; a veteran jockey will try to block out the galloping hooves around him and the hysteria of the crowd by mentally ticking off the time fractions in which he thinks his horse is running the race.

The athlete, in short, fights his daemon psyche by getting his mind off it.

In this section, we try to come to grips with how athletes fight the loneliest battle, the one the crowds don't see: the internal one.

The main thing is to keep going. If I get blocked, I claw my way in, **1** even if I have to crawl. I don't give a damn who's coming—the competition gears me up. I don't hate. I don't see how an individual can hate you one minute, then shake your hand the next and say, 'I don't hate you no more.'

> Defensive end **Deacon Jones** of the Los Angeles Rams' late 1960s "Fearsome Foursome."

I begin psyching up the day before. I build up in my mind the idea **2** that the opposing team hates me and is actually going to try to hurt me, to cut off my career. So I build up this hatred and the idea that 'I'm going to hurt them first.' I never go out to deliberately disable someone—they have a family and kids and a career like us too. But when you play rough football, someone's going to get hurt.

> Los Angeles Ram tackle, **Roger Brown**.

The pitcher has to find out if the hitter is timid. And if the hitter **3** is timid, he has to remind the hitter he's timid.

> Telecaster **Don Drysdale,** reminiscing about his headhunting days.

But my big mistake was what I said to Joe [Louis] before the fight. **4** Some newspaper guy asked me to call Joe up and when I got him, I told him, 'Hey, bum, get in shape. I'm gonna eat your eyes out for grapes.' I think that made him get in shape for me.

> Two-Ton **Tony Galento,** explaining how he tried to unnerve Louis before their championship fight in 1939.

People don't seem to understand that it's a damn war out there. **5** Maybe my methods aren't socially acceptable to some, but it's

what I have to do to survive. I don't go out there to love my
enemy. I go out there to squash him.

Jimmy Connors, in 1973.

6 Inside me, I just go crazy. I mess up a backhand and tell myself,
'You creep,' and maybe throw my racquet to vent my emotions.
Then I see one coming and visualize just where I'm going to hit it,
and the shot's perfect—and I feel beautiful all over.

Billie Jean King, queen of all the clay courts she
surveyed in 1974.

7 I turn mean with a 6-stroke lead. I'm not happy with a 2-shot win.
I want more. I want to demoralize them. People used to say I
didn't have the killer instinct. Well, most people don't know me
very well.

Johnny Miller, no mean duffer in 1975.

8 What I do is mentally picture myself pitching to a batter and strik-
ing him out. Then, I work myself into a hate mood and make it a
personal battle between me and the batter. When my adrenalin is
really flowing, I try to channel it into something positive—like getting the s.o.b. out.

Itinerant relief pitcher **Al Hrabosky,** known as the
"Mad Hungarian."

9 I like to fall a little behind in a race and survey things. If the
tempo is too fast, I'll hold my position. If it's too slow, I'll
take off. Whether I'm in the lead or not, I feel I'm always in
control.

Long-distance runner **Rick Wohlhuter,** after a 26-
victories streak in 1975.

10 I consider myself the fastest man alive. I have to believe that in
order to compete at this level.

Sprinter **Steve Riddick,** winner of 15 out of 16 heats
during the 1976-77 winter indoor season.

11 The public pressure was the big thing that drove me out of it.
Every time you stepped on the line, you were expected to perform
at your peak. The public recognizes adulation, but they don't realize the responsibility that goes with it.

World-record miler **Jim Ryun,** on why he dropped
out of professional racing.

12 I think I feel emotions more than most players. I have a drive, a
burning desire to win every time I step on a court . . . . I don't have

the serve of Martina [Navratilova] or the speed of Rosie [Casals], so I compensate.

> **Chris Evert** in March 1977, before she was eliminated in a lackluster performance at Wimbledon.

A race horse is a hypersensitive animal. He can sense if a jockey isn't **13** feeling well, is upset or scared. The hands and reins the jockey uses on a horse are like a telephone people use to communicate. It's a very delicate situation between jock and horse. A rider's attitude has a lot to do with the way a horse runs.

> **Patrick Day,** perhaps the first jockey to parlay meditation into more winning mounts.

It gives them a lot more to think about. When Gaylord [Perry] was **14** throwing it, we used to walk up and down the dugout saying, 'Forget about it, hit the dry side.' He'd throw it twice and you'd be looking for it on 116 pitches.

> Former Baltimore Orioles manager **Earl Weaver** in 1977, on the effectiveness of throwing the spitter, even when you don't.

Just to think about [Dick Butkus] was intimidating. I'd come up **15** over the ball and instead of thinking: 'I'm going to take three steps at a 45-degree angle and cut him off and I'm going to knock his knees out from under him,' I'd wonder: 'What's he going to do to me now? Where is he?'

> Center **Bill Curry,** who spent 10 years in pro football (1965-75), describing the "terrifying presence" of linebacker Dick Butkus.

He's [Bert Jones] arrogant. He's always smiling at you and jump- **16** ing around. He knows he has the officials protecting him. It's one of the tactics he uses to try to tick people off. You try to whack him and the official sees it. You never win, he always wins.

> **Carl Barzilauskas,** former New York Jets tackle, explaining why ex-Baltimore Colt Bert Jones was the quarterback he wanted to sack most.

On this team I don't have to be a hero, stopping a lot of shots. My **17** job is to stop the rare tough shots, so the other team can't get inspired by a goal. If I do that, I can psychologically suffocate an opponent.

> Former Montreal Canadiens goalie **Ken Dryden,** en route to his portion of the 1977 Stanley Cup.

We sometimes have to hold closed meetings before a game to get **18** ourselves interested.

> Former Montreal Canadiens coach **Scotty Bowman,**
> two-thirds of the way through the 1976-77 season, in
> which his team lost only eight regular-season games.

19 I didn't let my last game bother me at all. If you do that, you
become a mental midget.

> Former Philadelphia 76er All-Star guard **Doug
> Collins,** following a 1977 playoff game in which he
> scored only 12 points. Next time out, he tripled his
> output.

20 When I got hot I started to call for it. Sometimes you get to be
selfish and say 'Give it here.' But the guys were looking for me. In
the playoffs, you go to the hot hand and milk it.

> **Ibid**.

21 I am the best. That's my belief. If people think I'm cocky, it's just
because I'm highly competitive. It's one of the things I need to feel
to keep my edge. I just want the respect of the hitters.

> Former California Angel ace **Frank Tanana,** before
> the 1977 season.

22 If you can break your opponent's will, you can make him give up.
If you hit hard on every play, it starts to work on the opponent's
mind. And if you keep doing it, he's going to forget some defense.
When you get a guy thinking survival above all else, you sense
you've got him and maybe the rest of his team, too.

> New York Giant draft choice and ex-Stanford tackle
> **Gordon King,** the fourth collegian chosen in the
> 1978 draft.

23 He's a very easygoing big guy, and that's why he is fighting the
battle of the minors. He's just not tough enough. He's one of the
strongest players I've ever seen, but he doesn't have any aggres-
sion in his soul.

> Philadelphia Flyers general manager **Keith Allen,**
> describing much-traveled Mike "Suitcase" Korney,
> who had skated for 13 teams over a five-year span.

24 I don't know what happened, my legs went, I don't know why. I
almost had him. I never thought he would be that tough. Normally
when I hit a guy, he goes down. I think the title kept him up.

> South African challenger **Gerrie Coetzee,** after
> being knocked out by former WBA champ Mike
> Weaver in a seesaw slugfest in 1980.

My temperament wouldn't allow me to play tight end in the NFL   **25**
like I did in college. I like to inflict the pain instead of taking it.
> Houston Oiler linebacker **Robert Brazile,** in 1980.

Hitters always have that fear that one pitch might get away from   **26**
him and they'll wind up D.O.A. with a tag on their toe.
> New York Yankee pitcher **Rudy May** in 1981, on the
> intimidating effect of teammate Goose Gossage's ris-
> ing fastball.

Right then and there I found out that he [Randy Jones] couldn't   **27**
pitch at Shea. I've seen it happen to pitchers before. They hate to
pitch in certain parks and they worry about it. But I never seen a
pitcher who had this kind of problem in his own park.
> New York Mets manager **George Bamberger** on
> Randy Jones, looking back to spring of the 1982
> season. A Cy Young Award winner with San Diego,
> Jones had a 3-15 record at Shea Stadium in his two
> years with the Mets.

We had a golden opportunity to show we had risen to their level of   **28**
confidence and we didn't do it. We could have faced the same
situation with a dozen other clubs and gone out in the third period
and just blitzed them. But against the Islanders, we have so much
more to prove. We're certainly not afraid of them talent-wise, but
to be a winner, you have to beat a winner.
> New York Ranger defenseman **Andre Dore,** after the
> Islanders overcame a 3-0 deficit and came back to win
> over their local rivals, 4-3, in an early 1982-83 season
> game.

Rivalry

Rivalry is as integral to sports as fire is to cooking. When New York
Giant manager Bill Terry asked reporters looking for a story if
Brooklyn was still in the league he didn't expect to unleash such a
Pandora's box of reaction. But he had violated one of the cardinal
rules of winning: never stir up a dormant opponent. In fact, Brooklyn

was not only still in the league, but they managed to knock the Giants out of the pennant race. It is a lesson many have learned and practice: go out of your way to say nice (or at least soothing) things about those who can hurt you.

During and immediately after the Depression, rivalries were taken more personally: the annual Army-Navy game, Pitt vs. Fordham, NYU's Violets and Villanova, the Yankees and whichever team rose to challenge them. Even in the ring, where the largely synthetic ethnic hype had worn pretty thin by the 1930s, there were suddenly the two Louis-Schmeling confrontations with their undisguisable ideological implications, the Brown Bomber vs. the Aryan Superman, 15 rounds to the death.

With the postwar expansion, rivalries became more blatantly financial, a struggle for turf and the sports dollar. Could New York support three baseball teams? Boston two? Washington one? What about the Sun Belt, the South, the Northwest?

When both the Giants and Dodgers pulled up roots and decamped for California (giving birth to late box scores and not knowing outcomes until the following day), sports fans sensed that the era of great team rivalries was in eclipse. There was still, of course, head-to-head rivalry between individuals: Ali and Foreman, Evert and Navratilova, Bart Starr and Len Dawson, Nicklaus and Watson, Billy Martin and the world. Terms like "fierce competitors" and "gamers" were heard more often now—for players like Enos Slaughter and Pete Rose, George Blanda and Gordie Howe, Jerry West and Willis Reed.

The sense of rivalry had lost some of its connection to rooted place or home team or tradition, and been transferred to the level of the one-on-one encounter.

1   After our [the New York Giants] last game in Brooklyn during the '51 season, the Dodgers had a comfortable lead, and Jackie was banging on that door [separating the team locker rooms] with a bat and screaming, 'You guys are finished! We'll never see you again!' One of the guys yelled back, 'Robinson, you're a no-good nigger bastard!' And Monte Irvin looked up at him and said, 'I guess that goes for me, too.' There was a terrible silence . . . .

The thing is, they did see us again, in the playoffs. When we got to Ebbets Field before the first game, the Dodgers were taking BP [batting practice]. Our guys elected me to be spokesman. About six of us went up to the cage, very quietly. I said, 'Hey, Jackie, look who's here.' I'll say one thing for him. He never turned around. He just kept swinging.

Ex-New York Giant **Bill Rigney** in 1982, recalling the blood rivalry between the Giants and Dodgers 30

hit his dramatic home run in 9th inning of final playoff game.

Oddly enough, I think I shared more of my appreciation for championship basketball with my opponents, especially with those who were good enough themselves to elevate games to that special level I sought. Throughout my career I spent a lot of time off the court with Wilt Chamberlain, Elgin Baylor and Oscar Robertson. We never talked much about basketball, which in itself was a relief, and we had nothing to prove to each other, which helped us relax. We never became intimate friends, but I always enjoyed being with them, because they made the game so much fun for me. I felt we shared a special kind of camaraderie, like professional soldiers.

2

> **Bill Russell,** recalling the championship years in the 60s with the Boston Celtics and the competitors who were good enough to transcend team rivalry.

Why should I worry about batters? Do they worry about me? Do you ever find a hitter crying because he's hit a line drive through the box? My job is getting hitters out. If I don't get them out, I lose. I've got a right to knock down anybody holding a bat.

3

> **Early Wynn,** justifying his oft-thrown high inside pitch. Pugnaciousness and talent got Wynn 300 wins, and a niche in the Hall of Fame.

If you want to know how competitive a player is, you ask for a 'gut check.' 'Give me a gut check on this guy.' The answer will be that the kid is or is not a *competitor.* That's the biggest word, competitor. The scout will say, 'This kid is looking for something to hit; if it moves, he hits it. My God, I'm telling you this kid is a *competitor.*'

4

> **Anonymous football scout** giving George Plimpton the inside story on what the scouting organizations look for in a prospect.

After you hit 80 [stolen bases], the other players gun for you. The first baseman slams you with his mitt on pick-off attempts, the pitcher concentrates on getting you instead of the batter, and the catcher isn't even behind the plate. On my last steal in 1962 [the year Wills set a record with 104 stolen bases], the catcher was over in the batter's box waiting to throw me out.

5

> Fleet **Maury Wills,** former Los Angeles Dodger, praising Lou Brock's record (118 steals in 1974), which lasted until Ricky Henderson stole 130 bases in 1982.

6 I'm egotistical. I realize that. People say I'm a low-key guy, but I
want that title back. I'm jealous of Muhammad Ali for having it.
Man, I really hate not being champion.

> **George Foreman,** in 1976, 15 months after his loss
> to Ali in Zaire.

7 I want the Reds to win the pennant, 'cause we're gonna win ours. I
just don't want any team in the National League . . . . I want the
Reds. I want to take Pete Rose's ugly face and stick it in the mud.
And when we win, we're gonna pop off like they did.

> **Billy Martin,** New York Yankees manager in January
> 1977.

8 The dunk has come back. It's more than just a basket. It's like a
slap in the face [to the defender]. You do it on the playgrounds
and you try to do it again and a guy will low-bridge you. 'Cause
you're hitting at his pride. A slap in the face is worse than a punch
 in the face.

> Former Philadelphia 76er guard **Fred "Mad Dog"
> Carter.**

9 North and Hood both promised to sell sails to me . . . . Then North
reneged. I called him right to his face a no-good, lying S.O.B. He
compromised the principles of good sailing. It's never been done
before in the history of yachting, and it's a new low in sportsman-
ship. I hope he sinks. No, don't use that. I just want to beat him.

> Maverick **Ted Turner** raking his yachting rivals over
> the coals before the 1977 America's Cup. Turner got
> the best revenge—he won the race.

10 Last year I was assaulted by George Steinbrenner's Nazis, his
Brown Shirts. He brainwashes those kids over there and they're
led by Billy Martin—Hermann Goering 2nd. They've got a convicted felon running the club. What else do you expect?

> **Bill Lee,** a Boston Red Sox pitcher in 1977, who
> injured his shoulder the previous year in a fight with
> the Yanks' Graig Nettles.

11 The National and American leagues, it's been like the Civil War.
The two leagues have got to start communicating and exchanging
ideas and get to the point that one league doesn't say, 'The National suggested this, bleep it,' or 'The American League suggested that, so let's axe it.'

> **Unidentified baseball official,** following 1977 own-
> ers' meeting that considered, among other matters,
> interleague play.

Those huckleberries in the National League didn't want to do any-   **12**
thing that the American League wants to do.

>   Yankee broadcaster **Phil Rizzuto,** commenting on
>   the alternating designated hitter rule for World Series
>   play, during a New York-Toronto telecast.

We all know he's the best, but the attitude of the younger players   **13**
is, if they have their day, they're going to best him. They don't
want to finish good, they want to win.

>   Twenty-five-year-old **Ben Crenshaw,** speaking of
>   Jack Nicklaus during the 1977 Masters, won by 27-
>   year-old Tom Watson.

I'd been living off the fastball and a kind of mediocre curve. If the   **14**
curve wasn't working, they'd get pretty choosy about which
fastball they wanted to hit. I'll tell you, you can't live off a fastball
alone.

>   Kansas City pitcher **Dennis Leonard,** explaining why
>   (with Marty Pattin's help) he developed a slider.

I'll follow the S.O.B. [Bjorn Borg] to the ends of the earth.   **15**
Everywhere he turns he'll see my shadow.

>   **Jimmy Connors,** solemn vow after losing to Bjorn
>   Borg at Wimbledon in 1978. He's been following him
>   ever since, and caught up with him (temporarily) in
>   1982.

It's [football] a guessing game. A game of strategy. Me as   **16**
commander in chief, out there against their commander in chief,
probably a linebacker, calling all the defensive signals. It's a battle
of minds between the two of us.

>   Pittsburgh Steelers quarterback **Terry Bradshaw** in
>   1980, looking at football as a military campaign.

I've never walked on the field when I thought I was going to be a   **17**
backup quarterback.

>   **Ken Stabler,** after signing with the New Orleans
>   Saints in August 1982, presumably as Archie
>   Manning's backup. Soon after, Kenny became number
>   one quarterback and Manning was traded.

Both of them needed the ball and they didn't complement each   **18**
other well. There was only one ball and it didn't work out.

>   Seventy-sixers' coach **Billy Cunningham,** on why the
>   teaming up of Julius Erving and George McGinnis did
>   not bring Philadelphia an NBA title.

19 Look, if a guy stands in my crease and wiggles his rump in my face, what does he expect? The puck hits him, goes into the net, he does a little dance with his hands in the air. I say, if you want the luxury of a dance, you're gonna have to suffer a little pain.

> New York Islanders goalie **Billy Smith,** meting out frontier justice in 1982.

20 At Wimbledon there's an A locker room, where all of the top-seeded players dress, and a B locker room, which the qualifiers and the junior players are assigned to. Most of the guys in the B locker room are living on a shoestring, eating cheap food and sharing a tiny flat in Earl's Court with four or five other players. But that gives them a tremendous feeling of camaraderie—it's us against them. I've seen a player come back after beating someone from the A locker room, and everyone will stand up and cheer him.

> Veteran qualifier **Erik van Dillen,** who has been in and out of the top ranks of tennis, in 1982—the year Bjorn Borg was disciplined by being dropped temporarily into the "qualies."

21 We like the challenge of playing the No. 1 team in the country. It may show that we have no sense but we're looking forward to it, anyway.

> Houston basketball coach **Guy Lewis,** before his team's Final Four NCAA championship tournament match with North Carolina in 1982. Lewis was right on both counts; the Tar Heels prevailed, 68-63, and went on to clinch championship against Purdue.

22 There's no power shortage at Shea.

> **New York Mets slogan** for 1982—a subtle swipe at their more successful intracity rival. On the power front, the Mets had added George Foster while the Yanks were losing Reggie Jackson.

23 I know how crazy I made myself in 1979. I know these titles are not worth making yourself crazy for. I am not that same person I was then. But I want it, the title. How can I stop now?

> **Laffit Pincay Jr.,** winner of five Eclipse Awards (outstanding jockey of the year), in October 1982. Pincay has earned more money than any other jockey in five of the previous 11 years by helicoptering from track to track in California to ride day-night double-headers.

Pressure

In sports, pressure can come from so many different sources: from management, from coaches, from the team itself, from the fans, hungry for victory. It can instill and nurture a fear of failure, a fear of letting the team down, of letting the fans down. In differing circumstances, it can impel a player to excel or render him numbly inept.

Even worse than the external pressures to perform are the internalized ones. Then it is the waiting and the thinking about disastrous possibilities that becomes the innervating enemy. It leads to such physical symptoms as nervousness and nausea, sweating and dizziness. It is the mind doubting what the muscles know they can do, the mind saying, "Yes, you can do them—if I let you . . . ."

Both Joe DiMaggio and Roger Maris have admitted that the only time they found peace during their record-breaking hitting accomplishments was when they were actually on the playing field—in the eye of the storm, so to speak. Being in the game was a relief from the hobgoblins of insidious thought. DiMaggio used to try to find refuge in the last row of the virtually empty Radio City Music Hall on afternoons the Yankees weren't playing, a lone figure fleeing from the pressure cooker of fame. For Maris, probably because of the asterisk next to the historic "61," it went on for years after he broke Ruth's record, and in a very real sense shortened his career.

Pressure, in short, kills. Think of that the next time a player sets a new record or supersedes an old one. Note that among the first things he says will be: "I'm glad it's over . . . ."

Putting affects the nerves more than anything. I would actually get nauseated over three-footers, and there were tournaments when I couldn't keep a meal down for four days. **1**
      Byron Nelson, in 1970.

Oh, the poor kid. He's going to get an ulcer now. **2**
      Laura Quilici, mother of newly named (July 1972) Minnesota Twins manager Frank Quilici.

The joy of winning doesn't motivate me anymore. It's the fear of losing. **3**
      Shot-putter **Randy Matson,** a former world champion, just prior to failing to qualify for the 1972 Olympics.

4 The games were the easy part. Those hours were the only times
when I got any relief from the pressure.

> **Roger Maris,** reflecting on his 61-homer season a
> dozen years later.

5 Every day I went to the ball park—in Yankee Stadium as well as
on the road—people were on my back. The last six years in the
American League were mental hell for me. I was drained of all my
desire to play baseball.

> **Roger Maris,** in early 1977.

6 I not pressing. I just in slump. I too old to be pressing. This just
one of those things. Tomorrow another day. Got to go day by day,
that's all.

> **Tony Perez,** Cincinnati first baseman in 1975, after
> four hitless World Series games. In the fifth game,
> then 0 for 15, he hit consecutive home runs.

7 A big stone had dropped from my heart. The whole nation trusted
me, and I won.

> Austria's **Franz Klammer,** after setting a new world
> downhill skiing record in the 1976 Winter Olympics.

8 I had bad days on the field. But I didn't take them home with me.
I left them in a bar along the way home.

> Former Cleveland pitcher **Bob Lemon** (207-128), at
> his Hall of Fame induction ceremony.

9 I love it. I feel most relaxed when the pressure is the greatest. It
reduces the situation to where you can see the result immediately.
You either make the play or you don't.

> **Mike Newlin,** a Houston Rocket guard in 1976.

10 There's no pressure here. This is a lot of fun. Pressure is when
you have to go to the unemployment office to pick up a check to
support four people.

> Kansas City Royals third baseman **George Brett,** in
> 1977.

11 Pressure is everything. We teach the girls that they can't slow
down in training for even a day, because their roommate or somebody else will eat them up alive in competition. They've got to be
careful, or their best friend will beat them. Lie down for a day, and
you're *finished.*

> **Don Peters,** coach at Grossfeld's School of Gymnas-
> tics in Milford, Conn., which specializes in training
> young girls for the Olympics.

I had a checkup today and the doctor said I've got some tension   **12**
problems, which is an NBA coaches' disease.

> Thirty-eight-year-old **Larry Brown,** stepping down
> as coach of the Denver Nuggets in 1979, despite a
> very impressive overall record (272-158).

The pressures to win are getting unreal. Football and basketball   **13**
are the income producers, and if you don't sell tickets, you're out
of a job. So a coach who needs a player real bad will bend the
rules a little to keep him eligible. Once you bend them a little, you
bend them a little more.

> Former L.S.U. football coach **Charlie McClendon** in
> 1980, on the faking of college credits and transcripts.

The administrators don't have the guts to say, 'You're going to   **14**
have to win seven games a year, and you're going to have to go to
a bowl game every year, and you're going to have to win the conference every five years, and one other thing—you have to fill the
stadium to 90 percent capacity. And then you can stay.'

> Former Wisconsin football coach **John Coatta** in
> 1982, remembering the spoken and unspoken
> demands of a big-time college program in the late 60s.

I'm just going to try to keep telling myself that I'm hot. The thing I   **15**
don't want to do is put pressure on myself. But it's hard not to
think about what I'm hitting. My average is in the papers every
day and every time I go up to hit in Royals Stadium, it's up there
out in center field on the scoreboard that's as high as a six-story
building.

> Kansas City's **George Brett,** on the media focus on a
> man hitting .400, in late August 1980. Brett stayed
> close till the last week of the season, and finished with
> a .390 average.

The horse is still a baby and it's so dark out there. Then the   **16**
bright lights of the infield [totalisator boards], he just shied away.
I was getting some water down my goggles, but it was tough conditions for everybody out there.

> Jockey **Eddie Maple,** riding favorite Akureyri in the
> 1980 Remsen Stakes, against a driving rain. The fea-
> ture race for two-year-olds was won by Pleasant
> Colony, but darkness and downpour forced cancella-
> tion of ninth race.

Just getting in front of the camera in front of millions of people is   **17**
pressure in itself. To take an announcer's comment—one line in
an entire broadcast—and then take it out of context and make him

look foolish, is ridiculous. I mean, everything's ad-libbed. Johnny
Carson is reading off cue cards.

> Veteran sportscaster **Al Michaels,** during the 1982
> National League playoffs, commenting on some of the
> flak he has gotten over the years.

18 We have Little League syndrome with gymnastics parents. I've
heard mothers say to their daughters: 'We're paying all this money. Why can't you win?' I've had to tell mothers to stay out of the
gym and leave the coaching to me. I tell them to give the child ten-
der loving care and don't belittle her if she isn't performing well. If
the mother won't do that, it's time for the child to get out of
gymnastics.

> Coach **Dick Mulvihill,** who is training teen-aged
> gymnasts for the 1988 Olympics.

19 In four minutes of free skating you're being judged on a whole
year of practice. Not many sports put you through that, being the
focal point of the entire arena. You've got to look like you're
enjoying yourself and accept the judges' decision and not throw a
tomato at them. It's tough.

> **Peggy Fleming,** a world figure-skating champ at 17,
> Olympics winner at 19.

20 Qualifying is not as easy as many people think. They say, 'You
play the qualifications, an easy three matches.' But it doesn't
work that way. The concentration and preparation is so much different, and there are a lot of good guys in the qualifications. And
say you get through the qualifying, you feel like 'Jeez, I've played
these three matches, now I've got to play a tournament!'

> **Bjorn Borg,** after losing to Dick Stockton in the
> second qualifying round of the 1981 Alan King-Caesar's
> Palace Tennis Classic in Las Vegas.

21 I think everybody's vulnerable to coming apart at one time or
another, Somebody said to me the other day that if it got to
Reggie Jackson last year, with all the thick-skinnedness he had,
they didn't see why it shouldn't get to me, too. It's like a guy who
has a job putting five screws in a car. When he's got his headphones on and is listening to music with nobody bothering him, he
can punch those five screws all day long. Then he takes the
headphones off, the boss comes along and bothers him and he
misses four out of five.

> **Bucky Dent,** who lost his job as New York's regular
> shortstop in early 1982 when the Yanks acquired Roy
> Smalley. In midseason, playing poorly, he was traded
> to Texas.

I don't care who you are, you're going to choke in certain matches. **22**
You get to a point where your legs don't move and you can't take a
deep breath. I've done it. Sure I have. I did it at the beginning of the
fifth set against Ilie Nastase in the 1972 Open. I could feel it happening. You'd start to hit the ball about a yard wide, instead of inches.

> **Arthur Ashe,** former captain of the American Davis
> Cup team, talking about pressure during the 1982
> U.S. Open.

The professional athlete has more stress than the average person. **23**
Every third athlete suffers an adverse effect from stress. They are
more stress-resistant than the average person but still, every third
of them breaks down.

> Psychiatrist **Gregory Raiport,** after Garry Tem-
> pleton, then with the St. Louis Cardinals, was
> hospitalized for psychiatric observation late in the
> 1981 season.

Winning

"We know how to win." George Brett made this oracular declaration
with one month to play in the 1982 season and Kansas City leading
the American League by a slim one-half game. Ironically, this statement was made only a few days after rumors that Brett himself was on
the trading block.

Presumably what Brett meant was that since the Royals had
"been there before," they'd be able to handle the pressures of a tight
race. But California, the main challenger, was loaded with veteran
players who'd also "been there before," and would be unlikely to
"choke." And, indeed, the Angels edged out Kansas City.

Mystiques about winning are laced with terms like the ones in
quotes above. Fans and players alike believe them and repeat them to
each other with religious fervor.

Oddly, only in football (among the major sports) is there a
maxim that flies in the face of all this codified winning and losing. "On
any given Sunday," it begins with measured judiciousness, "any NFL
team can beat any other NFL team." This egalitarianism seems
curiously out of place in a bruising game like football, which has no

time for niceties. Yet in no other major sport is there a similar deference to the acknowledged possibilities of upset victories. Maybe this has something to do with numbers: football squads run to 45 men and the traffic can get pretty heavy out there.

Still, it was also football that gave us the imperishable words of Vince Lombardi on winning: that it is the only thing (See: "Hall of Fame," pp.206). Maybe that inflexible position paper is the mother lode for all the other mystiques about winning.

Boxing, where the traffic is light, provides a democratic antidote to Lombardi's tight-jawed dictum. The last thing the referee says after the ring opponents touch gloves and get ready to square off is: "And may the best man win."

Fair enough.

1 To tell a competitive athlete who is training three and four hours a day, day in, day out, year after year, to be not concerned with victory is liberal snobbery. Or at best it is the remark of someone who simply doesn't understand the agonistic struggle that is an integral part of the competitive sports experience. It is just as wrong to say winning isn't anything as it is to say winning is the only thing.

Jack Scott, mentor to agonistic athletes, in his unique role as Oberlin's athletic director in 1973.

2 His [Jack Sharkey's] chin was there to hit, what else could I do? A fighter must protect himself at all times, it says.

Jack Dempsey, recalling his 1927 defeat of Jack Sharkey, which won him a rematch with champ Gene Tunney. Dempsey, losing badly after seven rounds, "accidentally" fouled Sharkey, and as Sharkey turned to complain to the referee, Dempsey threw his knockout punch.

3 There was no way Jack [Nicklaus] could have made that putt, because I was standing right behind him mentally clutching his club.

Pete Brown, who won the 1970 San Diego Open after Nicklaus blew a four-foot putt.

4 —How many lanes in the pool, Mark?
—Six.
—How many lanes win, Mark?
—One.

Arnold Spitz, training his nine-year-old son Mark to be an Olympic swimmer. Mark got in the right lane.

5 I wanted that undefeated season more than anything I ever wanted in my life. I'd give anything—my house, my bank account, anything but my wife and family—to get it.

Former Ohio State football coach **Woody Hayes,** after losing 16-13 to Michigan State in 1974's last game. Hayes also lost the Rose Bowl bid—and his composure. He hit a fan.

Once you start keeping score, winning's the bottom line. It's the **6** American concept. If not, it's like playing your grandmother, and even then you try to win—unless she has a lot of money and you want to get some of it.

> **Al McGuire,** who coached Marquette to the 1977 NCAA championship.

I have to get mad to win. Billie Jean's the same way. And today I **7** didn't see the fire in her eyes.

> **Chris Evert,** after eliminating veteran Billie Jean King in the 1977 Wimbledon. But apparently Chrissie couldn't sustain her anger against Britain's Virginia Wade, who went on to win the cup.

The match is still going on as far as I'm concerned. There is no **8** winner. The match is still on my mind.

> **Jimmy Connors,** in refusing to accept his loss to Guillermo Vilas, after the controversial finish of the 1977 U.S. Open tennis championship. Connors strongly protested a belated foul call by a side lines- man on the final point of the fourth set.

Nobody wants a tie. The only time you want a tie is when you **9** come from behind with the Canadiens.

> Philadelphia Flyers' **Bobby Clarke,** back in the years when Montreal dominated the ice.

Talent is overrated. You win with character. In a short series, **10** talent might prevail. Over an 82-game [basketball] season, charac- ter prevails.

> Former player's agent **Lewis Schaffel,** who moved on to become general manager of the New Orleans Jazz.

In this game, you have to be a finisher. I call it 'finishing,' and you **11** don't learn it in Miss Hewitt's School for Young Ladies.

> Former light-heavyweight champ **Archie Moore.**

Winning is the epitome of honesty itself. **12**

> Former Ohio State coach **Woody Hayes,** carried away by his own rhetoric in September 1977. The

following afternoon Oklahoma beat the Buckeyes 29-28, on an honest 41-yard field goal with three seconds remaining.

13   What can I say? He's a totally different horse since he started drinking beer and put on that extra 150 pounds.

> Trainer **Billy McKeever,** explaining why Good La Quinta, a 5-year-old gelding, had suddenly turned to winning ways.

14   We came back from so far and beat the No. 1 team in the nation . . . . It happened so fast they didn't even know what was happening. They came in so confident, but in the overtime they lost all their composure. Too much confidence, you know? They were worried about their ranking. I mean, we weren't even ranked, and they were out there saying to themselves, 'I hope these chumps don't beat us.' Well, guess what?

> Diminutive Ohio State guard **Todd Penn** in 1978, following the Buckeyes victory over top-ranked Duke in overtime, 90-84, after trailing by 17 points with 13 minutes to play.

15   To go out on the field after all these years and expect to whip somebody else's tail for a change, that's a fun feeling, I'll tell you.

> **Don Money,** with the hard-hitting Milwaukee Brewers in 1978, after nine straight seasons with losing ball clubs.

16   Well, you saw . . . he was their best player . . . I can't explain it . . . sometimes you get mad . . . I get mad if I think someone is damaging my team . . . .

> New York Cosmo **Carlos Alberto,** after deliberately kicking Dallas Tornado star Omar Gomez on the back of the knee in a close game in 1980, knocking him out of action. The Cosmos went on to win.

17   There were 400,000 people at the track who watched me totally dominate and win the race. There were millions more watching on television. And not one person could say I didn't win that race. I just physically outran Mario Andretti and everybody else. I have no guilty conscience about anything I did. I'm just a helluva tough guy who played it close that day. That's what I'm paid to do. Nobody would pay me a lot of money if I was conservative. You play it as close as you can in this sport.

> **Bobby Unser,** looking back on the 1981 Indianapolis 500. Unser won the race, then was penalized and placed

second for passing other cars during a caution period.
After many months of controversy over the infraction,
the penalty was lifted and Unser was once again declared the winner.

I didn't want to win it by sneaking in the back door, but I did   **18**
sneak in the back door. My pride told me to play but my common
sense told me not to. I went with my common sense over my pride.
I'm glad it turned out that way. Robin [Yount] has probably won
everything else this season so why couldn't he let me win this? I'd
like to have played, but I wanted to win the batting title more.

Kansas City Royals **Willie Wilson,** who sat out the
last day of the season to win the American League batting championship with a .3316 average. Milwaukee's
Robin Yount went 3-for-4 (two home runs and a triple) that day, ended season with a .3307 average.

With Namath and Ali, it [egocentric behavior] was not falsely modest
but exciting. It seemed like an over-reaction to our image of the modest, self-effacing athlete. But now, it has become totally
obnoxious.

I went to two high school all-star games recently where the   **19**
kids had no affiliation or stake in the game. It was a chance for
them to show how good they are . . . . Instead, the kids were like
thugs. They needed to show their virility. I see that behavior in
the colleges and pros. The gestures and the putdowns of the
opposition. It's come to symbolize excellence. I try to tell my kids
the game is for fun, not humiliation.

Vic Gatto, Tufts University football coach, in 1982.

Losing

The two sports situations that seem to evoke prolonged thought are
preparing for a crucial game and losing a game, any game. Losing
makes the athlete stare down at his socks and wonder if he should
have bothered pulling them on that morning.

But there's "honorable" losing and "dishonorable" losing.
When the Canadiens were kings of the rink, no one apologized for losing

to them. Tying them was practically a victory, as the Flyers' Bobby Clarke pointed out, because they were "unbeatable." On the other hand, when Tampa Bay finally beat an NFL team in 1977 after 26 straight losses, the other team's coach said he was "ashamed," not only for himself and his players but for everyone in the organization. Why? Did he really expect that Tampa Bay would *never* win? Did he think that they had learned nothing from all those agonizing losses? All he cared about was the "dishonor" of losing to an expansion franchise that had never won before. Now that Tampa Bay has become more "respectable," opposing coaches no longer threaten self-immolation after getting trounced by the Bucs.

So much for dishonor. Another despicable side of losing is its supposed built-in contagion factor, and here a more viable case can be made. Losing, athletes firmly believe, begets more losing. The New York Mets, who haven't been contenders for a while, have announced that they are "going to get rid of the losers" at the end of 1982. Does this ensure another miracle in '83? The acquisition of two solid starters might better solve the problem. On the other side of town, a rash Rick Cerone blamed the Yankees lackluster play on the acquisition of so many players from losing teams all at once—forgetting that he himself came from last-place Toronto. Should teams trade only with contenders?

There are, of course, ballplayers who can fire up a team. Every winning team seems to have at least one. But winning is much more complex than that: it has to do with bringing together the proper combination of players who know how to pick each other up when things get tough, and equally important, how to submerge individual dazzle for the sacrificial team effort.

But if an athlete is drafted by a last-place club, how many swings around the league does it take before he is forever tainted as a "loser"? Is there no such thing as individual character, individual temperament? Is losing chronic, like herpes?

These are but two of the many mystiques about losing that spin the wheels of athletes and coaches, fans and sportswriters. For even more impenetrable mystiques, see the introduction to "Winning," page 49.

1   This team has shown me ways to lose I couldn't believe. You've got to look up and down the bench and say, 'Can't anyone here play this game?'
> New York Mets manager **Casey Stengel,** looking over his "Amazins" in the early 60s.

2   Show me a good loser, and I'll show you a loser.
> **Red Auerbach's** favorite acerbic comment on losing from his earlier coaching days.

Some days you eat the bear. Some days the bear eats you. Yesterday   **3**
the bear ate us.
> Favorite saying of **Preacher Roe,** back in the 40s
> and 50s when he was throwing the old dipsy doo for
> the Brooklyn Dodgers. The bear didn't eat Roe too
> often—in 1951, for example, he was a spectacular 22-3.

I don't want anybody in bed by midnight. Everybody is to go out   **4**
tonight and get loaded.
> Brooklyn Dodger manager **Charley Dressen** in the
> 1950s, after his team blew four straight to Philadelphia.
> The strategy worked; the Dodgers got back on track.

In 1967, Wilt [Chamberlain] and the Philadelphia 76ers beat us,   **5**
because they were better. They almost ran us off the court, and I
got an instant taste of the 'loser' syndrome. Though the Celtics
had run off an unprecedented string of eight consecutive championships before 1967, the fans in Boston hooted me that summer
in the streets. 'What happened to you guys last year?' 'All washed
up, eh?' 'I knew it couldn't last. You guys don't have it anymore.' I
had to blink my eyes.
> **Bill Russell,** in his 1979 book, *Second Wind.*

I'll be playing this one over in my mind for a long time. It's the   **6**
first time I've played a game over in my mind since my rookie
year, when I learned you shouldn't play a game over in your mind.
> New York Knick and Rhodes scholar **Bill Bradley,**
> after his team lost to the Lakers in the fourth game of
> the 1972-73 NBA playoff finals.

I want him like a hog wants slop.   **7**
> Heavyweight **Joe Frazier,** asked if he hoped to fight
> Muhammad Ali again, after his defeat in their brutal
> 1975 championship fight.

Ask him, [Willie Stargell] he saw it [the pitch] better than I did.   **8**
> **Jon Matlack,** with the New York Mets in 1976,
> asked after a losing effort what kind of pitch the
> Pirates' Willie Stargell had belted for a grand-slam
> homer.

You go so far, work so hard, play so many games, and then you   **9**
can see what you want, but you can't touch it . . . . It's going to take
a while before I get back to reality. I'll be sitting somewhere next
week and somebody will be talking to me, but I won't hear them. I'll
be daydreaming, totally involved in the [lost] game; second-
guessing.

New York Islanders defenseman **Dave Lewis,** after his team's 2-1 loss to Montreal and elimination from the 1977 Stanley Cup playoffs. Local hockey writers agreed that the Islanders should have won the game and that Lewis had played superbly despite an injured knee.

10   Hey, I have everything to be happy about, but I'm not. In the eyes of the media and my peers, I'm having a very good season, perhaps my best. I'm leading the league in scoring, but happiness in pro basketball is determined in the won-and-lost column, and we're not winning. Statistics are for losers.
> **"Pistol Pete" Maravich,** All-Pro guard of the 1976-77 New Orleans Jazz.

11   I hate to lose more than I like to win. I hate to see the happiness on their faces when they beat me.
> **Jimmy Connors,** runner-up to Bjorn Borg in the 1977 Pepsi Grand Slam tennis tournament, a match-up and result repeated at Wimbledon that same year.

12   We bring out the best in everybody.
> Seattle SuperSonics coach **Bill Russell,** who resigned after the 1976-77 season. His team finished last in their division, after a second-place finish the previous year.

13   I would rather not make any comment. We are all very ashamed of what happened. Ashamed for our people, our fans, the organization, everybody. It's my worst coaching experience.
> Former New Orleans coach **Hank Stram,** following the Saints' 33-14 loss to struggling Tampa Bay (0-12 in 1977, 0-26 as a franchise).

14   It's like Noah's wife told him. She said, 'Noah, honey, it's going to stop raining one of these days.'
> Chicago Cubs 1977 rookie pitcher **Mike Krukow,** after his fourth consecutive shelling, this one a 21-3 loss to the Cardinals. Noah's wife was right; Krukow went on to become an effective starting pitcher for the Philadelphia Phils.

15   This time of year, you get to ride a lot of cheaper races. Some of the horses just don't have it. Yet, when a trainer who has been giving an agent lots of horses to ride eventually offers him poor stock, the agent just can't say no.
> Seventeen-year-old jockey **Steve Cauthen,** after los-

ing 22 straight races in November 1977. The following day Cauthen had six winners, tying a track record.

All weekend the country watched other losing coaches standing on **16**
sidelines eating their livers in deference to the official cant that it
doesn't matter whether you win or lose. Not Woody [Hayes]. With
what can only be called fool's courage, considering his age and
physical condition, he responded like an Ahab determined to put
one last harpoon into the white whale that was destroying him.
> **Russell Baker's** sardonic view of the Woody Hayes
> firing in 1978. After an opposing player intercepted
> the ball, Hayes ran out and punched him.

It's bad enough losing, but to get up in the morning, hurt, and **17**
read that you're just a club fighter or a journeyman, that hurts.
> **Sandy LeDoux,** heavyweight Scott LeDoux's wife, in
> 1980. LeDoux has fought Holmes, Foreman, Ken
> Norton, Mike Weaver, and Duane Bobick.

It's never a matter of sameness. There's always a new way to lose. **18**
> **Archie Manning,** New Orleans quarterback in 1980,
> claiming that the timekeeper's alleged clock
> accelerations had cost the Saints their eighth straight
> loss.

We all played poorly. It wasn't just one guy's fault. It was a real **19**
team effort.
> Former Purdue coach **Arnette Hallman,** after his
> team was eliminated from the 1980 NCAA semifinals
> by UCLA, 67-62.

It [a home-run pitch] was God's will. **20**
> What San Francisco pitcher **Bob Knepper** is alleged
> to have said after serving up a game-winning home-
> run pitch in a 1980 game. Knepper moved on to
> Houston the following year.

I don't need anyone to remind me of that race. I've got it on **21**
videotape. I've played it at home about 10 times and I keep waiting for the end to be different. But it never changes.
> **Rick Mears,** after winning the Pocono 500 in 1982,
> referring to the Indianapolis 500 in the spring, in
> which he finished second to Gordon Johncock by a
> tantalizing 16/100ths of a second.

I've never seen him [Gerry Cooney] so depressed. He keeps **22** apologizing to everyone for what happened against Holmes. He tells us how he let everyone down. He just won't go back to the gym. I'm worried about him. It's more improbable than impossible, but Gerry might not fight again. Right now I'm more worried about the person than the fighter.

> **Mike Jones,** Gerry Cooney's co-manager, two months after the 1982 Holmes-Cooney championship fight.

23 I walked to the dressing room [after the fight], and they had to carry him [Sugar Ray Robinson]. He wouldn't fight me a third time.

> Former welterweight champ **Carmen Basilio,** recalling his only loss to Sugar Ray Robinson. Basilio had won their earlier fight.

24 That's when I knew we were dead. It was Red's [Holzman] attitude. He told me that during an 82-game season a team is going to lose some games. He said that after a loss, he would still have the same thing for breakfast the next morning and the same car would be in his garage. That's not what I wanted to hear.

> **Sonny Werblin,** president of the New York Knicks, about his coach at the end of the 1981-82 season. Hubie Brown replaced Holzman in May.

25 I thought about it all summer. When you lose like that in the last game of the season, it has to remain with you. I remember I was jogging this August and I was thinking, 'Boy, I can't wait to get back to them.' Those things are hard to forget.

> Pittsburgh goalie **Michel Dion,** recalling the fifth game of the first round of the 1982 NHL playoffs. Penguins led 3-1 in the final minutes, when Islander coach Al Arbour replaced goalie Billy Smith, giving his power-play unit time to catch its breath. The Islanders tied the score and went on to win in overtime.

Glory of the Game

"All the years I played basketball I looked for that perfect game." Thus says Bill Russell of the Boston Celtics (11 times professional champions), in his book, *Second Wind.* The parameters of "perfect," Russell goes on to say, included not only his own excellence of play and ability to infuse that spirit into his teammates, but the magical thing that occasionally happened in the competitive interaction with the opposing team; each team, by its court wizardry, impelling the other team to reach and then exceed its peak perfomance. Russell candidly admits that in those moments even the idea of winning receded, seemed less important than "levitating" into an exalted level of play.

Interestingly, on a perfection scale of 100, Russell never graded himself higher than 65 for any given game. A tough taskmaster.

What comes up again and again in the quotes below are the distortions of time, space, sound, and color in the midst of the game action at its best. It is as though the external world of the athlete is transformed by his supreme effort and the intensity of the struggle around him, while, oddly, his internal world remains tranquil and untouched. It is in these rare and unplottable moments that the purity of the game and the reason for playing it are realized.

[The magic feeling] never started with a hot streak by a single player, **1** or with a breakdown of the team's defense. It usually began when three or four of the 10 guys on the floor would heat up; they would be the catalysts, and they were almost always the stars in the league .... The feeling would spread to the other guys, and we'd all levitate. Then the game would just take off, and there'd be a natural ebb and flow that reminded me of how rhythmic and musical basketball is supposed to be. I'd find myself thinking, 'This is it. I want this to keep going,' and I'd actually be rooting for the other team. When their players made spectacular moves, I wanted their shots to go into the bucket; that's how pumped up I'd be. I'd be out there talking to the other Celtics, encouraging them and pushing myself harder, but at the same time part of me would be pulling for the other players too.

> **Bill Russell,** remembering playing at the top of his game with the championship Boston Celtics in the 1960s.

Ladies and gentlemen, here is the result of event No.9, the one- **2** mile. First, No. 41, R.G. Bannister of Exeter and Merton College, for the Amateur Athletic Association, with a time which is a new meeting and track record and which, subject to ratification, will be a new ... European, British Commonwealth and world record. The time is three minutes and 59.4 seconds.

> **Norris McWhirter,** reporting the outcome of the one-mile race to the 1,000 spectators at Oxford in

1954, the day Roger Bannister broke the four-minute
barrier.

3   I felt like an exploded flashlight with no will to live . . . . It was as if
all my limbs were caught in an ever-tightening vise. I knew that I
had done it before I even heard the time . . . .

> **Bannister,** after breaking the four-minute barrier for
> the first time.

4   The Yankees have all the hits in the game.

> Telecaster **Mel Allen's** way of telling the New York
> fans during a Yankee-Dodger World Series game that
> Don Larsen was pitching a perfect no-hitter on Octo-
> ber 8, 1956, the only time it's ever been done. Recall-
> ing the telecast in 1981, Allen remarked that it was
> the only way he could think of to avoid the then-taboo
> phrase, "no-hitter."

5   Running into the line, you go into a different world. All around you
guys are scratching, clawing, beating on each other, feeling pain.
There are noises from the crowd and from the linemen, but during
that one moment, I never seem to hear them. Then, going back to
the huddle, the sound of the pads slamming together will still be
in my ears and I'll listen for the first time. The sensation gives a
real insight into the game. It's too bad more people haven't been
in there, where football is really played.

> **Larry Csonka,** All-Pro fullback of the Miami
> Dolphins in 1972.

6   During the run there is a panorama of feeling and sensation—
luscious colors, feelings of weightlessness, a sense of everything
being quiet and an overwhelming sense of accomplishment. And,
oh yeah, it's freaky as hell.

> **Jack McClure,** in 1972, explaining why he had given
> up stock car racing for drag racing.

7   We have sailed some lovely miles alone, the old girl and I, but I
don't go out on the ocean for the sake of being on my own. Solitude isn't what I seek. I must have a sense of purpose behind a
solitary sail and that overcomes the solitude. There are loners of
the sea, men who wish not to speak to others and who avoid all
ports of call because that is the cut of their personality . . . . But for
me, a single-handed sail is part of an idea that leads to something
other than solitude itself.

> **Alain Colas,** single-handed ocean sailor, speaking of
> the *Pen Duick IV,* in which he won the 1972 Plymouth

(England) to Newport (Rhode Island) transatlantic race in 20 days, 13 hours, almost six days less than the previous record.

There is no sense of being an infinitesimal, helpless speck in the **8** universe when you are sailing in solitude. This is because you become the center of your own universe, you give birth to your own island, to your own nation when you sail alone. Soon enough, you sail her right out of the ocean and into your own small circle of being.

> **Alain Colas,** in November 1978, shortly before he entered his last race, the new transatlantic race for single-handers, called La Route du Rhum. Colas was lost at sea.

I'd rather hit than have sex. To hit is to show strength .... God, **9** do I love to hit that little round sum-bitch out of the park and make 'em say 'Wow!'

> **Reggie Jackson,** with Oakland in 1974, the year after he earned MVP honors.

I knew he was hurt, and that if he did get up he'd be hurt some **10** more. When you land a good punch you can feel it in your arm, your shoulder, your hip, your toes, your toenails ....

> Heavyweight **Ken Norton,** after knocking out Duane Bobick 58 seconds into the first round of their 1977 fight.

What was the biggest kick? What was the best thing about coach- **11** ing? It was this: playing when nobody else was playing. Everybody else had gone home ... there was just your team and some other guys .... The championships were great, but that playing last was the best.

> New York Knicks coach **Red Holzman,** just before he retired (at management's request) after ten years of coaching, including getting into eight playoffs, over 500 wins, and two world championships.

I get a kick out of watching a team defense me. A player moves **12** two steps in one direction and I hit it two steps the other way. It goes right by his glove. And I laugh.

> Master batsman **Rod Carew** in 1979, on hitting it where they ain't.

I played the game with an innate smile. **13**

> New York Knick **Earl "the Pearl" Monroe,** hanging it up at 36 in 1980.

14 Winning in Scotland beats winning anywhere else. I'm a
traditionalist and a sentimentalist, and there's nothing like winning a championship in the birthplace of golf. This tournament is
what golf is all about. You cannot love golf anymore than you do
when you come down the 18th fairway of this golf course a
champion.

> **Tom Watson,** after winning the British Open for the
> third time, at Muirfield in 1980.

15 I've been watching these guys [the New York Islanders] for the
last six or seven years, since they've been very strong. I'm still in
awe of all those players. To stop them is just the most joy I can
experience.

> Pittsburgh goalie **Michel Dion,** talking about the team
> that had won the Stanley Cup three straight seasons.
> Penguins nearly upset the Islanders in the 1982
> playoffs, in which goalie Dion played with determina-
> tion and brilliance.

Real Pros

The real pro performs heroics that are frequently overlooked. He
doesn't usually make headlines or play spectacularly, though sometimes he does both. His true value lies in his unspectacular consis-
tency or his ability to fill in or give a discouraged team an unexpected
lift. He's the man you can depend on in a volatile situation, the man
who comes through when you most need him.

Phil Jackson in his "sixth-man" role with the Knicks; Cookie
Rojas, the most versatile—and peskiest hitting—Philadelphia Phil of
all time; George Blanda in his unique (and seemingly perennial) role
as interim quarterback/kicker for the Oakland Raiders are examples
of the real pro at his best.

There is also about these men a sense of sacrifice for the good
of the team, an unquenchable pride that commands the best from
them even when it's clear that the team may not truly value the
limited role they play so well. Former New York Ranger defenseman
Carol Vadnais and former Yankee Roy White come to mind—fighting
for a job (or just to stick with the team) nearly every year, hanging in

doggedly, excelling when the chips were down.

It is, of course, the players more than the fans who recognize who the real pros are. They (the players) have an intimate knowledge of the game which extends to its hidden aspects, to all those obscure corners of the action that the fans aren't generally aware of. Or care about. And that, generally, is the arena where the real pro operates.

There are two games out there. The one that gets televised is the   **1**
game with the ball. I may not play in that at all . . . . I'm playing where
the ball is not.
> Veteran tackle **Merlin Olsen** of the Los Angeles
> Rams in 1967.

I'd had it and this was the end. I wanted to hit the ball and get out   **2**
of there. [Jack] Fisher threw me a fastball and for the only time in
my life I didn't know whether I was ahead of the pitch or behind,
over the ball or under it. It flashed through my mind, 'This guy
thinks he can throw it past me.' Next time he threw, I was
swinging.
> **Ted Williams,** in the last at-bat of his career in 1960,
> facing Baltimore Orioles' pitcher Jack Fisher.
> Williams hit the second pitch out of Fenway Park.

I lost 24 games my first year with the Mets. you've got to be a   **3**
pretty good pitcher to lose that many. What manager is going to
let you go out there that often?
> **Roger Craig,** looking backward in 1968.

You have to analyze a hitter a bit more carefully than before. You   **4**
have to know exactly where to play him [on Astroturf] because
your range is drastically reduced. Only the smartest infielders will
survive on the stuff.
> Slick-fielding **Bud Harrelson** in 1970, when he was
> the anchor of the New York Mets' tight defense.

Now, what the hell. Do you think I'd admit to that?   **5**
> Retired NL ump **Augie Donatelli,** asked if he'd ever
> made a bad call.

On a good team there are no superstars. There are great players,   **6**
who show they are great players by being able to play with others,
as a team. They have the ability to be superstars, but if they fit
into a good team, they make sacrifices, they do the things
necessary to help the team win. What the numbers are in salaries
or statistics don't matter; how they play together does.
> Former New York Knick coach **Red Holzman,** des-

cribing what his 1976-77 team wasn't doing.

7 I think the players before were much smarter, but the guys today have more ability. The guys that played in the 1960s and early 1970s were thinking guys. When they got you down, you didn't come back.

> Former New York Knick **Earl Monroe,** looking at the changes.

8 A linesman is measured by how many plays the guy across from you makes. John [Hicks] had such a good game, you never heard Dave Butz's name mentioned. That's how you measure offensive linemen—by how few negative things are [said] against them. We're a lot like the defensive backs—if they do good coverages, nobody throws the ball in their direction and no one hears about them. Maybe that's why we're the lowest-paid position in football.

> Former New York Giant reserve guard **Bill Ellenbogen,** after a 1977 game, assessing teammate John Hicks and offensive linemen in general.

9 All world records can be knocked down two or three seconds if you can turn off your pain switch. The major portion of training is to put yourself through as much pain as possible. Then, in a race, you get to a point where that amount of pain doesn't bother you.

> Olympic swimming champ **Mike Bruner,** after winning the 1977 200-meter butterfly final.

10 If a jockey in Europe wins by more than three or four lengths, he's considered a bad rider. You have to think of the handicap races, where lengths mean extra pounds.

> Seattle Slew's jockey, **Jean Cruguet,** after coasting to a four-length victory in the Belmont Stakes to win the Triple Crown in 1977. Cruguet was responding to criticism that his horse was a full 5 and three-fifths seconds off the track-record clocking.

11 I hold my breath with her every week. Hell, she's racing on a wing and a prayer. She looks good during the race because she's so game. All her hurts, she throws them away when she sees the bright lights.

> Trainer **Lou Meittinis** about his veteran pacer, Paula Scott N, a consistent winner despite her bad legs.

12 If I had had the attitude that I had to play every day to be happy, I wouldn't be here right now ... I'd rather be a swing man on a championship team than a regular on another team.

> Versatile New York Yankee outfielder **Lou Piniella,** in 1978.

His best weapon is his chin.   **13**

> **Richie Giachetti,** Marvin Hagler's manager,
> speaking about former middleweight champ Vito
> Antuofermo in 1980. Champ Hagler agreed, calling
> Antuofermo "by far the toughest guy I ever fought."

He threw me some good pitches. He didn't try to finesse me at all. **14**
It just wasn't meant to be 32, because there was no way I
shouldn't have got a hit on those pitches.

> **Ken Landreaux,** with the Minnesota Twins in 1980,
> after hitting in 31 straight games, the longest
> American League hitting streak in 31 years.

3. THE MONEY GAME

Play for Pay

After free agency, nothing has changed the nature of sports as much as money. Stars always got big salaries (in some sports), but there was a ceiling beyond which no one aspired. When that ceiling hit $100,000 a year around World War II, few thought it would ever be exceeded. And still fewer achieved it. And there were also no perks then, and few opportunities for endorsements, commercials, and other off-the-field enriching ventures. You went out and played until you were hurt or too old, then you hung it up and went back to Mason City.

Then along came TV, and sports in America made the quantum leap into a kind of national theater. Contracting to show blocks of games on TV guaranteed a built-in audience and built-in income, both of which escalated upward in an inflationary and affluent period. Franchises boomed. Ballplayers, through their newly organized players associations, fought for and got more money. And then still more. Sports was no longer an antic career full of pitfalls and dead ends. For the lucky and talented few it was now a scholarship-paved road to an excellent livelihood—and a shot at becoming an overnight millionaire.

Naturally such profound changes in a relatively short period of time were going to affect the attitudes of the players themselves. A host of new questions arose. Were athletes worth so much?

Was the quality of play of these "pampered" athletes the same as in the hazard-strewn, no-guarantee past? Did signing a long-term contract sap a player's motivation? Could you relax for the first four years of a five-year contract, then go all out to establish that you still had it? Was team loyalty an archaic and contemptible concept?

These—and other issues raised by the influx of big money—remain unresolved.

1

It's a lot tougher to get up in the mornings when you start wearing silk pajamas.

> Former jockey **Eddie Arcaro,** who won 4,779 races and $30 million in purses over two decades.

2

Money is a great motivator. In a Dallas Cowboys' game, I saw Harvey Martin go down on a kickoff and break the blocking wedge. If I'd asked him to do that in college, I wouldn't have been able to find him for three weeks.

> **Bobby Fox,** assistant coach at East Texas State in 1976, where defensive end Martin played college ball.

3

Mr. Barrow, there is only one answer to that—Mr. Gehrig is terribly underpaid.

> **Joe DiMaggio,** recalling contract negotiations with Yankee general manager Ed Barrow, in which Barrow reminded Joe that 16-year veteran Lou Gehrig, at $44,000, was only earning $1,000 more than the young centerfielder.

4

There is no principle involved in my holdout. Only money.

> **O.J. Simpson,** as an unsigned rookie of the 1969 Buffalo Bills.

5

Maybe it is all just a matter of growing up. Fans do tend to be children. They try to pretend that the athlete of their fancy is out there doing what he excels at for some greater good or glory than a buck. That naive view is probably the nub of the problem, and the fault lies with the fan, not the athlete who always knew he was playing for the dollars and not much else.

> **Mark McCormack,** head of the International Management Group, a complex of companies that represents a wide array of athletes in golf, tennis, skiing, and team sports.

6

Team spirit doesn't apply here. This isn't the college world series. With 27,000 bucks on the line, I hate everybody.

> Former Oakland A's pitcher **Ken Holtzman,** during

the 1974 World Series.

7 People were mad at Don Gullett for seeking security, but I'm not sure he was wrong. There was a time when I'd play baseball for nothing, but not in the '70's.

> Cincinnati pitcher **Gary Nolan,** a 15-game winner in both 1975 and 1976, announcing in early 1977 that he was seeking a multi-year contract. He was traded in mid-season.

8 I am a professional. I run for money, not for times. I realize that people like to see Ben Jipcho run sub-four-minute miles, and Ben Jipcho enjoys running sub-four-minute miles more than anything else in the world—except counting money.

> Kenya's world-class miler and steeplechaser **Ben Jipcho,** on why he runs only fast enough to win. Perhaps because of attitudes like Jipcho's, the pro track circuit folded in 1976.

9 I don't understand it. How can you expect a $30,000 ballplayer like me to stop a guy who's making $300,000?

> Pro basketball guard **Wilbur Holland,** then with the Atlanta Hawks, explaining to club officials why New Orleans' Pete Maravich managed to score 40 points against him in a 1976 exhibition game. Holland was dropped by Atlanta and picked up by Chicago, where he became a mainstay of the Bulls.

10 I see players on other teams and, yes, on our team, who can't pass a puck backhanded, and they all want $100,000.

> **Stan Mikita,** formerly with the Chicago Black Hawks, four-time scoring champion and one of hockey's most dangerous shooters in his day.

11 The money is on everybody's minds these days, it seems. Some players today are making more money than our 25-man roster in 1952. Our payroll was about $200,000. And we had a pennant-winning team.

> San Diego Padre general manager **Buzzie Bavasi,** lamenting the inflationary quarter-century (1952-77), most of which he spent in Los Angeles.

12 One year I hit .291 and had to take a salary cut. If you hit .291 today, you'd own the franchise.

> **Enos Slaughter,** former St. Louis Cardinals star, who smacked the ball at a robust .300 clip over a 19-season span.

Catfish [Hunter], that's one, and [Don] Gullett, that's two   **13**
[superstars]. But what has this done to all those guys down the
line who have no business making $200,000 a year and those who
have no business making $100,000. What is it gonna do? I guaran-
tee you five years from now good, decent kids who came to play
baseball won't be anywhere near the same kids.

>   Former Cincinnati Reds' manager **Sparky Anderson**
>   in 1977, on how big salaries were changing the game.

The difference is that it used to be you got paid after you did it.   **14**
Now you get paid before.

>   Fiduciary conclusions about recent contract
>   negotiations by Cleveland Indians pitcher **Rick
>   Waits.**

SELL CAMPBELL AND BRING BACK THE $1.50   **15**
BLEACHER SEATS!

>   Fenway Park **bleacher sign** that greeted Bill
>   Campbell, one of the first free agents to sign a
>   million-dollar contract, in the relief specialist's first
>   appearance in a Red Sox uniform in 1977. Campbell
>   has since departed.

If you want to know why I'm coming back, I watched the   **16**
heavyweight fights in Las Vegas last week and decided I could do
as well as anyone I saw. There's a lot of money in boxing today.

>   Heavyweight **Jerry Quarry,** coming out of retirement
>   at 32 after a two-year layoff and hypnotherapy treat-
>   ments in 1977.

Let's be realistic about this, when I was scoring all those goals   **17**
nobody said I was underpaid. I'm certainly not going to give any of
it back. And where am I ever going to have a chance to make this
kind of money doing anything ever again? I don't deny the money
is important to my life. Why should I?

>   New York Ranger veteran **Phil Esposito** in 1978,
>   making $325,000 a year and not nearly as productive
>   as in his Boston Bruin years.

You could stack it up and a show dog couldn't jump over it.   **18**

>   **Pete Rose,** imagining what his four-year $3.2 million
>   salary with the Philadelphia Phils would look like in
>   one pile. The deal made him highest-paid player in
>   1978.

When we joined the Nets I took that [bonus provision] out of the   **19**
contract, and got money instead. I didn't want people coming into

the Meadowlands and thinking that 50 cents of every ticket they were buying was going to Otis.

> **Bob Woolf,** Otis Birdsong's agent, protecting his client's image in 1981. The basketball star's carryover contract called for a million a year plus the 50-cents-a-person bonus for every seat sold over 5,000.

20   It's tough to sit on that on-deck circle makin' $800,000 less than somebody hitting in front of you.

> **Reggie Jackson,** in February 1981, making $580,000 in his last year as a Yankee. The following year Jackson left Yanks and Winfield's aura, signed with California, where his contract called for big bucks plus a percentage of gate.

21   You saw it. I don't have to say anything other than to say we'll be out here at 11 a.m. tomorrow . . . . We've got to start looking good, and we will work until we get it right. When you're making $500,000 and $800,000 a year, there is no such thing as battle fatigue.

> **George Steinbrenner,** laying down the law to his high-priced athletes in spring training, 1982.

22   Baseball is in a state of transition. We are asking ourselves: 'What is the proper way to go?' I don't think you can judge what we've elected to do until the end of the season. We felt these three people [Griffey, Collins, and George Foster] weren't going to fit into our salary structure down the road. We tried then not to let 'em go for nothing. Collins walked on us, but [with] the other two we were able to get something.

> Cincinnati manager **John McNamara** in spring training, 1982, aware that his entire 1981 outfield would be playing in more lucrative New York. The Reds finished last for the first time in their history; McNamara was fired.

23   We are the game.

> **NFL Players Association slogan** in early 1982, in bid to win new collective bargaining agreement that would guarantee players 55 percent of owners' gross income.

24   I could have sat on the bench for the next five years and made more than a million dollars. But sitting on the bench on Sundays and feeling like you are the only man who is not contributing is something I couldn't do. The economics aren't worth it.

> Los Angeles quarterback **Pat Haden,** tired of being a fill-in for bigger men, who retired in June 1982, shortly

after the Rams traded for Bert Jones.

Higher education is a business, and I think Sherrill's contract is   **25**
part of that process.

> Board of Regents chairman **H.R. Bright,** justifying
> Texas A&M's signing of Jackie Sherrill as athletic
> director and football coach in 1982. Sherrill's six-year,
> $1.7 million contract is considered highest ever paid
> by an American college.

The whole situation regarding baseball salaries has changed since   **26**
I signed my present contract. At the time I was negotiating it, my
father, [brother] Bobby and I agreed that if it could get to the
million-dollar plateau, things couldn't get any higher. Now some
guys are getting $2 million who have never hit .300. I've done it
six times.

> Kansas City star **George Brett,** in the first year of a
> five-year contract at a reported $900,000 a year in
> 1982, seeking parity with the Mets' George Foster
> and Montreal's Gary Carter in the $2-million bracket.

Free Agency

As late as 1969, the average baseball player was getting $25,000 a
year, a high-water mark for all big-time sports except basketball.
Then Curt Flood challenged baseball's seemingly unbreakable
reserve clause, charging that owners treated their players "like slaves
and pieces of property instead of as human beings." In 1970 Oscar
Robertson, emboldened by the competitive presence of the ABA,
brought a similar class-action suit against the NBA. Athletes in other
team sports quickly followed suit, and the major sports revolution of
the century was on.

Flood lost, after long and bitter litigation, but the owners' victory proved to be only a delaying action against the inexorable march
of free agency. The end came almost overnight with the historic Seitz
decision (arbitrator Seitz was promptly fired by the owners), and free
agency quickly swept away all the vestiges of the "enslaved" past. At
last ballplayers belonged only to themselves—after serving out their
initial indentureship, of course.

At first the waters were tested tentatively by established stars like Andy Messersmith and Dave McNally. There was still a veiled threat of retribution in the air. But soon even journeyman players—utility infielders, relief pitchers, and overage pinch hitters—were opting for the free-agency route to greener pastures and long-term lucrative contracts.

Free agency spread rapidly to other team sports, and with it came the burgeoning of a new growth industry—the lawyer-agent with his retinue of accountants, tax experts and investment consultants. Athletes were no longer at the mercy of heartless owners. They found themselves in the enviable position of having a monopoly on a valued commodity (their God-given talents), with the strength of the players association behind them, while the owners (except for a few diehards) were vying with each other in the open marketplace to corral those talents. The balance of power had shifted considerably.

The two sports that remained relatively immune to free agency were hockey and football, where equalization and compensation effectively blocked the free movement of players. Pete Rozelle's unique and complex financial arrangement whereby all the NFL teams shared in TV and other spinoff revenues had created an insulated profit structure that was unaffected by such volatile factors as attendance at games. There was no need to scramble for individual players when the financial guarantees insured a team's full measure of income despite performance. It's no accident, then, that football players are among the lowest paid in professional ranks, and the most restive.

Among the casualties of the new freedom to move from club to club will be, unavoidably, the concept of team loyalty. Rare will be the player who plays out his career with one team in one town. Rarer still the aggregate of players, brought together with great care and planning, who will form the nucleus of a winning team and create a tradition, perhaps even a "dynasty."

R.I.P., dear old Siwash. Your sons have flown, in search of the Golden Fleece. And there is little or no compensation.

1 When it came to negotiating, what I wanted was someone to go in there and knock heads. If an athlete who has been pampered ever since he was a kid is inserted into a heavy business situation, he gets chewed up.

> Former pitcher **Andy Messersmith,** one of baseball's first free agents.

2 With all the great universities we have in this nation, you can't tell me that some of these pipe-smoking guys can't set up a two- or three-man regulatory committee to watch over these athletes. None of the agents should work on percentage. They should be paid by the hour like you hire a lawyer or an accountant. Nobody should own anybody, and some of these agents do.

> Former Marquette basketball coach **Al McGuire** in 1974, deploring both the recruiting practices at the high school level and the role played by agents with college athletes.

We've burned a few agents who've tried to disrupt our program **3**
I think it's a shame when people like that try to destroy something that you've worked for and they [the players] have worked for . . . agents have ruined a lot of these kids and misled them in many ways. That's why you see so many confused professional players right now, who went too soon, who weren't ready.

> Former Notre Dame basketball coach **Digger Phelps,** angered at the pressure put on star college players—in this case, his center, John Shumate—to graduate into the pros before they graduate from college.

The hardest thing for me is to realize that football is a business. **4**
Mr. Mara has been super to me and every time we sit down I feel like I'm trying to reach around and pick his pocket. Somebody has to be the rotten person in these dealings and I don't want it to be me, so I'll let an agent handle it . . . .

> New York Giants linebacker **Brad Van Pelt,** who'd played out his contract in 1976 and didn't relish renegotiating his own contract.

Powerful? I don't know what that means. In my business, when **5**
you go into a man's pockets, he won't like you. So some owners make us sound like greedy guys. But we didn't create the market. We've just pushed the market to capacity.

> Player's agent **Irwin Weiner,** who may speak softly but carries a lot of clout.

First, these guys are unhappy ballplayers to start with, and I don't **6**
want unhappy ballplayers around. Second, they want more money than they are worth. Third, you have to give up too much in compensation to get them.

> Boston Celtics president **Red Auerbach** in 1977, on why he wasn't interested in the free-agency market.

I'm a professional, like a doctor or a lawyer. A nine-to-five person **7**
can't relate to that, or to entertainers—and that's what we are. I work as hard and as long as Sammy Davis Jr., and he makes $7 or $8 million a year. Nobody bitches about that.

> **Joe Rudi,** one of the gypsy band of free agents who escaped from Finley and journeyed to California and Boston—and back to Oakland.

8   The rules of civilized practice do not apply in sports.
> Chicago lawyer **Arthur Morse,** who is on the side of both management and labor—counsel to hockey's Black Hawks and an agent for athletes in other sports.

9   If they could pay a guy who has a leg in a cast [Don Gullett] $2-million, they can pay me what I think I'm worth. There's a lot of money around for the guys who played out their options, and there should be a lot around for the guys like me who didn't.
> Ex-Yankee **Sparky Lyle,** who guessed wrong in 1977. Edged out by Goose Gossage, relief specialist was traded the following year.

10 I'm just one of the guys. I tell them, I don't want to talk to any agents. If you and I were going fishing you wouldn't send over an agent to find out what kind of beer to bring, would you?
> Atlanta owner **Ted Turner's** viewpoint on signing free agents in 1977. Turner's overzealous "fishing trip" in pursuit of free agent Gary Matthews shortly after got him a one-year suspension for "excessive eagerness."

11 A rule was not made in heaven that the swag was to be divided the way it has been. As the rules change, it will be divided differently, and baseball players will be rewarded in the same fashion as Hollywood stars, hotshot ad copywriters and people who can guess what the future price of soybeans will be. The lucky recipients of these muscular skills will begin receiving some of these economic rents.
> Economist **Paul Samuelson,** in the early days, explaining the dialectics of free agency.

12 The fact is, it's a business, and both sides are business people. The owners try to make a legitimate profit, and so do the players. As far as youngsters go, when they reach maturity, they'll understand better. It's one of those unfortunate things.
> Agent **Jerry Kapstein,** offering his own version of economic reality and team loyalty.

13 Some [agents] are respectable businessmen and some aren't. . . . There have been some head-to-head struggles and when it was over what started out as a perfectly legitimate blue-collar movement [among the ballplayers] suddenly became a system of superstars .... People such as Marvin Miller have pointed out that some of the ballplayers have given back to the clubs certain privileges that were won such as the right of first refusal. If you're negotiating a new contract, they're [the agents] giving the present club the right of refusal instead of letting the man be a free agent. And Miller has complained about this and that they can't do this, so they do it under the counter because this is one businessman dealing with another. It's ironic because the agents don't really care about the history of what led up to this.

> **Roger Angell,** author of *The Summer Game,* looking at free agency in 1978.

In negotiations it's a question of whether you think they are being   **14** fair with you or trying to stick it to you. I'd rather be represented by an agent when I feel they are trying to stick it to me.

> Cincinnati Reds pitcher **Tom Seaver** in summer 1978, a year after M. Donald Grant traded away Seaver's 20-game arm and outspoken nature.

I am in no position to say any one player is worth so much or not   **15** worth so much, but the salary escalation in total has been absolutely abnormal. It has gone up faster than in any other business I know anything about, and I told the general managers this thing has got to slow down.

> Player relations expert **Ray Grebey,** during the 1978 baseball players draft, sounding the alarm.

Larry [Bird] is worth a million and a half. That's what we'll ask   **16** when his contract comes up. Why not? They thought I was crazy when we asked a million dollars for Birdsong. So why not a million and a half for Bird? What's the highest a player is worth? Oh. A billion. That sounds about right. I'd say one billion dollars a year.

> Agent **Bob Woolf,** setting the ballpark figures for the Boston Celtics' Larry Bird in 1981.

Free agency [in football] doesn't work. The owners aren't going to   **17** bid for players. Why should a guy go out and increase his payroll? He's not going to make any more money. They've already got a certain amount for tickets, television, NFL properties. They're all in business together. It's not like any other sport.

> Oakland Raiders guard **Gene Upshaw,** who is also president of the NFL Players Association, in 1981. Players sought a percentage of gross income to meet the unique situation in football.

18 It's the last year of my contract and a move like that [playing second base] would affect my standing as a free-agent outfielder. If they ask me to play second base, I would ask to extend my contract or renegotiate it.

> **Joel Youngblood,** whom the 1982 New York Mets couldn't seem to find a position for, suggesting a new kind of tradeoff. The Mets finally found a place for him—in Montreal.

19 One agent—up New York way—offered me $1,000 a month if I'd sign with him last summer. Plus, he said he'd take care of my family. I told him, 'That's a lot of money, but everybody at my school is depending on me and I'm not going to jeopardize my career.'

> Mississippi State linebacker **Johnie Cooks,** first choice of the Baltimore Colts in the 1982 NFL draft.

20 If I had to pick a word to describe most of the agents I've met, I'd call them leeches. These guys offered me *everything* to sign with 'em. Money. Cars. Women. And drugs. *Any* kind of drugs. Four agents even tried to sign me while I was still playing [college] football, which is against NCAA rules.

> UCLA offensive tackle **Luis Sharpe,** just before the 1982 NFL draft. Sharpe finally chose his high school football coach as his agent.

21 I have watched the commercialization of sports. I think it's been a turnoff to the regular fan. In the old days the athlete said, 'I will subordinate my own interests to the team.' But now the athlete is more interested in his own statistics.

> Sports attorney **Bob Woolf,** commenting on the last decade's changing attitudes.

Unions

Universally they skirted the word "union"—like other high-paid professionals before them—and chose "association" instead. And it has been the players associations in all the major sports that have transformed them from high-paid professionals to very high-paid ones, among the highest, in fact. For all their failings—miscalculated strikes, bad public relations gimmicks, fan-alienating tactics, foolish demands—they've gotten the job done. In the 1982 football players' strike there was a good deal of dissension in the ranks about asking for 55 percent of the gross gate receipts originally, but no talk of breaking up the, ah, association. Not a chance, not after all these years of seeing how unity pays off.

The players' open-ended prosperity has prompted ambivalent reactions among the fans. On the one hand the players are idolized as carriers of the torch; on the other they are resented as pocketers of the loot. Whatever move they make, as a group, they get little sympathy. For the average fan a strike—or even talk of a strike—disturbs both his peace of mind and his TV programming, not to mention his occasional stadium outings. Aren't these guys getting huge salaries for working at something that the rest of us would call pleasure? And for such a short season?

Many of the fans interviewed during the last football strike commented that the players were already getting too much money. Ironic, considering that of the four major sports, football pays its players the least. And football players have the shortest average career span of the four. The fan's reaction revealed either a profound ignorance about the realities of what is probably America's favorite sport now, or more likely, a widespread indifference to the problems of men earning close to $100,000 a year—even if their careers are curtailed or injury-riddled or fraught with other hazards.

The football and baseball strikes of the last 15 years have demonstrated that when the chips are down the media throws in with the leagues, and promotes this public perception of the Mercedes-driving ballplayer. Hardly surprising, in view of the contractural connections between the leagues and TV and radio.

Coming to it late, the players have found that unionization can be a lonely and embattled business.

My job is playing football, not working at football. I like the money, sure. I treasure it. One of my dreams has always been to have control of $1,000,000 ten years after I enter pro ball. But if you go out only for money, you're not going anywhere. I play football. It happens to pay well. But I'm still a football player, not a football worker.

1

> **Mike Curtis,** Baltimore Colts linebacker in 1970, on why he didn't join the NFL Players Association strike. Curtis was the first "name" player to report to training camp.

Football is a rough game, and it's conceivable that a team that went against all the other teams in the dispute might find itself

2

suffering an unusual number of injuries.

> Former Oakland Raider **Ben Davidson,** commenting
> on players who did report to camp during the strike.
> He later denied that it was a serious threat.

3 It's not very smart to call your players a bunch of rotten fish and
then try to sell those fish to the fans once the strike is over.

> **Frank Cashen,** then a Baltimore Orioles executive,
> presenting an unorthodox management view of
> baseball's first general players' strike, which lasted 13
> days and shortened the 1972 season by ten days.

4 We think the laws of supply and demand would rule as they do in
other businesses. We call it free enterprise, which I guess is a star-
tling concept to the owners. They call it anarchy. I suppose in
their position they have to stick their heads in the sand and insist
there can be no alternative to the system they have created.

> NFL Players Association representative **Ed Garvey,**
> on the owners' attitude to the players' 1974 demand
> that football's reserve clause be eliminated.

5 I don't know a freer class of people on earth. This is the first time
in the history of labor negotiations that $100,000 players are driv-
ing Mark IVs or Cadillacs to the picket line.

> Miami Dolphins owner **Joe Robbie,** unhappy with
> the 1974 NFL Players Association strike.

6 Marvin Miller is one of the most respected, brightest labor
negotiators in the United States. It's only because of Miller that
baseball players have been able to earn the money they deserve to
earn. This, of course, greatly upsets the Old World sportswriters,
who've always sided with—and enjoyed the favors of—baseball
team owners. Miller has done nothing at all to hurt sport.

> **Howard Cosell,** dispensing plaudits and brickbats.

7 The first purpose of a union is not to keep salaries high for a few
players but to maintain as many jobs as possible. Beyond that, the
sport is as much our business as it is the owners'.

> **Bobby Clarke,** Philadelphia Flyers All-Star defense-
> man and president of the NHL Players Association in
> 1977, considered the most powerful of the sports
> unions. His remarks reflected the union's concern
> about the imminent demise of the league's Cleveland
> franchise.

8 The thing that gets me is that I'm included in any pension plan changes for 10 years after I stop playing, which means I still have an interest in all the meetings, and yet I'm not included in any meetings, and I don't receive any information about them. Yet a rookie, a kid in the bigs for 60 days, is in there voting.

> Hall of Famer **Al Kaline,** now a broadcaster, talking about the baseball union in 1981.

If there is a strike, I've got to support it. Just about everybody **9** does. I don't want to get into a personal war with 1,500 players, especially being a quarterback who stays in the pocket.

> **Cliff Stoudt,** Pittsburgh's reserve quarterback, finding a unique reason for reversing himself and coming out in support of the posposed 1982 players' strike.

One thing about this game. We get to see you on the field next **10** year. We will have a little additional incentive when we do.

> Letter from **Gene Upshaw,** president of the NFL Players Association, to Denver quarterback Craig Morton, after the latter criticized the union on the eve of the football strike.

I've never been able to figure out why fans side with the owners. I **11** suppose fans identify more with the players and if they can't get more money in their jobs, why should players? Sure, players have a glamorous life and make a whole lot more. Sure, it's insane and there's no rational relationship to anything else for all the money that comes in. But we're not talking about whether it's right or wrong. It's there and why should 28 owners keep most of it?

> Former Minnesota Vikings defensive lineman **Alan Page,** now an attorney and consultant for the NFL Players Association, during the 1982 strike.

They said they would spend it [career adjustment bonus fund] **12** over five years, but they won't tell us how. The members of the Kansas City Chiefs and the rest of the 1,500 members of our union would be outraged when they find the $1.6 billion they believe is going to players' salaries is being used to keep college kids from going to the USFL.

> Kansas City Chiefs **Tom Condon,** voicing the players' fears about the owners' divisive tactics during the football strike.

In major-league baseball, most players have been through the mill **13** as employees. Most were drafted out of high school or after a year or two of college. They played under substandard conditions in the minor leagues. They rode buses, got moved around, had no

minimum salaries or security. They lived in the real world and
it was an enlightening and educational experience.

The football player was the big man on campus. Then he
comes to the pros and the coach is a god. It isn't until after his
career that he pays his dues, when he faces permanent injury and
realizes he was the lowest paid athlete. Then he realizes he's been
a fool.

> Baseball union head **Marvin Miller,** contrasting the
> union attitudes of ballplayers in 1982.

Sports
as a Business

Despite all the hand-wringing and alarms about big salaries, free
agency, and spiraling costs, sports is one hell of a business. Let us just
cite three areas that reveal how golden the oversize egg really is:
recent franchise sales, fan attendance, and television revenues.

Franchises: In baseball, the White Sox were sold for a hefty
$20 million, the Mets for 21. Chicago hasn't won a pennant since
1959, New York since 1973. Why would anybody spend money on a
loser? Football's San Francisco 49ers showed little promise in 1977,
but still brought $18 million. Four years later the Denver Broncos
changed hands for a cool $30 million. In basketball, Dallas's newest
expansion franchise carried a $13 million price tag.

No franchise placed on the open market ever goes a-begging.
Prospective owners stand in line to bid, and bid record amounts of
money. To keep the record straight, there have also been old-line
clubs that have claimed multimillion dollar losses, and this may
actually be the case. But no owner has ever volunteered to open his
books to verify this. And their accountants are known to have more
moves than the slipperiest wide receivers.

Attendance: All major sports except basketball and soccer
show comfortably upward curves; baseball's is soaring, despite a
$1.50 to $2.50 average ticket sale increase across the board, and
hikes in anything else you might buy in or near a stadium.

TV revenues: Combined TV rights guarantee each NFL

franchise more than $14 million a year through 1987. Even if not one fan shows up in any stadium. On the average, baseball clubs derived one-third of their income from TV and this is expected to rise sharply to 50 percent in a few years. Only American-based hockey franchises may eventually suffer because of problems in televising hockey, while Canadian clubs in a crunch can count on local beer sponsorship to ensure their solvency.

But long before that happens cable and subscription TV will bail out many ailing franchises. There are already 20 million American homes with cable, with a projected 30 million by 1985. This will be an enormously lucrative addition to an already solid TV financial picture.

Sports franchises, in short, are in very good shape or they wouldn't be able to maintain their high-level salary schedules. In 1982 the average basketball player drew $215,000; in baseball, it was $193,000; hockey, $120,000; and the NFL was at the bottom with $90,000. And those, remember, were *average* salaries.

The higher salaries, a few reaching into the millions, have become a kind of fiscal lottery. Deferred payments over a period of time make it possible to bank half the money and let the interest accrue until it matches the other half. More bookkeeping legerdemain.

Finally, owning a team is not only potentially lucrative and prestigious—it is also one of the prime tax shelters in Reaganomic America. That is, if you are rich enough to get into the 70 percent tax bracket. Even if your team loses money, those same busy accountants can go on depreciating everything but the players wives' sweat suits.

Sports as a business? Ed Garvey of the NFL Players Association, hungrily eyeing the nearly $400 million in guaranteed TV revenue that the NFL owners will be divvying annually through 1987, calls it "pure socialism."

If all the people who will claim in the future that they were here today had actually turned out, we wouldn't have to be moving in the first place.   **1**

> New York Giants public relations man **Garry Schumacher,** after the team's last game at the Polo Grounds in September 1957.

If the pros keep taking our best players, college basketball will go the route of college baseball in the near future, a dead spectator sport. We won't be able to fill our gymnasiums, there will be no national television. Right now the pros have a beautiful farm system going, and it's free, and they are milking it dry.   **2**

> Maryland basketball coach **Lefty Driesell,** one of a 1975 American Basketball Coaches Association delegation that met with pro basketball authorities to discuss the

problem of star players being wooed out of college before
they graduate.

3   In modern society one earns what one is worth.
>   Italian soccer coach **Helenio Herrera,** in 1971, re-
>   sponding to the criticism that his $240,000 salary was
>   ten times that of a government minister.

4   It's not a pleasant thing to hear, but I did what I had to do out of
necessity. This is not a public utility. I can't ask for a fare increase
when things go bad.
>   Virginia Squires owner **Earl Foreman** in 1974,
>   answering charges that he had sold off top players, in-
>   cluding Julius Erving.

5   We're [the International Management Group] by far the most
powerful influence on sport in the world. We could turn any individual sport—golf, tennis, skiing—on its ear tomorrow. The position we hold in some of these sports is the ability to reconstruct
the whole edifice .... It wouldn't take much to change things
[in golf], just a nucleus of players to go off on their own and start a
second tour. We want to do what is best for our clients and the
game. What we try to do is hold a balance of sanity between a lot
of tugging forces.
>   **Mark McCormack,** head of International Manage-
>   ment Group, a complex of corporations that specializes
>   in athlete management, in 1975. McCormack has been
>   called the most powerful man in professional sports.

6   Remember after World War II, when boxing was on the networks
at prime time on Monday, Wednesday, Friday and Saturday nights?
When I started making the Wednesday night shows for Jim Norris,
we paid the main event fighters $185 each and for Fridays it was
$212. Four shows a week devoured all the talent. Today the
money demands have reached the point where boxing, like all other
professional sports, can't survive without ancillary income.
>   Former Madison Square Garden matchmaker **Teddy
>   Brenner** in 1976.

7   This is the first time the commissioner [Bowie Kuhn] has charac-
terized players as good or clubs as affluent. I think he was giving
us a warning, and it had to come. His reference to the Sun Belt is
a sign of the times. Most ball players, like track stars and swim-
mers, come from California and Texas and they want to go back
there eventually. That's our handicap in Montreal—110 inches of
snow a year. We have to face them with dollars.

> Montreal Expos president **John McHale,** after Kuhn
> had warned baseball's owners, gathered at their 75th
> annual meeting in late 1976, about the long-term effects
> of free-agent warfare.

My daughter Kelley, who is 5, is a friend of Ken Boswell's **8**
daughter Ashley, who is the same age. They hadn't seen each
other for a while, and Ashley asked my wife if Kelley had been
traded.

> Former Houston infielder **Jerry DaVanon,** on life in
> the big leagues.

The [NFL] Players Association? Don't make me laugh. What you **9**
have here is a collective bargaining agreement in which the owners
and union need each other. The owners were going broke, the
union had only 200 members. [Ed] Garvey needed dues payers,
the owners needed peace. So now they're sweethearts. This is
traditionally what happens in the labor movement in this
country—players' interests become subordinate to the union
interests. Then there's the press—they're club-oriented. I'm not
saying the press is bought by liquor and sandwiches and free
rides; it's just that they remain friends with the owners while the
players come and go.

> Player representative **Howard Slusher's** view of pro
> football at the end of 1977. Also a lawyer, Slusher
> sometimes advises his clients *not* to report to camp or
> play.

When a lawyer [Howard Slusher] encourages people not to per- **10**
form a contract, that is intolerable conduct. I've lost all my respect
for him and, what's more, I think he's hurt the careers of some
important players.

> **Chuck Sullivan,** vice-president of the New England
> Patriots, deploring Slusher's tactics.

Football opens doors. In three weeks our company has gotten **11**
more publicity than it has in the last 30 years. If we'd come here
to announce a $1 billion construction deal, we wouldn't have had a
camera . . . . Because of our company's nature, we'll get more
benefit out of this than any other owner in the NFL would. I went
down to San Mateo yesterday to look at two mall sites that were
brought to our attention just because of this.

> **Eddie DeBartolo,** explaining why he was willing to
> ante $18 million for the lowly San Francisco 49ers in
> 1977.

12 What did we get for him? We got somebody who'll pay his salary.

> Atlanta Braves owner **Ted Turner,** after selling sore-
> armed pitcher Andy Messersmith to the New York
> Yankees and unloading his $330,000 annual salary.
> Messersmith never regained his winning form.

13 I refuse to recognize that there is a market that's exclusively
Manhattan's. The football team, the soccer team, they crossed a
political boundary—but not a social one. We're not raiding New
York. We're creating—we're creating the Tivoli Gardens of the
metropolitan area.

> New Jersey Meadowlands Complex president **Sonny
> Werblin** in 1977, sounding like Robert Moses.

14 I can't compete with other owners in bidding, but I can compete in
other ways. We don't deal in dollars. We deal in dreams and chances.

> Maverick **Bill Veeck,** on how to run a franchise
> (Chicago's White Sox) without money. Veeck had let
> slugger Richie Zisk go the free agent route (at $295,-
> 500 a season) to the Texas Rangers.

15 Eddie Gottlieb, the owner of the Philadelphia Warriors, used to
remind Wilt [Chamberlain] that it was all hype; at least that's what
Wilt would tell me. I believed this about Gottlieb, for whenever
the Celtics played in Philadelphia he would scream to the newspapers in advance that I was a criminal goal-tender and that I had
to be stopped. When we arrived in Philadelphia I'd see these
headlines, and in the game itself he'd scream at the referees so
violently that he had to be restrained. I always thought he was even
more of a firecracker than Red Auerbach, until one night when he
came into our locker room before a game, took me aside and said,
'I assume you're not paying any attention to all that stuff about
goal-tending. It just helps to keep our seats filled and our flock
growing.' He was warm and humorous, and then he went out to the
arena, and in a few minutes was screaming about goal-tending
again like a madman.

> **Bill Russell,** on filling the house in Philly.

16 To gain permission to move, an [NFL] team must show it would
create no travel problems for its opponents. It also must show that
it would create no serious weather, gate or television problems.
And the league prefers stadiums where football doesn't conflict
with baseball. In the Los Angeles Coliseum, we would qualify on
all counts.

> **Al Davis,** justifying moving the Raider franchise from
> Oakland to Los Angeles in 1980.

If [San Diego owner Eugene] Klein and Rozelle worry so much about **17**
football leaving Oakland, why didn't they worry about football leaving
Los Angeles? We had a team in the Coliseum for 33 years. And justi-
fying the move to Anaheim by calling it 'suburban' is a sham. Orange
County is no more a suburb of Los Angeles than Baltimore is of
Washington. Politics dictates the whole operation of the league. The
NFL is rotten with politics.

>Los Angeles Coliseum commissioner **William**
>**Robertson,** with another viewpoint on the contro-
>versial move.

I don't feel any franchise should be held in perpetuity. If you have **18**
a policy that locks in teams to their communities, it could work to
the disadvantage of the teams. Stadiums could be neglected.
Crowds could decline and the profit picture deteriorate. I don't
see where it makes much difference to the league whether two
teams exist in the San Francisco area or in the Los Angeles area.

>Dallas Cowboy president **Tex Schramm,** looking at
>the franchise hassle—and the future.

It was different then. I had accomplished all my goals. Today the **19**
players can't quit. They may get tired hitting tennis balls, but they
make so much money from endorsements, they play as long as
they can.

>Former net star **Karen Hantze Susman,** contrasting
>the current tennis scene with her own playing days in
>the 60s.

It wasn't a million dollars. It was a lot, though, definitely more **20**
than I've made off of any endorsement. But the thing was—I just
didn't want to be remembered as the Preparation H man. Mr.
Seven-Up, maybe. Not the ballplayer with the hemorrhoids.

>**George Brett** in 1980, the year he almost hit .400 for
>Kansas City and got an offer to endorse a product
>connected with a problem that had been cramping his
>style.

Football is a joke. The Giants have been total mediocrity for 15 **21**
years; the Raiders have been a major factor; yet the Giants earn
more than the Raiders. No one can say we haven't put an exciting
team on the field. We've got the best record in football. It isn't fair
that we should be earning less than a lot of clubs that don't feel
any need to perform. They suffer no penalty for their
incompetence.

>Oakland Raiders maverick owner **Al Davis** in 1981,
>in his bid to get the franchise moved to Los Angeles.

22 It's hectic. It's a continuous battle for stability. You sweat out the free-agent thing in November. Then you make all the trades in December. Then you struggle to sign all the guys left in January. And in February, I guess, I can get down to sewing all the new numbers on the uniforms.

> St. Louis Cardinals general manager **Whitey Herzog** in 1981, on the off-season hassle of running a ball club.

23 The acts, activities or sports prohibited by the contract include the following: auto racing, motorcycle racing, piloting of aircraft, fencing, parachuting, skydiving or hang gliding, horse racing, boxing, wrestling, karate, judo, jujitsu, snow skiing, charity basketball games or organized competitive basketball, organized competitive football, bob sledding, ice hockey, field hockey, jai-alai, lacrosse, soccer, organized bicycle racing, motor boat racing, organized competitive polo, tennis, handball, rodeo, surfing with a surf board . . . .

> Partial list of **proscriptions in a standard baseball player's contract** used by one franchise in 1981.

24 . . . in professional sports, literally every action, every business judgment and every decision of a league is now subject to attack under the antitrust laws.

> **Pete Rozelle,** urging that the Professional Sports Bill of 1982 be passed. The bill would, in effect, give the NFL a virtual monopoly over pro football.

25 Rozelle may be amazed to learn that every other business faces exactly that same situation every day and that it is precisely the point of the antitrust laws.

> **Editorial reaction in** *Business Week* to Rozelle's position (see above).

26 It appears that we are well on our way toward the very considerable losses over the five-year period 1980 through 1984 that I predicted last year. It is clear that our industry continues to operate in a precarious financial condition.

> Former baseball commissioner **Bowie Kuhn's** glum view of the game's prospects in mid-1982. Presumably only nine of the 26 franchises made money in 1980, though the complex nature of their financial structure and their refusal to open their books make this a debatable conclusion.

27 We're in the midst of growing pains, no doubt. We've introduced a new sport in this country. But all you have to do is look at

playgrounds and schoolyards across the country to know the
future is going toward soccer. When you have seven million kids
playing soccer you have a product you can sell.

> Chicago Sting owner **Lee Stern** in 1982, against a
> background of slipping attendance in the North
> American Soccer League.

Pegging basic compensation to gross receipts would give players   **28**
something to work for, make them more responsible for building
up the league.

> Seattle SuperSonics owner **Sam Schulman,** urging
> the NBA to emulate the NFL's revenue-sharing finan-
> cial setup.

Please, not here, not now, don't fight for free. This is for big   **29**
money.

> Promoter **Don King,** talking straight and protecting
> his interest, at a 1982 prefight press conference at
> which heavyweight Larry Holmes took an open-
> handed swipe at challenger Gerry Cooney.

Owners

In the beginning they were the old-line families—the Wrigleys, the
Maras, the Comiskeys, the Stonehams, the Rupperts. They lived in
the house on the hill. They were wealthy and patient and seldom did
anything ostentatious. They knew how to build, how to wait for
results, how to win—or lose—gracefully. They sent baskets to the
poor at Christmas.

And then it all changed. New leagues, new franchises, new
ways of doing business made sports as chaotic as trading in futures.
New kinds of owners appeared, a new breed, in a hurry for results.
People who had made money quickly, a great deal of money, and now
wanted all the things that come with money. Prestige. Splash.
Recognition. The best seats in the theater, the best table in the
best restaurant.

But always money. Buying a club, for all its glitter, was part of
the corporate money wheel It was part of what their accountants
called "the overall fiscal structure." It had to produce—quickly—and

in the meantime it could be a dandy little tax writeoff.

They cared less about the game as such, in part because they knew less about the game. Essentially it was like any other business, wasn't it? You had a product, you marketed it, you made a profit. Why all the fuss about outmoded traditions?

When free agency came along the new breed were among the most avid bidders for talent on the loose. You need a relief specialist, you buy one. Looking for quick results, most of them got burned. Some, shaking a fist at the league, dumped the franchise and went back to pork backs and selling insurance. They didn't know that great teams aren't jerry-built in three weeks, like World War II Liberty ships.

In the last two decades half the baseball clubs have moved or been sold. Many other sports franchises have changed hands or expanded into new areas. The new breed has uniformly replaced the old, but they could learn a thing or two from them.

1 Sonny [Werblin, owner of the New York Jets] used to come to training camp in Peekskill, N.Y. in a black limo that had a bar set-up in it. One day he arrived just as a hail-storm started, and [Jet coach] Weeb Ewbank was so scared of him that he wouldn't end the practice. And these hailstones like damn baseballs are coming down. And I remember afterward, Paul Rochester, who was a defensive tackle, was complaining: 'Goddamn, we're down there with these hailstones bouncing off our butts, and Weeb won't send us in 'cause Sonny's sitting in his limo drinking a bloody Mary.'

> Football writer **Paul Zimmerman** about Sonny Werblin, in the days when Sonny was the Daddy Warbucks owner of the overhauled New York Jets.

2 We were losing our war with the San Francisco 49ers and we had to do something. We needed somebody who wanted to win so badly, he would do anything. Everywhere I went, people told me what a son of a bitch Al Davis was—hell, that's why I wanted him.

> **Wayne Valley,** Oakland Raiders owner, in 1963.

3 It took us 50 years to build this wonderful world. And it's very painful to see it attacked. But if it becomes necessary to maintain our management position, we may just have to give up a year of football.

> Chicago Bears owner **George Halas,** about the NFL strike in 1970. The strike was short-lived; in August a four-year agreement was signed.

4 The owners are intent on making the players eat dirt. They want the players to bend down and kiss their shoes . . . . I told the players that they are up against unscrupulous people who are used to living above the law.

> **Marvin Miller,** head of the Major League Players
> Association, during the 1972 baseball players' strike.

Sports becomes for them diversions, more financial success, or a **5** tax writeoff. They get great competitive advantages from the Government, either directly or indirectly, while the fan faces nothing but higher ticket prices and even higher parking, hot dog and beer prices.

> Senator **William Proxmire** in 1974.

This is my 14th year in football. I feel very deeply. I love the game **6** as do other owners. There isn't another owner in the National Football League that is in it for a buck. I promise you that. They're in it because they love the sport.

> Cleveland Browns owner **Art Modell,** during the
> 1974 football strike.

I'd like to hang the owners by their thumbs. They're just 32 jerks **7** who thought they'd be millionaires overnight. They only told us one truthful thing out of 50,000 lies. That was the fact that we were going bankrupt.

> Kicker **Chuck Collins** of the defunct World Football
> League Detroit Wheels, in 1974.

The line had always been that we were a part of this big happy **8** family. We were always the 'sons' of management. Well, that's not the way it was, or is, not at all. Let a problem come up, like the soreness in my back, and the Mets moved quick to make a good deal for me before word got out that I was hurting. But that's the way it should be. Baseball is primarily a business, and the Mets acted in their best interest. My only objection is, let's quit kidding about it.

> Relief ace **Tug McGraw,** shortly after the
> New York Mets hastily dealt him
> to Philadelphia in 1976.

Tom [Seaver] now wishes to renegotiate his contract that he was **9** so happy with a year ago. Our board of directors voted unanimously against renegotiation. The contract is the fundamental cornerstone in our country, and baseball as well.

> Statement issued by former New York Mets general
> manager **M. Donald Grant** in 1977. Against stormy
> fan opposition, Seaver was finally dealt to Cincinnati,
> where he got bigger bucks.

10   I've got players I put complete confidence and faith in and I've
found that those players don't give a damn. They don't care about
anythng but drawing a paycheck.
> **Brad Corbett,** principal owner of the Texas Rangers
> in 1977, after dipping heavily into the free-agent market.

11   I like a little conflict. I think it's needed because with the 162-
game schedule and the players always around each other, tempers
are bound to get tight. They need an outlet. If they keep it inside
them, they're going to bust.
> Yankees owner **George Steinbrenner** in 1978,
> establishing his style.

12   The more we lose, the more often Steinbrenner will fly in. And the
more he flies, the better the chance there will be of the plane
crashing.
> **Anonymous New York Yankee player,** during
> the early days of the Steinbrenner
> ascendancy.

13   [Baseball] owners are not like each other and are not united. It's
the most unbusinesslike group of businessmen you can imagine.
Every move they have made in the last 15 years has been almost
without exception totally self-destructive. They fought the players
association tooth and nail, and the reason they did this was because they were incapable of ruling themselves.
> **Roger Angell,** author of *The Summer Game,* in a 1978
> interview.

14   We are constitutionally opposed to the creation of young sports
millionaires.
> **Detroit Tigers front-office position** on free agency
> in 1978. Tigers ranked 22nd among 26 clubs in total
> payroll.

15   Basically, there is a bunch of [garbage] out there.
> Remark attributed to Cleveland Indians president
> **Gabe Paul,** about the 1978 free-agent roster, which
> included many veteran players.

16   Freedom of speech isn't carte blanche when you're taking someone's money.
> New York Jets president **Jim Kensil** in 1979, after
> firing linebacker Bob Martin for critical
> remarks about the front office and the
> team's esprit de corps.

The greatest turn-on for a successful businessman in this country is **17**
the theater and owning sports teams, and the theater is a poor second.
It sounds corny, but the average guy is Walter Mitty. An owner has a
paper-box company and has a million dollars but goes into a restaurant and he can't get the number one table. With a team, he gets
the table.
> **Earl Foreman,** commissioner of the Major Indoor
> Soccer League.

George Steinbrenner, to me, is the best owner in baseball. He **18**
wants to win. Gee whiz, he's dynamic, he's good for baseball. If
more owners were like George, there'd be more controversy, more
excitement and more seats filled in all those parks.
> Veteran Yankee outfielder **Lou Piniella,** in October
> 1980.

I'm like Archie Bunker, I get mad as hell when my team blows one. **19**
But there are five million Yankee fans just like me sitting in front
of their TV sets with beer and hollering the same thing when
Ferraro sends Randolph home and he's out. I want this team to
win, I'm obsessed with winning, with discipline, with achieving.
That's what this country's all about, that's what New York is all
about—fighting for everything; a cab in the rain, a table in a restaurant at lunchtime—and that's what the Yankees are all about,
and always have been.
> **George Steinbrenner,** explaining it all in 1981.

Give me a bastard with talent. **20**
> **Inscription** on a pillow on the couch in
> George Steinbrenner's office in Yankee Stadium.

There is a time limit on a man's effectiveness, and if a man has not **21**
done it [won a championship] in five years, then he won't do it in ten.
> Houston owner **John McMullen,** after firing general
> manager Tal Smith in 1981, the year the Astros won
> their first divisional title.

We've got a lot of new players now who came from clubs where **22**
they never got that feedback, where they maybe have never seen
the owner. It takes time to learn to deal with that and be secure in
your mind. You find players on other teams who enjoy seeing the
Yankees lose because they know George [Steinbrenner] will chew
us out. They can't believe what we have to go through.
> Second baseman **Willie Randolph,** on what it's like
> to be young and a New York Yankee in the
> Steinbrenner years.

23 I know that in 1955, when the players came to my father [Art Rooney] and asked whether they should join the union, he said that if the union could negotiate a pension for them, then they should join. I think we've always had a good relationship with our players. We treat them as people and human beings. When they tell us they are union members, it doesn't upset us. It's too bad too many people on both sides get hardheaded.

> Pittsburgh Steelers owner **Dan Rooney,** at the outset of the 1982 football strike.

24 I think I'm pro-union. At this stage in our league history, we need it. It gives us and the players a chance to discuss things instead of winding up in court. I disagree with everything the union is doing but I also think it's wrong for the prominent players to hold themselves aloof from the union. If they disagree, they should try to change it.

I loved the old days, when a player signed a contract on the kitchen table in his mother's home. Now, I'm detached because we have a general manager and players have agents. Still, once a player signs, he must still love to play the game. That hasn't changed.

> New Jersey Giants owner **Wellington Mara,** during the football strike.

25 They're [football players] getting a major piece of the pie, but they're not satisfied. They want the whole pie. Professional sports is the only business I know where it's a public disgrace for ownership to show a profit. Aren't the owners entitled to make a profit? . . . The players are doing very well. They just want to do well-er. You spell it G–R–E–E–D.

> New Jersey Giants general manager **George Young,** in the seventh week of the 1982 football strike.

Sports and TV

On a summer Sunday in 1979, John J. O'Connor, television critic of the *New York Times,* asked almost plaintively at the end of a column on sports and TV hype, "Can the torrent of silly words from American sportscasters be reduced to a bearable trickle?" The answer is no. We cannot hope for a diminution, John. Just keeping it at the current level for any length of time would be an acclaimable victory.

Ironically, less than two months after the O'Connor column the Entertainment and Sports Programming Network was launched on cable TV. Quickly dubbed ESPN, it was to be (and is) an around-the-clock seven-days-a-week sports channel, and on its very first day that September it managed to present: professional softball, college football, soccer, wrestling and hurling. The accompanying commentary may not have been at the inflated level of the networks, but just think of all that additional overnight word tonnage. An immediate success despite its makeshift schedules and professional shortcomings, by 1981 it had crept into nine million American homes and was still growing at a healthy rate.

The sudden appearance and, more significantly, the upward spiral in subscribers no doubt shook up the networks a bit. But it did not create panic in an easily panicked industry. Sitting on their lucrative contracts with professional football, baseball, and basketball, the networks felt pretty secure, even when ESPN extended its mandate to Australian football and rodeo. They could nibble the corners, it was felt, but they couldn't get at the sandwich proper.

This could be correct, or it could be creeping complacency. Wiser network heads recollected the year 1970, when everybody thought ABC was making a mistake in introducing football on Monday nights. And despite the reworking of the same cliches week after week, despite Dandy Don and the Giffer, and most of all despite Howard Cosell's shifting scenario of what really is happening on the field, America's Monday night lifestyle has been altered irrevocably. In 1977 the Cowboys and the Cardinals almost edged out *The Godfather* in the ratings. *The Godfather I,* that is, the one with Brando in it.

"Unquestionably," Cosell declared about this time, "TV is saving sports, although I'm not sure sports is worth saving."

One example of what he meant, we suppose, was that time at the Super Bowl when they had to kick off twice because the camera had missed the first one. Or maybe he was thinking of the tight game in which CBS switched to the movie *Heidi* before the conclusion of the game. Or the unexplained time outs when nothing is happening on the field; or the time Woody Hayes attacked a player and seven cameras were pointed elsewhere.

Or maybe he meant programs like "The Superstars," "Challenge of the Sexes," or "Sports Spectacular," or that other one—what's it called—"The Wide Wide Mouth of Sports"?

The season should consist of only 60 games, all of them on weekends.   **1**
Former ABC-TV president **Thomas Moore's**

concept of the perfect (for TV) baseball season.

2 At the annual sales meeting, when I announce
our TV advertising schedule they scream and beat their chairs on
the floor.

> **John P. Kelley,** advertising director for
> Goodyear Polyglas tires, in 1971. His company moved
> its TV advertising, directed primarily at men, out
> of general entertainment shows into live sports events
> in the early 1960s.

3 There never has been one like me before, and there never will be
one like me again.

> **Howard Cosell,** in 1967. Cosell can claim one other
> distinction: he is the only personality who has ever
> come in first as both the most popular and least
> popular sportscaster in the same poll.

4 The college game isn't sick . . . . Big as pro ball has become, the
pros still refuse to televise a game live into a city in which it is
played. Even the Sugar Bowl is blacked out. We play UCLA and
Notre Dame and draw 80,000 to 90,000 even though the game is
being televised right across the street.

> **John McKay,** football coach at USC in 1971. In
> 1976 McKay moved into the pro ranks himself.

5 Sports are the greatest thing that ever happened to TV, the only
honest thing that goes on. And I don't just say that because we've
got the field surrounded. As the overall quality of TV continues to
deteriorate, sports will become even more effective. There's no
such thing as too much sports on TV.

> **Barry Frank,** vice-president of International
> Management Group in 1975. IMG both manages
> athletes and packages sports programs for all three
> major networks, including "The Superstars" series,
> "Challenge of the Sexes," and other tournament
> sports specials.

6 If people watch soccer on television now, they'll be . . . bored
silly. Television has to perfect some ideas for this sport, like how
to handle the instant-replay concept in a game that never stops.
On television soccer looks like a bunch of guys chasing a big
balloon around.

> **Dick Berg,** general manager of the NASL's San Jose
> Quakes, explaining his team's lukewarm position on
> TV coverage.

I find soccer an exciting sport, with long-range potential as a   **7**
television attraction.

> **Barry Frank,** a vice president of CBS Sports in May
> 1976, just after his network had signed a three-year
> contract with the NASL.

Barry Frank is confident that he can achieve the ratings with auto   **8**
racing or golf; he is not confident that he can achieve it with
soccer.

> NASL commissioner **Phil Woosnam,** on hearing that
> CBS had decided not to renew its option and had
> dropped its TV soccer contract for the second time.
> Previously, CBS-TV had discontinued its soccer
> telecasts after a brief trial in 1968, the first year of
> the league. Thus, CBS got in—and out—on the
> ground floor twice.

We hope we will eventually be able to transplant this sport [foot-   **9**
ball] to Japanese soil. And then television sets will sell like
hotcakes.

> **Seiji Nogami,** official of a Japanese firm that pro-
> duces football emblems and memorabilia, as well as
> TV sets, in 1975. At that time an estimated 4,000
> Japanese were playing football at college or on club
> teams.

Baseball has prostituted itself. Pretty soon we'll be starting games   **10**
at midnight so the people in outer space can watch on prime-time
television. We're making a mistake by always going for more
money.

> San Diego Padres owner and MacDonald hamburger
> king **Ray Kroc,** reflecting on the frosty October
> telecasts of the 1976 World Series.

If you're paid before you walk on the court, what's the point in   **11**
playing as if your life depended on it? Hell, if you've locked up a
bundle of money from a challenge match, you might as well take a
vacation the rest of the year.

> Former tennis pro **Arthur Ashe,** in opposing the so-
> called "Heavyweight Championships of Tennis,"
> when it was disclosed that athletes were to receive
> prearranged payments regardless of who won or lost.

You would think an award [the Heisman Trophy] of this stature—   **12**
and it's the top award in college football—could stand alone and
not need commercialism. My concern is that when you put anything

like advertising attached to it, you take away from the great
achievement and pride of the young man who wins it.

> Yale football coach **Carmen Cozza** in 1977, when he
> learned that CBS-TV had bought the rights to the
> 43rd Heisman Trophy award and was turning it into a
> one-hour show.

13   Have you heard [Phil] Rizzuto doing a commercial for the Belmont
Stakes? You ought to catch it. He says racing is the Number One
sports event.

> American League president **Lee MacPhail,** wryly
> taking the New York Yankees telecaster to task in
> 1978.

14   The game is in a serious decline. Television has all but wiped out
the minor leagues, where people used to learn how to play
baseball, I mean *really* learn: basics, fundamentals, hitting the cut-
off man with throws from the outfield, running bases properly,
sliding, bunting, tagging runners, all the things that made the game
as demanding and as beautiful as it used to be . . . . So, what
you've got now is a few good ballclubs, a lot of expansion teams
that are really minor-league squads in disguise, and hundreds of
kids reaching the majors with virtually no experience, training or
fully developed baseball skills. And the mediocrity is being
accepted mainly because it is being sold by the most powerful
interest in the country, the television industry.

> **Frank Robinson** in 1978, when he was managing the
> Cleveland Indians.

15   People forget that TV is not free. The consumer eventually pays
for those enormous rights fees, whether he's paying Russia for the
Olympics or the NFL for 'Monday Night Football.' The costs are
passed along through almost every product advertised on
television. One estimate is that several hundred dollars of
the cost of a new car represent TV advertising; it's a nickel on
every tube of toothpaste, and so on. So when we talk about the
price of TV sports going up, it's significant, because it affects
everything else.

> Assistant professor **David Klatell,**who ran a six-week
> seminar called the Institute on Broadcast Sports in
> 1978, the first in-depth academic study of sports
> programming on TV. The Boston University seminar
> was surprisingly well attended by sportscasters,
> executive producers, advertising execs, team owners,
> coaches, and government regulators.

And it's equally important to look at what television is doing to **16**
the definition of sports in this country. The trend now is toward more
and more 'junk sports'—shows like 'Challenge of the Sexes' and 'Battle of the Network Stars,' where Farrah Fawcett-Majors pulls taffy
against O.J. Simpson. Everybody we spoke to this
summer agrees on this: there is going to be a continuing
de-emphasis in traditional sports and a greater emphasis on
sports-as-entertainment. The network people and the advertisers all
say that this kind of program attracts more women. If you can get the
entire family watching sports you effectively double your ratings.
> **Ibid.**

I'm not going to put a girl on the air when she is wearing next to noth-   **17**
ing. It has gone too far. I'm not a purist but we're trying to sell football
games, not this kind of stuff. The less they wear the more they think
the cameras are going to zero in on them. If they are scantily clad they
won't be going on the air.
> ABC sports director **Chet Forte,** in 1978, crack-
> ing down on the "Monday Night Football" cheer-
> leaders.

C'mon now, gimme a break ... Okay, let's go to the videotape **18**
> Telecaster **Warner Wolf,** who moved over from ABC
> to CBS in 1980, still asking for mercy nightly, still
> going to the videotape in his ("Boom!") uniquely
> boisterous style.

We do cooperate with TV in some respects, but overall I would   **19**
say there's a pretty good balance. The print media accuse us of
doing certain things as a convenience for the networks. I personally feel these things are a convenience for the fans. Sometimes things that are in the public interest also happen to be in
the network's interest.
> NFL commissioner **Pete Rozelle,** making it all come
> out even.

We'll be playing hockey games in a studio. They're already work-   **20**
ing on getting crowd noises. You don't need a live crowd if you've
got so many people at home paying to watch the game.
> Toronto Maple Leafs owner **Harold Ballard,**
> predicting the future. Sixty percent of Canada's TV
> audience already had cable in 1981.

The Fans

"We're No. 1!" they chant, holding up a solitary finger. But are they? Not according to Ralph Nader or the NFL Players Association (whose slogan is "We're the game") or the media, or even the owners. The last three, it frequently seems, would like them just to pay their money and bear (more or less) silent witness.

But the fans seem to weather everything: shifting franchises; inadequate facilities; TV blackouts; ticket scalpers; and even free agency, which disperses their adopted heroes to alien cities. Theirs is but to do and die.

They sat in the rain and chanted "Let's Go Mets" for a team that lost over 100 games for seven seasons in a row; they rooted for Tampa Bay when it was 0-26; for the Cavs and Quebec and the Columbia Lions. They are the defeated and maligned who never entirely lose hope, and who live for reflected glory. "Wait till next year!" they cried out in Brooklyn—for nearly three decades.

But they're not always sweetly reasonable: they've thrown batteries at Dave Parker's head, dead fish on the ice at hockey games and they scream about the point spread after the two-minute warning. They can drive a player back to the Sally League with their taunts and obscenities. Still, their dogged loyalty is the financial foundation for sports in America. Contracts are signed on the basis of how many of them will sit in the Superdome on a given evening. They'll drive through three states to go to a game or pay $30 to watch a nontitle fight on closed circuit TV. They are the perennial spectators in a society that has more TV sets than bathtubs.

They are, for better or for worse, the fans.

1   At first there was a lot of mail from older people who didn't want me to break Babe Ruth's record. The young generation took notice of that and supported me. I think they want to see me have a record, not someone their granddads saw play.
              Hank Aaron in 1973, as he closed in on Ruth's long-standing record of 714 career home runs.

2   Maybe they're all on marijuana. Do you think it would happen if the first kid on the field got his head broken? I'm ashamed that I live in this country—but I'm not sure New York is part of the country.

Former Cincinnati manager **Sparky Anderson,** after
the near-riot in Shea Stadium during the final playoff
game in 1973. Mets beat the Reds, 7-2.

The fans are really getting on me. I can hear them screaming at   **3**
me—'Garland, you $2 million bum, when are you gonna start earn-
ing your money?' They don't treat me like a human being. It's like
they think I go out there and pitch with all the money in my back
pocket, like I've pulled the wool over their eyes.

            Wayne Garland, one of the first overnight
            millionaire ballplayers, languishing with a dismal 5-9
            record in the summer of 1977.

There's a different breed of cats coming out here. Instead of hoi   **4**
polloi, we're now getting Johnny Six-Pack.

            Forest Hills tournament ref **Mike Blanchard** in
            1977, on the changing tennis scene.

It's interesting to see the type of crowds we get. Now the Friday   **5**
night crowd is the one that has anxiety built up. They've been
working hard for a whole week. They're coming to get out. They've
been caught on the freeways. If you have a good Friday night, the
cheers are a few decibels louder. If you have a bad Friday night,
the people are rougher. Friday is no night to play badly. The fans
will crucify you . . . . The Sunday crowd comes out to take their
kids and see the stadium and the mountains in the background
and the palm trees . . . . You really have to be cheating them out of
their entertainment to hear a boo. Monday and Tuesday nights
you get the fans who really know baseball.

            Steve Garvey, assessing the fans in Dodger Stadium.

The arrogance of the owners and their lack of sensitivity toward   **6**
their fans is accelerating. They never ask the fans what they think
of the policies and rules these owners set. And the fans have a
right to know the full costs they are paying, as taxpayers, for the
municipal stadiums most of them can't get into, even if they could
afford a ticket.

            Ralph Nader, in announcing the formation of a new
            consumer group to be called FANS (Fight to Advance
            the Nation's Sports), in 1977.

Robert F. Kennedy Stadium was built by the taxpayers, but all its   **7**
65,000 seats are sold on a seasonal basis only. Many of these
seats are controlled year after year by the big corporations, some
of them with as many as 50 seats at their disposal to entertain the
politicians. What chance does the ordinary taxpayer have to see

the Redskins play there?
Ibid.

8 It'll be a relief to go home and get away from all the fan noise. You
might not hear individual comments, but you hear the noise. You
try to do the best you can. You try to tune it out. It's just wild
screaming, and they were on me constantly.

> Los Angeles shortstop **Bill Russell** in 1978, the year
> the Dodger fans decided he couldn't field.

9 Physically I'm sure I can play next year; the only question is, do I
want to put up with all the crap? When you lose, you walk down
the street and people come over and tell you, 'You're too old. Why
don't you get the hell out?'

> Battered 37-year-old quarterback **Fran Tarkenton,**
> facing the 1978 season with the Minnesota Vikings.

10 There are still some great matadors. But it seems to me that an
essential quality—the concern for a sacred rite, tragic in its
isolation—is slipping away. Mass spectacle is prevailing over art.
Now the bullfighters do what the public expects, and the bullfight
no longer has meaning.

> Spanish matador **El Viti,** in a 1978 interview with the
> French magazine, *Le Nouvel Observateur.*

11 There's a fan behind our bench in Pittsburgh who screams at
Dwight White the entire game. 'He stinks, get him off the field!' If
it wasn't for football, I'd be afraid to see what he would do in life.
I'm sure he comes out of a game as exhausted as the players.
There's a great element of society that uses football as a release.

> Pittsburgh Steelers tight end **Randy Grossman,** in
> 1979.

12 When I was still in Philadelphia, the Flyers were becoming renowned
for rough play. You had to watch the fans in the corners, the
expressions on their faces, when players were fighting in front of
them. There was something deep down emotionally going on
there. The players may be fighting, but those fans are ready to
come through the glass. And the players are getting paid to do it.

> Pittsburgh Steeler **Randy Grossman** on violence in
> hockey.

13 I consider *The Sporting News* the best reading material next to the
Bible.

> Letter to *The Sporting News* in February 1980 from
> **Jeffrey A. Snoke,** Poland, Ohio.

New York sports is different from every other city. The fans take   **14**
it more seriously here. They have this vicarious feeling of winning
after losing all day. New Yorkers are losing all day in the subways,
to the crowds, everything. So when they come home at night it's so
important for their team to win. A sportscaster in New York has to
understand that and it's tough if you're not from New York . . . . In
Los Angeles it's more like 'Hmmm, the Dodgers lost tonight.
Where do you want to eat?' In New York, a loss can ruin someone's day.

> WPIX's **Jerry Girard,** a telecaster definitely in the
> New York mold.

There's one guy at Shea Stadium who told me the other day he   **15**
has 100 of my autographs. I know he's either selling them or trading them off. Why else would a guy want 100 autographs of the
same player?

> Atlanta Braves coach **Bob Gibson,** a Hall of Famer
> who's just as tough off the mound.

O, Sovereign Owners and Princely Players, masters of amortiza-   **16**
tion, tax shelters, bonuses and deferred compensation, go back to
work. You have been entrusted with the serious work of play, and
your season of responsibility has come.

> **A. Bartlett Giamatti,** president of Yale
> and a devoted Red Sox fan, in an appeal to end
> the paralyzing baseball strike of the summer of 1981.

There was so much out there I couldn't pick it all up . . . I don't   **17**
know why the do it [throw coins]. I just take it as a compliment
and go out and pick it up. Today the people were yelling, 'Reggie,
please pick it up!' It's almost like they touch you when you pick up
their quarter.

> **Reggie Jackson,** after a September 1981 game dur-
> ing which he picked up $82.56 in coins and $1 bills
> tossed from the stands. Unsigned by Steinbrenner in
> 1982, Reggie carried his hatful of money to a new
> team, the California Angels.

Steinbrenner sucks! Steinbrenner sucks! Steinbrenner sucks!   **18**

> Obscene **chant** of disgruntled fans after Reggie hit
> dramatic home run against old teammates in his first
> appearance in Yankee Stadium in a California
> uniform in April 1982.

I was booed in Cincinnati, but not on every pitch. I'll endure it but   **19**
I'll be prepared for it next year. The fans are like a 10th man
against me.

against me.

> **George Foster,** at the end of a dismal first season
> with the Mets, learning what it's like to play in New
> York. Going into the last week of the season, Foster
> (who had signed for $2 million per) had batted .184
> since the All-Star break.

20 There are two groups of fans. The first type understand the
economic battle between the employee and employer. The second
group are the know-nothings. They are the hard-hat mentality who
think these are lazy, spoiled bums playing a boy's game for a
fabulous salary. And there are some who see what blacks in sports
are making and they say, 'Look at me.' Don't think it doesn't
bother them.

> Baseball union head **Marvin Miller,** in 1982.

21 I tried to watch Canadian football for a while, but it didn't have
any interest for me. Finally, I gave up, hung some pictures for my
wife and went down to the local field and watched a girls' soccer
team. That and dinner will be Sunday.

> Cincinnati football fan **Louis Merrill,** on how he
> spent the first Sunday of the 1982 football strike.

Gambling

Team-sport gambling is illegal in 49/50ths of the United States. Yet
on a typical fall weekend in Nevada, $15 million is bet on pro football,
and another $5 million on college games. That means that more than
$300 million is bet legally on football between Labor Day and the
bowl dates that mark the end of another season.

Football is the most popular gambling sport in Nevada, home
of the point spread, but the other sports (both team and nonteam)
also get their share of play. In fact, the operation is so big that Nevada
has an agency that no other state has yet: a state Gaming Control
Board.

Is the rest of the country sitting by, idly speculating about
whether the best bet that week is the Steelers and 3? Well, no. It is
estimated that across the nation $50 billion is bet annually on team
sports alone. This represents a major sector of the underground

economy, a vast reservoir of itchy money looking for action. And finding it, one way or another.

Of course in about half the states gambling is not strictly an under-the-table activity. Horse or dog racing or jai alai are legal and bettable and exist side by side with the illegal (but still bettable) team-sports action. It's sort of a two-tier system.

What distinguishes team-sport betting from straight betting on dogs or thoroughbreds (besides its illegality) is the concept of the point spread. Jimmy the Greek usually gets credit for having invented this tricky betting equalizer. It introduces subtleties that touch upon mathematics, psychology, and personal honor. What you're betting on is not so much one team against another but that the oddsmakers are wrong in assessing that the Vikings are a touchdown and a field goal better than the Cardinals on a given Sunday because Wojezschowicz sprained his thumb.

This is why the new stadium chant in the closing minutes of the game is no longer "Go Buccaneers!" or "Get 'em, Packers!" or even "Deee-fense!" but "Cover the spread!, Cover the spread!"

The people at ABC are the best friends our industry has this side **1**
of the Jersey City police department.
> **New York bookie's** assessment of one year of "Monday Night Football," in 1970.

They tell me $50-billion a year gets bet illegally on team sports. **2**
That's a gang of money, and we're all kidding ourselves if we don't think so. Why shouldn't government share in it?
> **Paul Screvane,** former president of New York's OTB, in a bid to extend the scope of legalized betting to team sports in 1975.

Government shouldn't be running sports betting any more than it **3**
runs the commodity market. I can't see civil servants making lines and point-spreads and putting up the state's money. The potential for a ripoff is enormous.
> **Shannon Bybee,** member of the Nevada Gaming Control Board, which supervises licensed bookies who run the state's lucrative sports betting operation.

It [gambling] has to be run by ex-bookmakers that know the busi- **4**
ness. You just can't take some square people into a business like this. It would have to be run by a group that put up the money and took the risks. They'd either win or lose. What they'd be is one big legitimate bookmaker.
> **Ash Resnick** of the Tropicana Hotel in Las Vegas, in 1975. Resnick's words proved prophetic: by 1982,

New York's OTB was saying it would be losing money within three years.

5 Once we drove to Philly to see the races at Liberty Bell. But we got shut out because the jockeys refused to run on a frozen track. I was furious. So myself and a few other guys headed to the airport and chartered a plane to Ohio. We found a track open there.

> **Stan the Analyst, an Aqueduct regular** once and now a Fortune 500 company executive, on the lengths that compulsive gamblers will go to to find the action.

6 It is clear that [New York Knick Earl] Monroe's shot [which scored a basket for Portland] was nothing more than a spur-of-the-moment act. He himself describes his action, which had no effect on the outcome of the game, as a 'whim.' The NBA is satisfied that this incident was unpremeditated, and the matter is closed.

> **NBA statement** following inquiry into a 1977 New York-Portland game in which Knick Earl Monroe scored a last-second basket for the Trail Blazers, reducing margin of victory to 108-104. Monroe explained that he thought the time had run out, but bettors who had given 5½ or 6 points on the Knicks had other thoughts about both Monroe and the loose play of the Knicks in the closing minutes of the game.

7 Pro football is the biggest gambling sport there is. It's the biggest sport on account of the tube. People like to bet what they can see.

> **John Quinn,** director of race and sports betting at Las Vegas's Union Plaza Hotel, in 1981.

8 The injury list [issued weekly by the NFL] insures the integrity of the game.

> **Jim Heffernan,** director of public reltions for the NFL. Heffernan's statement is really a tacit acknowledgment of the prominent role gambling plays in pro football watching.

9 George [Anderson] is a good friend of mine. Kenny's [Stabler] a good friend of mine. Tom's [Keating] a good friend of mine. I know a lot of the Raiders, and never once have we talked about betting football. I didn't hang around them because of gambling. I hung around because they were my friends.

> **Samuel "Fat Sam" Reich,** well-known San Francisco bookmaker, in an interview following the 1981 NFL inquiry into links between Oakland Raider players and gambling interests.

I'm John Unitas .... You know I was the best on the field because **10**
my record proved it .... With all due modesty, I achieved that
record by handicapping and analyzing the opposition before every
game. Outthinking and setting up the other teams and their
coaches makes beating the Las Vegas line look like child's
play ....

> Football **magazine ad** for the "John Unitas All-Pro
> Football Report," a gambling tip sheet that offers
> both pro and college football selections for $50
> annually.

People wrote me to say, 'Well, gee, all these people who looked up **11**
to you are kinda disappointed that you'd take a turn . . . to this
type of situation.' But I'm not doing anything wrong. I'm not doing
anything illegal .... All I'm doing is merely giving information to
people. If they so decide to bet their dollars on it, that's their
business.

> **John Unitas** in 1982, defending his tout-sheet
> connections.

Recruiting

It all started with recruiting, assembling the young men and women
who will represent dear old Siwash on the playing fields of the nation.
In a more virtuous age, the Ivy League schools promulgated the ideal
of the scholar-athlete, a sort of Joe Namath in horned rims. But as
Frank Carver, former University of Pittsburgh football coach, once
said, "You don't go to bowl games with pre-med students." Well, the
sad truth is that you don't—and this has led to the latter-day,
innocent-sounding special admissions programs, the lowering of
academic standards and the introduction of compensatory incen-
tives used to recruit the athletically endowed undergrad nation-
wide.

What follows is a scenario for the new breed big-time coach,
for whom recruiting has become the number one priority:

First you gotta recruit the kid. You fly up to Michigan,
have coffee with his folks, take them to the shopping mall, take
the old man fishing. Play it modest that you're a big-time coach.
They'll know. Others have already been there from other schools.
Suggest that there's a lot of drug-dealing in those schools.

If you can't get him in on a special-admissions basis, you can always get a transcript faked. You expect a kid who can run the football to get straight A's? Did you?

Sign him to one of those one-year renewable athletic scholarships. Why overburden him with the full four-year package? Will that help his grades?

Make sure his academic program is balanced, though. Steer him toward some sensible courses, like "Safety with Hand Power Tools," "Jogging," "Ozark Folk Heroes." Watch out for courses like "Main Currents in American Thought" or "Europe Since 1914." Too many hours in the library.

But don't rush him. He wants to carry nine credits, let him. More time for practice. He can always make it up with correspondence or summer courses. Maybe you'll even be able to wangle fifth-year eligibility for him if he's real slow.

Keep an eye on him, however. Don't let him get lonely for home. Some gung-ho alumnus wants to buy him a stereo or some clothes—hey, no problem. You can't expect a ghetto kid to come to college with an embossed blazer, can you?

Then there's transportation. You did promise to co-sign a promissory note so that he can get at least a Toyota. The kid's gotta have wheels.

But there are some things you gotta be very careful about, coach. Hard drugs are definitely out, period. You can turn a blind eye to a few uppers before games, you can always say you thought the assistant coach was handing out vitamins, but you gotta crack down on cocaine. Definitely verboten.

Listen, coach, just in recruiting this kid you're exposing him to the best environment he's ever been in. And a free education. Plus he'll get a crack at the pros—if he manages to stay off the injury list. Is it the school's fault—or yours—that his chances of making it to the pros run about 2 percent? Shoot, you didn't make those odds, did you?

1   No prospect is more than 4½ hours from your campus by jet today, and the trend is to go after the super-prospect regardless of where he is from. When I was at Oklahoma we began with a recruiting budget of $3,000, and I don't think we ever had more than $7,500. Now that wouldn't pay your phone bill.

> **Bud Wilkinson,** by 1968 the former coach of the University of Oklahoma Sooners dynasty.

2   Just give every coach the same amount of money and tell him he can keep what's left over.

> **Abe Lemons,** 1971 basketball coach at Oklahoma City, dispensing advice on how to win in the recruiting sweepstakes.

One of these days the NCAA might put in a rule that says you **3**
have to have one player a year on your team from your home
state.

> **Abe Lemons,** five years later, at the University of
> Texas.

I try for good players and I try for character. If necessary, though, I **4**
settle for the player.

> Vancouver Canucks general manager and ex-coach
> **Phil Maloney,** laying down his recruiting philosophy
> in 1974.

Sometimes it's frightening when you see a 19-year-old kid running **5**
down the floor with your paycheck in his mouth.

> **Bob Zufplatz,** basketball coach at Boston College in
> 1975, on the pressure cooker aspects of the college
> recruiting syndrome.

A surprisingly small number of blue-chip players really get an **6**
education—among NBA players, fewer than half have college
degrees even though the majority spent four years in college.
Thousands of lesser players end up with neither a degree nor a
career in pro ball.

> Former Boston College basketball coach **Bob Cousy**
> in 1976, on one of the evils of recruiting.

Frankly, we're panicking. We'll do anything to get Albert **7**
[King] . . . the sky's the limit.

> **Recruiter** for a top 1977 college basketball team.
> King was perhaps the nation's most-sought-after
> schoolboy athlete.

What's funny, though, is some of these guys travel hundreds of **8**
miles to see me play and then after the game they act like
they're afraid to talk to me. I'm only 17. They're adults. But they
usually just say something like 'Nice game' and that's it. If that's
all they want to say, I don't understand why they come.

> **Albert King,** who decided on the University of
> Maryland because coach Lefty Driesell's recruiters
> talked a good game.

If we're going to spend thousands of dollars a year on athletic **9**
scholarships for women, we want to attract the best. That man-
dates evaluating those players, finding out what kind of people
they are and what kind of homes they come from.

> USC athletic director **Richard Perry** in 1978,
> defending aggressive recruiting practices even when

they violate Association for Intercollegiate Athletics
for Women rules.

10 This women's basketball, it's getting to be a big deal, isn't it?
> **Mrs. Eleanor Olkowski,** mother of June Olkowski, a
> 6-foot forward for St. Maria Goretti High in
> Philadelphia, in 1978. Mrs. Olkowski found herself
> serving coffee regularly to a succession of women
> coaches from Rutgers, Old Dominion, Penn State, and
> other basketball schools.

11 We felt that certain individuals, whether football players or
musicians, deserved a chance to prove themselves in our environment, right alongside people who would normally make it.
Remember, the special admissions procedure included everyone
from legacies to oboe players to basketball players.
> **Lee Stetson,** University of Pennsylvania director of
> admissions, justifying Penn's special admissions pro-
> gram under which 15 percent of each freshman class
> is set aside for students who do not meet the univer-
> sity's stringent academic standards.

12 The original idea of the Ivy League, calling for competition from
students drawn from the normal student population of each
school, should be reaffirmed. We hope through mutual agreement
of the Ivy schools to live up to the ideal of the scholar-athlete, that
these special admissions can be dropped in the near future.
> A 1979 **report of the University of Pennsylvania
> Senate Advisory Committee,** recommending finan-
> cial cutbacks in the school's athletic program and
> reductions in the special admissions program.

13 When you get a middle class kid who wants to got to Princeton
and you tell him, 'Hey kid, you know you're going to have to pay
some of the load, you're going to have to work your way through,
because you don't qualify for financial aid and we don't give
athletic scholarships,' his old man will look at you like you're
crazy. Just plain nuts. Especially when one of those big-time
schools turns up with a boatload of money, a full ride.
> Princeton basketball coach **Pete Carril** in 1979, on
> Ivy League recruiting.

14 Everybody needs players. You need a tackle, you need an extra
lineman. It's up to these kids to go where they won't be misused.
They could wind up as another body on a depth chart.
> Temple assistant coach **Frank Massino,** looking over

the 85 stranded players at the Villanova Field House
when that college decided to give up football after 87
years in 1981. Forty player-hungry colleges sent reps.

I decided to come to Carolina because Dean Smith is a sincere **15**
person. I felt very comfortable with him. Unlike other coaches, he
didn't talk too much about basketball, he stressed how I would
grow up to be a person at Carolina, not just a basketball player.

> North Carolina's **Sam Perkins** in 1982, just before
> the Tar Heels finally won the National Collegiate
> tournament.

When I was a coach, I recruited a kid to come out and play foot- **16**
ball. I recruited him as a football player first, because I knew my
job depended on it. Not that I didn't want to help them improve
academically. But the academic aspect of it, that came second. I'm
sorry to say it, but that's the way it was. You're not going to go out
and recruit a great scholar who can't play the game. And sometimes, they don't go hand in hand.

> Former Wisconsin coach **John Coatta,** recalling in
> 1982 that he spent most of his coaching time on the
> road recruiting.

When you're being recruited, it's a whole different world. It's like **17**
window shopping, all glamour and bright lights. But once you get
in and try to buy the merchandise, it's different. You feel power-
less to do anything. The school has locked up all the angles, and
there's a no-return policy on the merchandise. It's like the lamb
staring the tiger in the face.

> **Thomas Vines,** University of Maryland Baltimore
> County senior, who quit the basketball team when
> practice sessions conflicted with his academic
> schedule. His athletic scholarship was revoked in
> early 1982, five days before his final semester.

Future Shock

What does an athlete do when his playing days are over? The answer
to this question—a part of the darker side of the sports world—has to

do with three factors: money, image, and self-esteem.

● Money. Salaries have skyrocketed, so this is no longer the problem it once was. Or is it? Playing careers are short (the average baseball player's is six years; in pro football, it's only four) and athletes, being human, get caught up in the lifestyle of their contemporaries at close to peak earnings. Then comes that sudden drop to the economic neighborhood where "ordinary" people live. Very sobering, even to the least realistic of men.

One solution, of course, is to catch on in the same sport in a more modest capacity; scout, assistant coach, minor league batting instructor and the like. Another is to have invested the money you made in your best years wisely. (But then one recalls that even a champ who made as much money as Joe Louis was led up the garden path by bad counsel, and had trouble with the IRS for years.) The best solution is to have planned for another—and longer—career. But for every Doc Medich, Nick Buonaconti or Bill Bradley there are probably 50 athletes who slip into quiet oblivion.

● Image. When an athlete is no longer an athlete, what is he? A prospective sporting goods salesman? An unemployed jock waiting for the phone to ring? A one-time celebrity whose name is only hazily recalled? That guy in public relations whose job is to go to lunch with people? A has-been? An ex-pro who works with kids? An alcoholic?

Ten or 15 years later than the rest of us, the athlete once again faces that complex and never totally answerable question: Who am I? And unless he's built a life both apart and parallel to the one on the playing field, he's in trouble.

● Self-esteem. This is the toughest area. His on-field accomplishments are behind him and recorded. Now he must look at his former life, evaluate it, decide what the curve of his future is. Does he value what he has done, what he has been? If he was once "more" than other people, is he "less" now? How does he readjust to being just another human being?

These are just some of the nagging problems that face the man who knows his playing days are on the wane.

1 How much do these kids have in their pension kitty now? Ten or fifteen million? Maybe they can turn some of it loose for us old guys.

> **Marion Motley,** the crunching fullback of Paul
> Brown's great Otto Graham-led Cleveland Browns.
> Though he had a career average of 5.7 yards per carry,
> he never earned more than $11,500 for a year's work.

2 The anti-intellectualism of baseball has been diminished. People are slowly discovering tht there *is* life after baseball.

> Ace relief pitcher **Mike Marshall,** a Los Angeles

Dodger in 1974 and throughout his career one of the free
spirits in the game.

I guess I'm starting to realize how much my ego, my whole sense   **3**
of self-esteem was tied up in basketball. Like when I was a player
and I came here [New York]. I felt great, people saw me as Jim
Barnett, the player . . . now I wonder how they see me.
> Guard **Jim Barnett,** cut after 11 years by the New
> York Knicks after the 1975-76 season, on the fleeting-
> ness of fame.

They took me right out of the casket.   **4**
> **Jim Barnett,** pleased at being signed as a free agent
> by the Philadelphia 76ers in 1977. Before the
> season's end, he was reinterred.

I wanted to do other things, and golf takes so much of your time,   **5**
doesn't it? I was keen on tennis and fishing and I wanted to stay in
touch with my friends.
> Seventy-five-year-old **Lady Heathcote-Amory,**
> recalling in 1977 why she'd only played competitive
> golf for nine years. *The Encyclopedia of Golf* ranks her
> as "the supreme woman golfer of her age, perhaps of
> all time," and Bobby Jones, after a 1935 match with
> her, praised her as the best opponent, regardless of
> sex, he'd ever faced.

I put my whole heart and soul into baseball, then, one day, it was   **6**
all over. When you leave baseball you leave part of your childhood
behind.
> Former Dodger **Sandy Vance,** who pitched for Los
> Angeles in 1970 and '71, before his arm went dead.

It's stupid to stay six years in baseball and get out with nothing.   **7**
All I can say is, 'I've been in the big leagues and I've played with
the Mets.' I don't think you can get too far in life saying that.
> **Randy Tate,** a young minor league pitcher with con-
> trol problems, who quit baseball in 1977. Two years
> earlier, he had come within five outs of pitching a no-
> hitter.

There is a little gear behind your brain, and any time the front   **8**
wheel of the bike makes a funny slip or the back wheel slides,
which is about three times a lap, this little gear tells you that you
are falling down. Well, when you're 18 that gear doesn't even
work, but when you're 31 or 32 it's working so well that you aren't

comfortable at the speeds you have to go to win. When that
happens to me, I'll probably look for something else to do.

> Motorcycle racer **Kenny Roberts** who, at 29, has won
> races during a single season on all five American
> Motorcycle Association types of courses, from dirt
> tracks to hardrock-racing tracks.

9   Years ago, there was more room for a player like me in the minors.
Then they had not only kids but old guys hanging on. When I was
starting out in the minors an old player told me: 'Son, there's two
kinds of ballplayers—prospects and suspects. And suspects don't
like prospects. So get me a beer.' But now everybody down here is
up and coming.

> Former Yankee pitcher **Jim Bouton** on the perils of
> the comeback trail, circa 1978.

10   I guess this means they fired me. I'll never make the mistake of
being 70 years old again.

> **Casey Stengel,** dropped as manager of the
> Yankees in 1960 after losing the Series
> to Pittsburgh. Stengel had won 10 pennants for
> New York.

11   Our goal was an image, and that image was success. We wanted an
image that would last. When success waned on the golf course, as
we knew it had to someday, it wouldn't matter. In the minds of the
buying public, Johnny Miller would still be a success. A name that
sells products. That's the way it has worked. It's like building an
ark. You build it before it gets wet. It's much harder working in
the rain.

> Agent-promoter **Ed Banner,** on the making of the
> Johnny Miller, golf pro, image.

12   They run me out of my home. I played hard all those years for
'em, but when they used me up, they run me out.

> Slugger **Willie Horton,** on having given the best
> years of his playing life to the Detroit Tiger organiza-
> tion. Traded to Texas in 1978, he soon drifted out of
> baseball.

13   There is a built-in discipline to playing any sport, a structure that
keeps you within certain bounds. I played hockey for 25 years. All
of a sudden, I couldn't play anymore. The discipline was gone.
And it was easy to drift away. Suddenly I was no longer Bernie
Parent, the hockey player, but I wasn't prepared to be Bernie
Parent, the human being.

Former Philadelphia Flyer goalie **Bernie Parent,** who
had to turn to Alcoholics Anonymous for help soon after
his retirement.

In 1961, instead of exploiting my home runs, and Mickey   **14**
Mantle's, they did everything they could to downgrade them.
They acted as though I was doing something wrong, poisoning
the record books or something.
    Now they talk on the radio about the records set by Ruth
and DiMaggio and Henry Aaron. But they rarely mention mine.
Do you know what I have to show for the 61 home runs? Nothing,
exactly nothing.

> **Roger Maris** at the 1980 All-Star Game, looking
> back bitterly at 1961.

The doctors had to tell me: 'Lay back, give us the ball and let us   **15**
run with it.' The future? I can't think about it.

> **Dan Lloyd** at 26, whose career as a feared linebacker
> for the New York Giants was suspended in 1980 by
> lymphocytic lymphoma. Lloyd beat cancer, tried for a
> comeback in 1982, but didn't make it.

I can think of three managers who weren't fired. John McGraw of   **16**
the Giants, who was sick and resigned; Miller Huggins of the Yankees, who died on the job; and Connie Mack of the Athletics, who
owned the club.

> Sportswriter **Red Smith,** offering solace to Boston's
> Don Zimmer at the end of the 1979 season. Zimmer
> hung on for another season, then joined the inner cir-
> cle of rotating managers, caught on with Texas in
> 1981, only to be bounced again in 1982.

I called Mr. Irsay [Baltimore Colts' owner Bob Irsay] last year and   **17**
told him, 'I know you're going to make some changes . . . and I'd
be more than interested in talking to you concerning the general
manager's position.' He said, 'I'll get back to you after the season.'
I haven't heard from him since.

> **Johnny Unitas,** who passed for 290 touchdowns in
> 18 seasons, 17 of them with Baltimore, trying to get
> back in the game in 1982.

I would like to work in hockey again. Maybe I shouldn't say this,   **18**
but I will. I've never heard from the New York Rangers. That was
my favorite team. I promoted hockey for them. I never missed a
banquet. I thought maybe I could be a scout for them in the
Montreal area. They knew I was available.

Diminutive **Camille Henry,** who scored 256 goals for the Rangers in the 1960s (fifth highest in the team's history), and who now works as a night watchman.

19 Most people are dead at my age. You could look it up.
Casey Stengel, at 75.

4. THE IMAGE GAME

Image

Image, a very modern concept for athletes, has to do with four more or less contemporary phenomena: 1) the show-bizification of sports; 2) the assigned hero-or-villain role of the participants (umpires, referees, wrestling, and Howard Cosell spring to mind); 3) open hostility by players toward the fans and/or the media; 4) media saturation.

Ruth and Cobb didn't bother much about their "images." Neither did Jack Johnson or Red Grange or Babe Didrikson or Bill Tilden or any of the other pre-electronic greats. They let their records speak for them. Then came the winking eye that sees all, between commercials.

Media saturation makes it possible for a tennis player (let us say) to publicly give the finger to 70,000 fans while millions gasp. No word of mouth is needed to pass on the news. He is now Tennis' Bad Boy. Watch for him next week in the French Open, when he plays against that other one, the foreigner, who throws his racket, bullies linesmen and can swear in five languages and seven Slavic dialects. It should be some kind of match!

Athletes have probably always been hostile toward fans (who exploit them) and the press (which bedevils them). But no one knew about it. Now, no sooner does a player come into prominence than he

115

must be assigned a nickname, label, or identifying tag. And so: "Broadway Joe" Namath; Mean Joe Greene; George Brett, All-American Boy; Earl "the Pearl" Monroe; "Clyde" Frazier; Jack Nicklaus, Mr. Nice Guy; Reggie Jackson, Mr. October.

    Truth or media hype?

    Neither. Just images for the shadow play of competitive sports.

1 Dressing a pool player in a tuxedo is like putting whipped cream on a hot dog.

> The legendary **Minnesota Fats,** after learning that he wasn't being invited to the 1972 world championship pocket billiards tournament in Los Angeles, a black-tie affair.

2 Next to Sinatra, I have the most hostile press in America. I have been called a company pimp, a prostitute and a man with no trace of decency or morality. I have been vilified by people I have never even seen.

> **Howard Cosell,** in 1975.

3 My life is a living testimony and is an incongruity and a contradiction to what America has hitherto here asked for success. I am a black ex-convict from the ghetto, an ex-numbers runner, and now I'm sitting at the top of 30 Rockefeller Plaza. It's a testimony that can only happen here in America.

> Boxing impresario **Don King** in 1975, on the fall and rise of Don King.

4 I can do without the unhuman looks people give me. Even kids do it. When I tried to do some teaching in the off-season, the kids said, 'Hey, man, you're a football player, not a teacher. We don't want you here!' I'm just an object.

> Pittsburgh Steeler defensive end **L.C. Greenwood.**

5 It makes me cry, the way they treat me on this team. The Yankee pinstripes are Ruth and Gehrig and DiMaggio and Mantle. I'm just a black man to them who doesn't know how to be subservient. I'm a big black man with an I.Q. of 160 making $700,000 a year, and they treat me like dirt. They've never had anyone like me on their team before.

> **Reggie Jackson,** when he was the new boy in town in 1977.

6 He's an animal as a competitor with a good nose for blood . . . more savage than anyone since Gonzalez. The vulgarness—the cursing, the finger, the stroking of his racket like he was masturbating—that's all part of it.

> Tennis player **Gene Scott,** about Jimmy Connors.

Many times at the beach a good-looking lady will say to me, 'I want to touch you.' I always smile and say, 'I don't blame you.'   **7**

> **Arnold Schwarzenegger,** voted "Mr. Universe" several times, and an occasional movie star.

I guess you could say I'm the redemption of the fat man. A guy will be watching me on TV and see that I don't look in any better shape than he is. 'Hey Maude,' he'll holler. 'Get a load of this guy. And he's a 20-game winner.'   **8**

> **Mickey Lolich,** former Detroit Tigers pitcher, whose best year (25-14) was 1971. He also won three games in the 1968 World Series.

The man came to us one day and said, 'I want short hair, no beards or mustaches and you'll wear ties and suits in public—or it'll cost you $100 a day.' When he puts it that way, how can you resist?   **9**

> **Ted Simmons,** when he was with the 1977 squeaky-clean St. Louis Cardinals. "The man" was manager Vern Rapp.

The big argument now is that we're entertainers; people are interested in our salaries, and in what we do off the field. I don't like that sort of attention. Entertainment is planned, but when we go on the field, it's spontaneous, the game happens. There's nothing planned about it, and we're still under the same pressures as ballplayers years ago.   **10**

> Former New York Yankee **Roy White,** now playing in Japan, commenting on the baseball player's changing image.

I know it was obnoxious of me to flash the victory sign to the Charlotte people after the game. I mean they had enough heartache. But it's just part of my sandpaper. The coaches around now, they either want to kiss me or spit on me.   **11**

> Former Marquette basketball coach **Al McGuire,** after a last-second victory over North Carolina at Charlotte in the 1977 NCAA semifinals.

I'm like an old tin can in an alley. Anyone who walks by can't resist kicking it.   **12**

> Former New York Mets owner **M. Donald Grant,**

alluding to the continuing criticism he was receiving after the Seaver trade.

13 I'm such an ogre in the United States. Even my father asks why I insist on being such an ogre.

> New York Yankees owner **George Steinbrenner,** in April 1977.

14 I never asked him that. I don't think a normal father would ask him that. I never thought he was an ogre. He'll always be a little boy to me.

> **Henry Steinbrenner,** George's father.

15 I was an official jockey the first time I got on a horse.

> **Steve Cauthen,** when asked how it felt to lose his 5-pound apprentice's allowance.

16 I felt more then [after defeating Ken Norton] than when I got the decision in Las Vegas. I was so happy I thought I was gonna cry. But I kept things in, and I just waved. It wouldn't be right for a world heavyweight champion to be crying.

> **Larry Holmes,** after quickly dispatching Ken Norton in their June 1978 bout for the fractional heavyweight championship of the world.

17 I'm tired of hearing people ask me, for 13 years, how much I weigh. What's the difference? I never ride that pine. I play 158 games a year. The guys with the beautiful bodies are always hurt. Nobody ever says, you can pole it; you can picket. All they say is, what you weigh?

> First baseman **George Scott,** who used to pole them for Boston and Milwaukee.

18 I'm the bad guy. You got your good guys, your Dr. J. You got your pie and ice-cream guys. I'm no pie and ice-cream guy.

> Basketball enfant terrible **Marvin Barnes,** embracing his role in 1978.

19 Dallas is a squeaky-clean city. Roger Staubach is Mr. Straight. Nice, clean, bright uniforms and stadium. Pittsburgh? They call it a shot-and-beer town. Hard-working guys with stumpy legs. A team with mean-looking black uniforms. Nothing squeaky-clean about Pittsburgh. It's good guys versus bad guys.

> **Rocky Bleier's** pre-Super Bowl assessment of the rival Cowboys and Steelers in 1979.

Let's face it. These athletes aren't angels. They're not the nicest peo- **20**
ple in the community. They're young, self-occupied and have violent
urges. The bulk of athletes have more of a sense of supermen about
themselves than do the fans. They're plagued by the need to be
supermen. They are driven men.

> Boston psychiatrist **Stanley Cheren,** whose specialty
> is psychosomatic medicine.

If they want somebody to play third base, they got me. If they   **21**
want somebody to go to luncheons, they should hire George
Jessel.

> **Graig Nettles,** sassing Steinbrenner and ducking an
> offical welcome-home luncheon in 1979. He was fined
> $500.

When I was a boy, every girl in England had to play tennis, or she   **22**
wasn't asked away for the weekend. That's all gone and the clubs
have declined in number, but the interest has survived that and
grown and grown and grown. Now the game has a high quantity of
good-looking athletes, the pop singer sort of thing. It has sexual
appeal to all classes of people. There is a new strata of society
that identifies as much with it as the aristocracy.

> Former tennis player and current fashion designer
> **Ted Tinling,** on the escalating Wimbledon mania.

It's wrong thinking to try to demean the [baseball] players and the   **23**
Players Association. As owners we should be boosting the players.
We need the players. We need the players to be respected and
liked across America.

> Baltimore Orioles owner **Edward Bennett Williams,**
> on the eve of the 1981 baseball strike.

When you give a man a three-year contract when he's 38 years   **24**
old, then you've got to expect leadership from him. Lou [Piniella]
is like a child who tests you with how many times he can go to the
cookie jar. The type of individual he is, once in a while he has to
be belted good.

> Yankee owner **George Steinbrenner,** seeing himself
> as Keeper of the Cookie Jar, chastising Sweet Lou for
> reporting eight pounds overweight in the spring of
> 1982.

I'm tired of being treated like Little Orphan Annie.   **25**

> **Lou Piniella** striking back, after being fined $7,000
> for reporting overweight and leaving the "A" team
> without permission. The fine was later reduced to

$500—provided Piniella stayed below 203 on Steinbrenner's precision-calibrated scales for the rest of the season.

26 Never seen a team like this. We're just a bunch of rich orphans the Cowboy [Gene Autry] took in.

> **Reggie Jackson's** team portrait of division-winning California Angels during the 1982 playoffs. Though the team had four former MVPs and an embarrassment of other high-priced talent, they were nevertheless eliminated by Milwaukee.

27 Shoot, I'd rather be the No. 10 pitcher on the Yankees than a starter in Cleveland.

> New York Yankee reliever **Ron Davis,** on learning that John Denny had passed up a Steinbrenner bid to re-sign with the Indians. Shortly after, Davis was traded to Minnesota.

28 Nobody knows I'm human. That's my image problem . . . What makes him [Arguello] a gentleman? Helping up Boom Boom Mancini? Who knocked down Mancini in the first place? And Mancini was just a 19-year-old boy who'd never had a big fight before in his life. I'm just as much a gentleman as he is, but there are no gentlemen in the ring. People don't come to see gentlemen fight.

> WBA junior welterweight champ **Aaron Pryor,** in defense of both his title and his dignity against challenger Alexis Arguello. Pryor TKO'd Arguello in 14 rounds.

29 I'm excited to see what I can do, to discover talents I never knew I had. I want to see the next chapter. Is this the perfect Cinderella story? Will I be the true athlete I think I can be?

> High hurdler **Renaldo "Skeets" Nehemiah,** who signed on as a wide receiver with the San Francisco 49ers in 1982.

30 We as athletes are already fighting the stereotype of being dumb jocks, and now, you add to that we are also drug addicts.

> Cornerback **Carlton Williamson** of the San Francisco 49ers, angrily reacting to reports of widespread drug use in the NFL.

31 I haven't been this hungry in three years, since just before I won the title. I feel naked without my title. I feel like a little kid running around without no clothes on.

Former champ **Matthew Saad Muhammad,** after winning by a TKO over Pete McIntyre in 1982, in the light-
heavyweight division.

Well, you know what they say about race drivers. They are too   **32**
lazy to work and too honest to steal. I guess that question [why he
continues to race despite arthritis] might be one for a psychiatrist.
Johnny Rutherford, who has won at Indianapolis
three times.

It's like living in your own secure little world. The [hockey] net is   **33**
your cocoon. You have your protective equipment and de-
fensemen to watch over you. It's a chance for a shy person to be
onstage.
Diminutive goalie **Chico Resch,** with the Colorado
Rockies, before they moved the franchise to New
Jersey.

BIC Corporation has tapped the terror of tennis to tout its dispos-   **34**
able shaver . . . taking full off-court advantage of [John] McEnroe's
feisty image, the 30-second commercial opens with a seemingly
familiar on-court confrontation between McEnroe and an umpire.
Press release from the BIC Corporation in 1982,
alerting the news media to its forthcoming print and
TV ads using John McEnroe in a familiar stance.

Celebrity

In the world of sports, celebrity can reach an extraordinary level of
intensity because the mass media machine churns out instant fame,
creating heroes for a nation in which they seem to be in distinct short
supply, both in and out of public life. Athletes today enjoy the same
degree of fame as movie stars because, like them, they are never out of
the public eye—and mind. For example, even before Reggie Jackson
had hit a baseball at Yankee Stadium, he was exercising the First
Amendment to assure his ever-expanding fame. "I didn't come to
New York to become a star," he declared after signing his lucrative
contract. "I brought my star here." This from a player with a .267

lifetime average with two previous teams.

Not surprisingly, Jackson's flamboyance made both the fans and the press hypercritical of his performance, especially his fielding, but Jackson made amends with a good year at the plate.

By contrast, other athletes seem to thrive on the controversy their utterances and antics incite. Muhammad Ali was the reigning figure in this department, but every sport has its headline-grabbers. "I'm good copy," says high jumper Dwight Stones, generally accompanying anything he says with the prediction that he is about to set a new world record.

Is this bad? Not if you're the "right" kind of star. Top-notch performers in the glamour sports—usually those associated with winning teams—are rewarded for their fame with indecently large salaries plus the opportunity for endorsing products. Their images are stamped on our culture for as long as their celebrity is worth exploiting. Or even longer. Fels Planetarium in Philadelphia named a distant star after the retiring Willie Stargell in 1982.

But fame is fleeting, as we know, and yesterday's hero may suddenly plummet to complete obscurity. "The fame of men ought always to be estimated by the means used to acquire it," wrote La Rochefoucauld long before Abner Doubleday laid out his first diamond, and the sage athlete recognizes that his celebrity belongs to the sports pages, which are hardly the most important record of man's achievements on earth. The exceptions—the Babe Ruths and Bobby Joneses—survive the dazzle, the tub-thumping, and the river of foolish words written about them, and do finally achieve a kind of immortality.

1   Too many people think an athlete's life can be an open book. You're supposed to be an example. Why do I have to be an example for your kid? *You* be an example for your kid.

> Hall of Famer **Bob Gibson** in 1970, when he was pitching for St. Louis.

2   I often get calls at the most impossible hours from women who just want to let me hear the sound of a kiss.

> **Giacomo Agostini,** world motorcycle champion, speaking in 1970.

3   Cosell was crazy about being in the movie. He's a tremendous ham, a cartoonlike character. He comes across that way on TV, too. He's the same way if you're eating dinner with him—he broadcasts the meal.

> **Woody Allen,** speaking about his film *Bananas,* in which Howard Cosell made his film debut.

Chris is riding the crest of a wave, and I hope she enjoys it. It's the best **4**
time of her life. But I also pity her: she hasn't a free moment to herself.
Chris no longer belongs to Chris Evert. She belongs to the public.
> **Billie Jean King,** in 1971, on the 16-year-old who
> was soon to be her successor.

Around the world I'm better known than Joe Namath. But in the **5**
States I'm a nobody.
> Chess champion **Bobby Fischer,** one of the more
> memorable high school dropouts of our time.

I'm the world champion but I don't feel any different than that fan **6**
over there. I'll still walk in the ghettoes, answer questions, kiss
babies. I didn't marry a blonde or go nude in the movies. I'll never
forget my people.
> **Muhammad Ali,** after the 1974 Zaire fight with
> George Foreman.

Leave me alone. I'm a lineman. I want to be obscure. **7**
> Ex-Baltimore Colt offensive tackle **Dennis Nelson,**
> fighting off the press after a 1973 game.

I'm only an average superstar. **8**
> Canadian Football League Rookie of the Year
> **Johnny Rodgers** in 1973, whose lack of size offset
> his accomplishments—Heisman Trophy winner in
> 1972—in the NFL drafting deliberations.

The super athlete is getting closer to the top entertainers of 10 **9**
years ago in image and financial structure. The athlete has gone
off the sports pages and their investments and businesses have
become subjects for the financial pages and national trade
publications.
> **Larry Fleischer,** executive of the NBA Players'
> Association.

The way you look up there [on the victory stand] is the way people **10**
remember you for the rest of your life.
> Track star **Marty Liquori,** accounting for the disap-
> pearance of his beard and mustache at the 1976
> Olympics.

It gets to be frustrating. People are always pushing that on me. **11**
I've got to keep it in the back of my mind. In fact, I don't even
think about it unless people ask me about it. It's over now. I can't
live with that hit for the rest of my life.

Former New York Yankee **Chris Chambliss,** whose ninth-inning home run won the 1976 playoffs against the Royals.

12 I guess I'm not the same. I don't like to say it, it's weird, but I feel sort of different since I got my picture in the newspapers . . . Like I'll be driving my car and some guy will cut me off, you know, and I'll think to myself, just who is this guy, cutting me off? When did he ever get his picture in the paper? It's like I know I'm not just a nobody anymore.

Tennis star **John McEnroe,** who got all the way to the semifinals at the 1977 Wimbledon before losing to Jimmy Connors.

13 I'm going to be famous one day. Sports is a shortcut to fame. Look at them Chris Everts and Billie Jean Kings getting to do all them commercials. That's what I want to be.

Maryland boxing trainer **Pat Coleman,** a gal in a rush for glory.

14 It's just amazing. It's much bigger than I ever expected. Everywhere we go people stop us and actually thank us for being such a good couple for their kids to look up to. They don't think we fight. Sometimes I don't think they think we're human. We'd have to get divorced to get off this pedestal.

Chrystie Jenner, six months after her husband Bruce won the 1976 Olympics decathlon championship. The adulation—and money— were promptly forthcoming; so was the divorce and getting off the pedestal.

15 But when I read stuff about me getting spoiled, I just turn the page. And what really bothers me is when people start writing about me like I was a god. I don't have any magic. I have to prove myself like everybody else, as a race rider and as a person.

Jockey **Steve Cauthen,** quoted at unusual length (for him) in *The Kid* by Pete Axthelm. The book had the good fortune to appear just after Cauthen won the Triple Crown atop Affirmed.

16 I think that many of them [fans], when they're in the stadium, are privately gratified over the distress or defeat of a famous athlete. I think it pleases this kind of fan to know that even famous and monied heroes have to bow to the humiliations of life. Maybe the fan isn't aware of it, but I've been to too many stadiums and heard

too many crowds to question it.
> Former Minnesota Viking quarterback **Fran Tarkenton** in early 1977, following a season in which he set several NFL career passing records.

If I come to New York, they'll probably name a candy bar after me.   **17**
> **Reggie Jackson,** casting himself in the Ruthian mold.

My gum company made a $40-million profit last year, and I can't get the financial writers to say a word about it. But I fire a manager and everybody shows up.   **18**
> **Philip K. Wrigley,** the late chairman of the famous chewing gum company and owner of the Chicago Cubs, commenting on American media priorities.

In Italy, I am hero. On slow days the papers sent reporters to my house to ask me questions and put my answers on front page. I was highest-paid player in all Italy—$200,000 a year, no tax. Everyone wanted to marry Chinaglia, to be part of Chinaglia's clan. In Italy, there are 52 million people, and all they care about is soccer. I would hear them chant, 'Keen-Al-Ya, Keen-Al-Ya,' through streets. Here I got nobody. It bothers me, it wouldn't bother you?   **19**
> **Giorgio Chinaglia,** making money with the New York Cosmos, but missing the adulation back home.

In all my years as an umpire, I've never had a person come up to me and say, 'Are you Nestor Chylak, the umpire?'   **20**
> The late **Nestor Chylak,** after 23 years as an American League umpire.

It's a difficult situation to deal with. I want to play professional tennis, which brings me into the public eye, but I don't want to be in the public eye. I've had my fill of being ogled and exploited and used.   **21**
> Transsexual **Renee Richards,** who went from being Dr. Richard Raskind, male ophthalmologist, to being a 6-foot 2-inch female tennis pro, in 1978.

I still don't know why they asked me to do this commercial.   **22**
> Marvelous **Marv Throneberry,** better known for his barstool commercials than for the way he played first base for the "Amazin" Mets.

The day I checked into our hotel here a guy held up his hands and   **23** said, 'Don't hit me now.' I get that everywhere I go. I bet 30 people have done that . . . . But some guys are hoping I will. One night in New Jersey four different guys in four different places tried to goad me. I finally had to go home. It must have been full moon.

> Yankee manager **Billy Martin** in 1980. Despite his less strident managerial role in Oakland (from which he nevertheless got fired), the myth of Billy the Kid persists.

24　I get more fan mail now than I ever did. I get letters now that almost make you cry. They tell me that looking up to me gave them inspiration to become what they are.

> **Mickey Mantle** in 1982, 14 years after he retired from baseball.

25　Steve [Scott] gets more attention in New Zealand than here. If Steve were getting big money for this race, if this was called 'The $500,000 Fifth Avenue Mile,' then you'd see people get excited. People just want to see athletes competing for money.

> New Zealand's **John Walker,** former world-record holder in the mile, speaking about America's Steve Scott, who has run the mile in 3:47.69, the second fastest ever. Scott finished second to Tom Byers, who ran the Fifth Avenue Mile in 3:51.35. Walker himself was third.

26　There's been a disappearance of fame and an emergence of celebrities. Little McEnroe earns 10 times as much as the Chief Justice of the United States, and will be forgotten as soon as he stops playing. You hear an announcer saying at a tennis match, 'On this serve rests $40,000.' Imagine saying that about a sonata performed by Serkin.

> Historian **Henry Steele Commager,** in 1982.

Superstars

The term "superstar" first appeared in the late sixties or early seventies. Why wasn't "star" enough any more? For the same reason that olives are now graded giant, mammoth, and colossal. Small, medium, and large are out; they no longer adequately describe our overinflated world. Dave Winfield makes more money in nine days than Ruth made in his best year, whether he plays or not. Otis Birdsong used to get a million a year plus 50 cents a head for every Meadowlands customer over 5,000 for every game—until his agent decided that was conspicuous accretion and got the extra money written directly into his contract. Everyone wonders what a Willie Mays would get if he were a 20-year-old phenom out of Alabama today. Or a young Sandy Koufax.

And so we find ourselves in the age of the superstar in most sports, a few of whom are genuine, many of whom are the fortunate victims of team circumstance and/or corporate greed.

Q.: How do you cut a superstar down to size?

A.: With a simple stroke of the pen: sign him to a 10-year no-cut no-trade contract at 2 mil per year.

He [John Unitas] scares you more than any quarterback because **1** of that long bomb threat he holds in his hand. You can't intimidate him . . . . When he throws on third down and long yardage, he just defies you to stop it. When he sees us coming, *he* knows it's going to hurt and *we* know it's going to hurt, but he just stands there and takes it. No other quarterback has such class.

> One of the **"Fearsome Four"** of the Los Angeles Rams (Brown, Jones, Lundy, and Olsen), speaking for the group on the Baltimore Colts' John Unitas.

It's like rushing the passer in football. You don't know whether to **2** go in after Alcindor or drop people back like linebackers to cover his receivers.

> Former Stanford basketball coach **Howie Dallmar** in 1969, resorting to football analogies to describe the threat of Lew Alcindor's full-court passes.

Everytime you make a move to the hoop, you run right into that **3** giant oak tree [Lew Alcindor]. You just can't make any penetration, and you can't beat anybody by taking 20-footers all night.

> Baltimore Bullet forward **Jack Marin,** during his team's losing effort in the 1971 NBA finals against the Alcindor-led Milwaukee Bucks.

[Bill] Walton is playing as well right now as any center who ever **4** played, and Kareem is playing about the same—better than any center has played.

> Former Los Angeles Laker guard **Lucius Allen,** assessing the awesome matchup of Portland's Bill

Walton and teammate Abdul-Jabbar in the 1977 NBA
playoffs, won ultimately by Portland.

5 I don't lose when it comes to championships or money. I lose some
exhibition games. But nobody scores on me unless I want them to.
Paul Haber, perennial handball champ, in 1970.

6 We used to start with Jackie Robinson and the manager would say
you gotta keep him close at first, then he would say you gotta keep
him close at second and then he would say you gotta keep him
close at third because he likes to steal home. When you go over a
guy base by base, you know you're in a lot of trouble.

Former catcher **Joe Garagiola,** recalling in 1975 the
anti-Robinson strategy sessions before Cardinal-Dodger
games.

7 Throwing a fastball by Henry Aaron is like trying to sneak the sun
past a rooster.

St. Louis Cardinals pitcher **Curt Simmons,** who was
one of the best in 1971.

8 Chess is in his fingertips. That's the difference between a master
and a truly great grandmaster. The master will study for hours
and perhaps make the right move. But Fischer will toss out the
moves on his fingertips, and they will be unerringly correct ones.
He has a sense for what is correct, what is beautiful and what is
true.

Larry Evans, grandmaster, on Bobby Fischer.

9 When he [Jack Nicklaus] plays well, he wins. When he plays badly,
he finishes second. When he plays terrible, he finishes third.

Golfer **Johnny Miller,** in 1973.

10 I don't think. I just chase. I could cut through the infield and she
still beat me.

Ex-jockey **Braulio Baeza,** whose mount finished nine
lengths behind undefeated Ruffian in a 1974 race.

11 He's the only guy who puts fear into me. Not because he can get
me out, but because he could kill me.

Reggie Jackson, with Oakland in 1975, paying
homage to Nolan Ryan's fastball.

12 Randy's pitches are too good to take—and not good enough to hit.

Bob Skinner, a slugger in his day and 1976 batting
coach for the Pittsburgh Pirates, on the pitching

legerdemain of the Padres' Randy Jones. Jones was
perhaps the first "junk" pitcher to win a Cy Young
Award.

Greaseball, greaseball, greaseball. That's all I throw him, and he **13**
still hits them. He's the only player in baseball who consistently
hits my grease. He sees the ball so well, I guess he can pick out
the dry side.

> Veteran pitcher **Gaylord Perry** on Rod Carew's bat-
> ting prowess.

Rick goes his own way. Superstars always do . . . . If Rick has a **14**
drawback . . . it's that he's not very patient. He can't understand
why a guy can't play the game the way he does. That is a fault of
all superstars. You may say of these people that they aren't
regular guys. Well, they aren't.

> **Al Attles,** Golden State Warriors coach in 1977,
> about the Warriors' Rick Barry.

He certainly had the ability to pick up the puck, charge the length **15**
of the rink and score with everybody going nuts. In the other
team's end, if one of his four teammates didn't have the puck, he
had it. When he was on the ice he had the puck 50 percent of the
time, and he was almost always on the ice. He absolutely controlled games. He was amazing.

> Former teammate **Don Awrey** on Boston Bruin
> Bobby Orr, before knee surgery.

But you couldn't ever mess up Unitas, he was different, he was **16**
cold. He never even acknowledged you were there. You could be
yelling at him and he never even looked at you. He had no reaction at all. At least not until he completed the pass. Then he gave
you that smile. That damn smile.

> Linebacker **Dick Butkus** on Johnny Unitas in 1979,
> when they were both inducted into the Pro Football
> Hall of Fame.

When you tackle Campbell, it reduces your I.Q. **17**

> Washington Redskin tackle **Pete Wysocki** in 1979,
> on the risks of intimate contact with Houston Oiler
> back Earl Campbell.

Everyone says that he [Bjorn Borg] can't volley because his **18**
ground strokes are so good. He has learned how to volley. It is not
textbook, but who cares. It is such hard work playing against him.
So many balls come back. It's like taking too many body punches.

You are tired by the end.

> **Brian Gottfried,** after losing to Bjorn Borg in the 1980 Wimbledon, which Borg went on to win.

19 Every time we play the Celtics I talk about Larry Bird. I don't know how to defend him. You give him the outside shot and he'll hit that. You play him tight and he'll go around you. You double team him and he passes off.

> Indiana coach **Jack McKinney,** about the Boston Celtics' high scorer.

20 I never hit a shot, even in practice, without having a very sharp, in-focus picture of it in my head. It's like a color movie. First I 'see' the ball where I want it to finish. . . . Then the scene quickly changes and I 'see' the ball going there . . . . Then there's a sort of fade-out, and the next scene shows me making the kind of swing that will turn the previous images into reality.

> **Jack Nicklaus,** detailing the "visualization" technique that helped make him one of the world's great golfers.

21 I couldn't possibly prepare for that move. All I could think to myself was, 'Which one of his 150 moves is [Mike] Bossy going to use this time?'

> Pittsburgh Penguin goalie **Michel Dion,** talking about the New York Islanders' best threat to score. Bossy's move on the play was to pass off to Bryan Trottier at the last second—who scored.

22 He [Jim Thorpe] was the greatest athlete who ever lived. Lovely fellah. What he had was natural ability. There wasn't anything he couldn't do. All he had to see is someone doin' something and he tried it . . . and he'd do it better. He had brute strength . . . stamina . . . endurance. A lot of times, like in the decathlon, he didn't know what he was doing. He didn't know the right way to throw the javelin or the discus but it didn't matter. He just went there and threw it further than anyone else.

> Ninety-year-old **Abel Kiviat,** silver medal winner in the 1912 Olympic Games in Stockholm, recalling the prowess of Jim Thorpe 70 years later.

Dreams Come True

The athlete is part dreamer, and the dream lies somewhere in the process of perfecting his skills. Part of growing up is training the body to perform those functions that normal life situations demand of it. Beyond that lies the performance of acts and coordination of reflexes that require greater dexterity in situations we create and call games. For most young people the challenge of this performance beckons; it is there to be met and mastered, but most fall short. For a few the challenge becomes a style of life, a goal, even a gauntlet. We call them athletes.

The dream lies not only in the striving for ultimate (and unreachable) perfection but in the exhilaration of playing in and of itself. To feel the readily triggerable response of your dormant reflexes, the reserve of strength or skill in your muscles, to know the layers within layers of things you can do to move the ball across the court or through the uprights is, as Willis Reed put it, "the world." Perhaps it is as close as man gets to feeling totally physically alive.

The validation of the dream, for the athlete, is seeing his name or number up there on the scoreboard. It is the tangible proof, if proof is needed, that the dream and the reality have met in the same place and time. To play against your peers and know you are one of them is as far as the dreams of childhood can carry you; and though the athlete knows the dream must end, he knows also that its pursuit has been his closest brush with immortality.

I've got your mother on the line. Tell her you won the Heisman Trophy.   **1**

> **Charley Callahan,** sports information director at Notre Dame in 1956, as he handed an open phone to Paul Hornung.

The body builder is the sculptor of his own body. Whatever   **2**
Michelangelo, Rodin or Da Vinci imagined in their minds and put together on stone or marble, this is what the body builder made possible in reality. He builds a body like that of the Greek statues.

> **Arnold Schwarzenegger,** perennial "Mr. Universe" and star of the cult movie *Pumping Iron.*

3   It's the Peter Pan complex. It's a desire not to grow up. It's like living in never-never land, playing the same game at 31 or 32 you were playing when you were 8 years old.

> Offensive lineman **Bill Ellenbogen,** cut by his fourth pro team in the fall of 1976, on why he was looking for a fifth.

4   I saw him [Hitler] for the first time at the trials of the 100-meter run . . . I wanted to win one event and that was the 100 meters. It was considered the event which could make you known as the world's fastest human. I had looked forward to that for nine years and when I had done it, I never looked into the official box. My heart was too filled with joy with what I had done.

> **Jesse Owens,** recalling in 1976 what it felt like to win at the spectacular 1936 Olympics in Berlin.

5   To go against Jack Nicklaus, to go against the greatest player who ever played, in my opinion, and to win, that has to be the greatest thrill for any golfer. Very few people have ever had that experience, and I consider mysef very fortunate. It is my greatest thrill in golf.

> Twenty-seven-year-old **Tom Watson,** after shooting 268 to win the 1977 British Open by one shot over Nicklaus's 269 and establish a new record. Earlier in the year Watson had narrowly edged Nicklaus in the U.S. Masters as well.

6   It was one of those days you dream about. Every hole seemed to be 6 inches wide.

> Pro golfer **Tom Purtzer,** after a sparkling 66, in the third round of the 1977 Los Angeles Open.

7   The glory of the game is as a player. When you bounce that ball with your sneakers on—that's the world.

> Former Knick great **Willis Reed,** on the occasion of his being appointed coach of the team.

8   Naming the gym after me is like the college giving me a bunch of roses in the month of December.

> **Nat Holman,** first a great player with the Original Celtics and then a great basketball coach, being honored at 81 by New York's City College (now CUNY).

9   I wasn't nervous, I didn't have butterflies, but I could hear my name called clearly. I was thinking of how many times I had seen that ritual on television at home, on opening days, at All-Star games, at World Series. Now it was happening to me. It was a dream.

New York Mets rookie outfielder **Lee Mazzilli,** on opening day, 1977.

It was like a fairy tale. It was a feeling of everyone loving you, **10** everyone being appreciative, as if all my friends had hit the homer with me.

> Former Yankee **Reggie Jackson,** after hitting a ninth-inning home run to beat the rival Red Sox in a crucial September game, 2-0.

I am very happy. God has been kind to me. Three World Cups and **11** now a championship in America. I can die now.

> **Pele** at 36, announcing his retirement from soccer, after the New York Cosmos won the 1977 NASL title.

I feel like a king. I've umpired for 32 years, worked 10,000 games **12** in all sports. Hell, don't I deserve one day behind the plate in a major league game?

> **Bob Roesner,** fill-in umpire in an August 1978 Baltimore-Seattle game, during the short-lived (one night) major league umpires' strike.

What makes it pleasing to get the game-winning hit is that **13** ordinarily, as a utility infielder, I'm always in the position to lose a game but never in one to win it. Most times in a close game they're gonna hit for me in the seventh, eighth or ninth.

> Former New York Yankee **Fred Stanley,** after getting the hit that won a July 1980 game.

I was excited. It was the longest [run] I've ever made. It's the most **14** lonely feeling in the world breaking into daylight and knowing you still have 80 yards to go.

> Oakland Raider halfback **Kenny King,** after a 1980 touchdown run of 89 yards. Regarded as a flop by the Houston Oilers, King became an Oakland standout.

They're on their way to becoming millionaires. The first black **15** millionaires in the history of Gastonia.

> Gastonia, N.C. community leader **James Ferguson,** referring to James Worthy and Eric (Sleepy) Floyd, early choices in the 1982 NBA draft and both from the small (population 48,000) North Carolina town.

Got 'em out, one, two, three. Ten pitches. My biggest thrill was **16** standing on the hill that night with my bald head shining in the moonlight and the national anthem playing. I was 64 years old.

St. Louis Cardinals pitching coach **Hub Kittle,** telling
how he pitched one inning for Springfield in 1980, giving
him the distinction of having pitched in six decades.

Dreams of Glory

. . . And then there are the dreams that are unattainable, or try to
reach too far, or go slightly sour. Sometimes they start out just as
nobly; just as often they are an afterthought, a what-might-have-been
addendum to a prosaic career.

Some of the quotes below read like parodies of the ones in the
"Dreams Come True" category, above. But sometimes reaching for
the moon—even a slightly bent and tarnished one—can add a sense
of purpose to an otherwise meaningless life.

1 Remember Captain Marvel? Well, I'm the comic-book hero in real
life. In a phony world, I stand for something simple and direct. I
love life, but I know that you have to take chances to make it
worth living. People look up to me for that. They wouldn't pay to
see just anybody do what I do.

Stuntman **Evel Knievel,** in 1974.

2 Our job is to destroy the offense, to crush the passer, foul up their
blocking and timing . . . Some day the four of us want to play the
perfect game: no points, minus yards on the ground and even off
their passing yardage by dumping their quarterback.

Merlin Olsen, referring to the Los Angeles Rams'
"Fearsome Foursome," and their unreachable dream
game.

3 I think of it very often. It's the way people will remember me for
the rest of my life. Like the promoter said to Rocky, it's a once-in-
a-lifetime thing. And I won their respect. I wasn't just somebody's
bum of the month.

Heavyweight **Chuck Wepner,** comparing his March
1975 fight with Muhammad Ali (in which he lasted all
but the last 15 seconds of the 15-round fight) with
the title bout that the hero of the movie *Rocky*
fought.

I thought they'd stop the game and give me second base.   **4**

>**Milt May,** Houston Astro catcher in 1975, after steal-
>ing his first base after five years in the majors.

It was the World Series to me. I was just as nervous. I wasn't over-   **5**
joyed, but I was pleased. Of the 97 pitches, all of them knuckle-
balls, I only threw 10 that didn't do anything. I wouldn't want to
be called up as a box-office attraction. I only want to go to the big
leagues if I could win up there. Knuckleballers go on and on. Hoyt
Wilhelm was still throwing them in the big leagues at 49, which
gives me a good 11 years.

>**Jim Bouton,** former Yankee pitcher turned author,
>then broadcaster, on his brief comeback attempt.
>Bouton resigned a $65,000-a-year TV job to pitch
>knuckleballs in the minors for $1,500 a month, and
>got back to the big leagues just long enough for a cup
>of coffee.

I played stick ball, every kind of ball . . . Mickey Mantle was my   **6**
idol. I wanted to be just like him, but I couldn't hit. I had the arm
to be an outfielder and I played shortstop, but I also wanted to be
a pitcher because the pitcher got his name in the paper and I like
to get my name in the paper. I'd play shortstop, but my best
friend would pitch no-hitters and get his name in the paper. So I
pitched until I could pitch better than he could.

>**John Montefusco,** San Francisco Giants pitcher in
>1975, who got his name in the paper when he was
>selected Rookie of the Year, and again the following
>year when he pitched a no-hitter against Atlanta.

You can work out the odds with a pencil and paper. Less than 900   **7**
black athletes are earning a living in sports—and not more than
1,500 overall, including coaches and trainers. By comparison,
there are perhaps 3 million black youths between [the ages of] 13
and 22 who dream of a career as an athlete. The odds are 20,000
to 1 or worse. Statistically, you have a better chance of getting hit
by a meteorite in the next 10 years than getting work as an
athlete.

>Berkley (Calif.) sociology professor **Harry Edwards,**
>taking a hard look at career prospects for blacks in
>sports in 1979.

Today was a sad day. Within an hour, I received four telephone   **8**
calls . . . telling of players I represent who had been placed on
waivers . . . [Jesse] Dark had a no-trade contract and will be paid
for the season. But the irony is there is nothing you can tell these

young men. They have spent their lives girding themselves to be pro basketball players and they have come up empty.

> Sports attorney **Norman Blass,** talking about the heartbreak of being cut at the beginning of the basketball season.

9   . . . I know I should not do it, many people say I should not do it, but it's a risk and what I would gain is immortality, four times world heavyweight champion. Two times world champion is great, three times is great, but a four-time heavyweight champion of the world, I'll be the greatest athlete of all times, not just a boxer.

> **Muhammad Ali,** with his eye on the title, coming out of retirement in 1980 at age 38. Larry Holmes beat him easily.

Scandals and Other Embarrassments

For the modern era it began with the infamous Black Sox scandal of 1919. The public was horrified that a World Series outcome had been tampered with and that the culpable Chicago players had actually conspired to throw games *for money.* Only stern punishment—lifetime suspension for the guiltiest—calmed an aroused public. Thanks to the Calvinistic response of Judge Kenesaw Mountain Landis, the good name of baseball was saved and the nation went to bed feeling that things had been put to rights.

Skimming history in newsreel fashion points up the great changes that have since occurred on the sports scene, illustrating what might be called the erosion of innocence. There was still a good deal of moral outrage when the basketball scandals of the 1950s broke. It was, for many, shocking. College boys in collusion with known gamblers to shave points. Poor boys who went to City College on scolarships, "A" students, some of them. Who would have believed it? What was the country coming to?

The country bumped through the 60s and its revolutions, probably our most unsettling decade of change. When the same thing occurred in the 1960s and the 1970s, once again in college basketball, the reaction was less vociferous. No one was happy about it, of course, it was certainly regrettable, but these things do happen. Where there's money to be made, some said, there's always a *certain element* that will find the one or two bad apples in a barrel.

Later still in the 70s, when several members of the then Oakland Raiders were found to be fraternizing with known gamblers (the phrase was very much in vogue by then), there was no great show of moral indignation. Pro football was a huge and lucrative enterprise by then, and the public was more concerned with the weekly point spread than vague intimations of corrupting influences. (Unless, of course, the latter directly altered the former.)

The NFL seemed more embarrassed than anything else, and relieved that the exposure never got beyond the austere pages of the *New York Times* and a few other newspapers. (By contrast, Leo Durocher had drawn a one-year suspension in 1947 just for being photographed sitting next to a known gambler.)

But despite the growing cynicism about the purity of sports, the feeling persists among most members of the public that the major sports are still relatively untainted. Hockey seems too rough a sport to be fixed; baseball, thanks to the afterglow of the implacable judge with the formidable name is sacrosanct; football and basketball seem more vulnerable to rumors of fixing, but there hasn't been much hard evidence, at least on the pro level.

Boxing and racing, however, are the two sports where people have generally felt that corruption was lurking just below the surface. Rumors—and the reality—of fixed races have plagued every major race track, the most recent big one being the Aqueduct and Saratoga meets of 1974 and 1975, during which exactas and triples were allegedly fixed. Eleven jockeys, including some of the best known in the country, have been accused of arranging the final order of finish. In any other sport this would be a major scandal. But only one ex-jockey has gone to jail while the inquiry drags on reluctantly.

One refreshing aspect in the case is the absence of the shadowy "known gambler." Since everyone around a race track is a gambler, known or otherwise, this wouldn't be news. Instead we have Tony Ciulla, the "master-fixer," who claims he personally fixed hundreds of races at 39 different tracks in the early 1970s. Even if he's exaggerating by half, that's impressive.

Meanwhile a cynical racing public is speculating on which one—or two—of the 11 top-ranking jockeys will take a fall in the backstretch before this drag-on investigation is finally quashed.

In 1979 jai alai and dog racing took the scandal spotlight. In Connecticut, several jai alai players were indicted for losing games at the behest of a gambler known both in Miami and Milford. At the same time, back in Miami, a behind-the-scenes computerized scam

was siphoning off perhaps $2 million at the Flagler Dog Track.
Several clerks and computer personnel had perfected a system by
which they could lower the trifecta odds on win pools as they floated
through the electronic limbo of the computer's memory bank, then
skim off the difference in the payoff total. Since only those happy bet-
tors holding winning tickets were affected, this was not discovered
and probably never would have been if one of the perpetrators' wives
hadn't told a friend in the strictest of confidence.

If Judge Landis had been alive to hear the light sentences
handed out to the culprits, he probably would have died of apoplexy.

1   It is plain from our investigation that at this time *Ring* [magazine]
lacks the credibility necessary for it to carry out its assigned role
in the tournament.... On the subject of active wrongdoing, we
were unable to find any evidence that [Don] King himself was
involved in kickbacks, false ratings or other similar irregularities.
The most disturbing action by King for which we were able to
acquire direct evidence of personal involvement was his clearly
improper payment of $5,000 to John Ort [associate editor of *Ring*]
which seriously compromised the integrity of the selection process.

> **Report** of investigation headed by Michael Armstrong,
> former chief counsel of the Knapp Commission, into
> alleged kickbacks and altering of boxing records for
> the U.S. Boxing Championships tournament in 1977.
> The four-month inquiry had been requested by ABC-
> TV, which had telecast the tournament.

2   We long ago abandoned frontier justice in California. No affront
justifies such retaliation. It sets a terrible example.

> Superior Court Judge **Edward Rafeedie,** in sentenc-
> ing Evel Knievel to six months in jail for beating his
> former press agent with a baseball bat. The press
> agent had written a defamatory book about the dare-
> devil.

3   Have you heard about the new cocktail called a Ringer? It's
Cinzano on the rocks but it doesn't look like it.

> **Joke** told at every race track in the country following
> the 1977 fix in which Cinzano, a Uruguayan stakes
> winner, was substituted for Lebon, a Uruguayan
> plater, for a $116 Belmont payoff.

4   There is not a university or athletic conference in this country that
would permit a coach to physically assault a college athlete.

> Ohio State University president **Harold Enarson,** in
> supporting the dismissal of Woody Hayes after he

punched a Clemson player during the 1978 Gator
Bowl game. The controversial Hayes had coached at
Ohio State for 28 years, and was on Big Ten proba-
tion for previous outbursts.

No mas, no mas, no more box.   **5**
>Roberto Duran, abruptly ending his second fight
>with Sugar Ray Leonard in the 8th round, in 1980,
>due to stomach cramps. It was later revealed he had
>eaten two 16-ounce steaks at dinnertime, and a
>"dinner" steak for dessert.

It was funny. They never would consider throwing games. *That*   **6**
they understood to be criminal. But shaving points they were able
to consider.
>Judge **Jacob Grumet** in 1980, recalling his role in
>the 1950 sensational basketball scandal in which five
>players on CCNY's championship team conspired
>with gamblers to shave points.

I'm the Boston College basketball fixer . . . . I paid three Boston   **7**
College basketball players during the 1978-79 season to shave
points—not to blow games—in nine games between Dec. 16, 1978
and March 1, 1979. The players were Rick Kuhn and Jim
Sweeney, who were in it from the beginning, and Ernie Cobb, the
star of the team, who was with us the last five games . . . . It cost
me $2,500 per player per game—except when they screwed up
and I didn't give them anything or cut them back. As a com-
plimentary service, I bet money for the players when they so
requested.
>Organized crime figure **Henry Hill,** now a govern-
>ment informer, in a cover story for *Sports Illustrated*
>in 1981. Hill's operation, carried out with several
>members of a New York crime family, is the most
>recent point-shaving disclosure in the continuing saga
>of fixed college basketball games.

I always wanted to be someone big. Instead I became a criminal   **8**
and a drug dealer.
>**Paul Mazzei,** before being sentenced to a 10-year
>federal term for his role in the Boston College basket-
>ball games. Mazzei had already been serving time for
>his connection with a Long Island international heroin
>ring.

A zillion people called and told me he [Feliciano] should be   **9**
allowed back. I don't want to play God or anything like that. But

since he was told to leave, and left without incident and he has behaved himself like a gentleman, he has served his time, and I think I am doing the right thing for him and his family. They have suffered enough.

> **Chick Lang,** Pimlico Race Course general manager, in readmitting former jockey Ben Feliciano to the track in a nonriding capacity in 1982. Feliciano was one of four jockeys banned from Maryland tracks for fixing races at Bowie in 1975.

10 The Canadian Football League is to blame more than Mr. Skalbania is. It was the league that allowed Mr. Skalbania to come into the league. The league should have been a little bit suspect, I think, because of Mr. Skalbania's track record with professional sports franchises.

> **Steve Mazurak,** CFL Players Association executive director, in 1982. Montreal Alouettes' owner Nelson Skalbania signed Vince Ferragamo to a $2.5 million contract, as well as nine other American pro football players—then sold the club out from under them. In a similar situation, in 1978 Skalbania folded the Indianapolis Racers of the World Hockey Association without giving refunds to season-ticket holders for the club's remaining games.

11 You ain't gonna believe this. But I got a plus-16 [on a lie detector]. I passed with flying colors. Four practice runs and two film runs, and I passed every time. I told them what I said that night—I didn't go putting' anything on the ball.

> **Gaylord Perry,** after appearing on a TV show called "Lie Detector." The 43-year-old Perry had been ejected from a game in Seattle and suspended for 10 days in August 1982 for throwing a "doctored" pitch. Perry is also the author of a book called *Me and the Spitter*.

12 Nobody in this country will hire me. I'm sure a lot of players are mad at me. Can't blame 'em. I fixed games. I hurt their sport. But I know of a lot of guys who fixed games and never got caught. So I'm not such a bad guy, am I?

> **Kirby Prater,** former jai alai player who fixed hundreds of games in Connecticut and Florida in collusion with Miami gambler Bobby Moore. Arrested in 1979, Prater received a suspended sentence; he now works as a plane cleaner in Miami International Airport.

13 I used to go to parties and everybody would ask the same

question: Is it fixed? I began to watch games closer and wonder how a guy missed a shot. Then I heard of someone betting a 1-2 perfecta 50 times and it came in cold. When the worse two players in the house won, I figured games were being fixed. I knew Bobby [Moore] and that's when I agreed to help him. I did it to make a nice, decent living.
Ibid.

Drugs and Alcohol

Like gambling, drugs and their use by athletes is a murky area of sports. A great deal is written about it, rumored about it, speculated on, but comparatively little of the hard evidence rises to the surface. Much of it, the public has come to feel, is squashed early on. But it can hardly be denied. In 1980 the *Los Angeles Times* charged that between 40 and 75 percent of NBA players use cocaine. And the league is not suing for defamation of character. If anything, it's probably since redoubled its security operations.

The creation of these security operations, launched in the 1970s in all major team sports except soccer, is a tacit admission that the problem is both severe and extensive. Using former FBI agents and other law-enforcement types, their undisguised role is to police the sport and keep the athlete away from the drug dealer and the drug scene. Inevitably, this had also led to rehabilitation programs for those already too far into drugs or alcohol to be able to back away without help. Nor does every major player seek or want help with his "problem." The few who have admitted to taking cocaine, for instance, claim it's only a "recreational" drug, never taken before games.

Drugs, of course, are not new to the sports scene. The use of painkillers to neutralize injuries has been going on for at least two decades; on the international level, world-class athletes have been disqualified for using muscle-building anabolic steroids. In the last two Olympics, in fact, there has been a still-unresolved controversy about distinguishing between massive drug buildups for competing athletes and the sophisticated sports medicine programs instituted in Eastern bloc countries. In Montreal it was even rumored that female gymnasts from those countries had received testosterone injections at various stages of their growth process in order to make them smaller, shorter, and more muscularly agile. Creating a race of super-pygmies, so to speak.

The drug scene is even more chaotic in horse racing. Drugs that are legal and commonly used in one state are illegal in another. Even the period of time that must elapse after, say, an anti-arthritic drug is used on a horse varies from state to state. One Kentucky Derby winner, Dancer's Image, had to forfeit the winner's purse several weeks after the race when traces of a drug whose use is illegal in Kentucky were found in his after-race urine.

One good thing about horses, though. None of them can claim that they're only doing it for "recreational" purposes.

1 At halftime, Dr. Cook [team physician] said if I just took this shot of Xylocaine in my leg, it would be all right to go back out and play. I took the shot, felt good for about 35 seconds, limped through the rest of the game, and spent the next six weeks in a cast on crutches.

> Former Portland Trail Blazer **Bill Walton,** during a 1976 game. Walton had experienced pain during warmups in his right leg. X-rays taken after the game showed he had been playing on a stress fracture of the right fibula.

2 Many athletes have told me that steroids very likely do have a positive effect on them. Is that positive effect because they are training and thus motivated, or does it really put on a lot of bulk and thereby make them stronger? That's what we've got to find out. I've yet to meet an Olympic or world-class weight lifter who hasn't felt it has been beneficial to his performance. Athletes would like not to take steroids. They don't feel good or right about it, but they're afraid not to, because they're concerned about what the next athlete might be doing.

> **Dr. Irving Dardik,** chairman of the U.S. Olympic Sports Medicine Commission, in 1978.

3 Anabolic steroids do not enhance athletic ability.

> **Warning added to The Physician's Desk Reference** about the use of Dianabol and other steroids in the mid-70s.

4 The most important influence creating the violence in football is the high-dose amphetamine. You actually become, for the peak effect of the drug, crazy. And it's the most murderous type of crazy that we know. It is the paranoid psychotic, the killer of presidents.

> Psychiatrist **Arnold Mandell,** who spent a season working with and observing the San Diego Chargers.

I've had cases, for instance, of young men who have had their legs **5**
buckle underneath them while taking a jump shot. I examined the
leg and there was absolutely nothing wrong with it. The natural
reflex arc of the leg had prevented it from landing in an awkward
and damaging position. The body had taken care of itself.

Send someone out there numbed and the body can't reflex
naturally. Yet, athletes will still take any chances or anything to
play because they want to.

> **Dr. Ernest Vandeweghe,** Los Angeles pediatrician
> and former New York Knick, in 1979.

Their [new drugs] effect on horses is horrendous. When they're **6**
loaded up, the horses lose their warning systems. They can lose a
spare wheel and don't know it. They'll run through a brick wall.

> **Arthur Stall,** chairman of the Louisiana Racing
> Commission, talking about new doping techniques in
> 1978. Widely used across the country, the new drugs
> are difficult to detect. One of them, Sublimaze, is 100
> times more potent than morphine.

Athletes are protected more than any group in the school sys- **7**
tem . . . . We have a state rule that anybody caught drinking
cannot participate for nine weeks. With an athlete, this rule is
overlooked.

> School district drug counselor **Mary Ellen Harris** of
> St. Louis Park, Minnesota, at a University of Wiscon-
> sin conference on sports and drug abuse in 1981.

I couldn't have said this then, but I'm grateful they traded me. I **8**
really do believe in my mind that if the Nets had not traded me, I
wouldn't be alive today due to the fact that I did a lot of driving
under the influence of alcohol. I was really scared of staying in
New York another year.

> Former New York Net **Bernard King,** in admitting
> he'd been an off-court drinker when he first came up
> to the pros.

Look, I like Billy Martin, I think he's one great guy and I certainly **9**
don't intend to pick on him. I'm not against him making commercials. I don't blame him at all. I'd take the money, too. It just
bothers me to see ex-athletes making these alcohol commercials
because professional sports isn't doing much, educationally speaking, to offset them.

> Former big leaguer **Ryne Duren,** an ex-alcoholic and
> now a rehabilitation consultant, on sports per-
> sonalities doing beer commercials.

10   Our coach [Joe Williams] had a rule—if you can't practice, you
can't start. That game was a big rivalry. [Florida] A&M was an all-
black school and I got 17 points in the first half. My ankle was kill-
ing me and they used some freeze-on [ethyl chloride] and sent me
out for the second half. I fouled out on purpose and I spent the
whole summer getting the ankle ready again.

> Varsity basketball player **James Bozeman** in 1982,
> revealing the illegal use of drugs and other abuses at
> Florida State University.

11   I know one thing. Guys [athletes] aren't afraid to do drugs.
Nobody's afraid to do drugs. I wasn't, because I knew one thing.
If I got caught, somebody was going to bail me out. It's just like
one of us driving down the road going 90 miles an hour. They
don't write us tickets. They let us off.

   That was one of my problems. Nobody ever made me be
responsible for what I was doing. They'd always get me off the
hook some way, so consequently I said, 'Hey, I can get away with
this stuff.'

> St. Louis Cardinals catcher **Darrell Porter,** who's
> had problems with both alcohol and drugs.

12   You need to start letting kids in college know the dangers. When I
was growing up, my daddy would talk to us about dope fiends,
people who fooled with heroin. If somebody had offered me heroin, I
would've killed him. But nobody ever talked to us about cocaine. I
went all through college and never heard much about cocaine.
Then I got down to Miami [as the Dolphins' No. 1 draft choice]
and people started telling me it's not addictive, that it's just something to have fun with. A young guy who comes from poor
surroundings, like I did, is easily influenced when he gets to the
pros. He starts going to parties with guys who are his heroes. And
if his heroes are fooling with it, he's gonna wanna do it, too.

> Ex-pro **Don Reese,** speaking through his agent, in
> 1982. In 1977 Reese was sentenced to a year in the
> Dade County (Florida) Stockade for selling cocaine to
> an undercover agent.

13   The athletes are doing just what society expects. Cocaine is a
crime of affluence. The kid has too much money. Heroes are doing
what they always did: Surrogates, fighting out the battles for the
public .... When I played, you fell over it. I don't think it's different than it ever was. Athletes hang around with people who tell
them, 'The rules don't apply to you.'

> Author **Peter Gent** (*North Dallas Forty*), who played
> with the football Giants until 1969.

My bottom line was zero; my alternative to a cure was death.   **14**
> Former Minnesota Viking lineman **Carl Eller,** talking
> about his $100,000-a-year cocaine habit in 1982.
> Broke and desperate, he took the cure, now works as
> consultant in the NFL's new alcohol and drug abuse
> program.

Cocaine arrived in my life with my first-round draft into the NFL   **15**
in 1974. It has dominated my life . . . . Eventually, it took control
and almost killed me . . . . Cocaine may be found in quantity
throughout the NFL. It's pushed on players . . . . Sometimes it's
pushed *by* players . . . . Just as it controlled me, it now controls
and corrupts the game, because so many players are on it . . .
> **Don Reese,** in a special article written for *Sports
> Illustrated* in June 1982, blowing the whistle on the
> NFL.

5. SPORTS LANGUAGE

Candor

One of the factors that impelled us to do this book was our mutual dislike of the daily media hype that invests sports, to which those in and around the game often generously contribute. Not blatant hyperbole—we have a category for that—but the everyday nonsense and frivolity that is supposed to juice up the action for the interpretation-hungry fans. As an antidote to this inescapable blather we quickly saw the value of the straightforward unalloyed response, frequently uttered unself-consciously or without intending to impress anyone. (Ruth's sassy remark about the incumbent President's "batting average" [found under "Hall of Fame"] could have appeared here as well, or the Chicago kid who asked Shoeless Joe to "Say it ain't so" when Jackson emerged from the Black Sox scandal hearings.)

How refreshing, then, to pick out the occasional (and unmistakable) genuine human response that is not readymade to fit into the programmed hoopla surrounding every sport. It is a salutary reminder that even among athletes, owners, officials, and coaches truth struggles against myth, hype, press agentry, and self-serving venality—and sometimes even filters through. Or if not truth, at least candor.

1   I'm very glad to receive the Klem Award, but I'll tell you the trut

Klem hated my guts and I hated his.

> **Beans Reardon,** former major-league umpire, upon
> receiving the 1970 Bill Klem Award, umpiredom's
> highest tribute.

As the season progresses, I get lighter, faster and more afraid.   **2**

> Former Houston Oiler **Jerry Levias** in 1970, on the
> physical and emotional rites of passage of a flanker.

We drink too much. We live too good. I don't consider myself an   **3**
athlete because I'm not in good shape. Arnie Palmer's not in good
shape. Bob Murphy sits on a walking cane between shots. Julius
Boros could be one hell of a player, but he's twenty pounds overweight and he doesn't want to fight it.

> **Bob Goalby,** who won the Masters in 1968, looking
> over the field in 1970.

There go half my friends.   **4**

> **John P. Cowand,** newly appointed (1971) Secretary
> and Deputy Commissioner of the Pennsylvania Har-
> ness Racing Commission, when told that henceforth
> he was expected not to associate with known gam-
> blers and other undesirable types.

We don't want to give the fan an opportunity to see if he can live   **5**
without baseball.

> A **Baltimore Orioles executive,** during the 1972
> players' strike.

Glamorous, huh? Singers can wear gowns to hide the bulges, and   **6**
wigs and make-up. But our bodies are seen the way they really
are. We come off the court sweating, hair dripping. Our life is
showering and changing. I change clothes five times a day and
wash my hair every day. It's a tough role to play, so you don't see
many femmes fatales in tennis dresses.

> **Billie Jean King,** on the glamorous life in big-time
> sports, in 1972.

We've stopped recruiting young men who want to come here to be   **7**
students first and athletes second.

> **Sonny Randle,** University of Virginia's football
> coach in 1975, elaborating on his school's grant-in-aid
> program.

Fact: As the top man in the organization there is no question as to   **8**
who is responsible for the Capitals' miserable record. I am.

> Half-page **newspaper advertisement** taken out by
> Washington Capitals owner Abe Pollin, in early 1976,
> when his team's record was 5-41-5, worst in the NHL.

9   I can't tell the pitches. I don't know the difference between a
slider and a curve. I know a fastball because it comes in rapidly.

> Former AL ump **Ron Luciano,** on why he preferred
> working the baselines.

10 Any time I got those bang-bang plays at first base, I called 'em
out. It made the game shorter.

> Retiring NL umpire **Tom Gorman,** in a sort of
> valedictory.

11 A guy who strikes out as much as I do had better lead in something.

> Philadelphia Phils' third baseman **Mike Schmidt,**
> who, in between striking out 149 times, hit 38 home
> runs, for his third consecutive home run title in 1976.

12 The two toughest saves were made by Gary Goalpost.

> Former New York Islander goalie **Glenn Resch,** on
> how he managed to shut out the Atlanta Flames.

13 I began the poetry and predicting rounds. And it worked. They
started coming with their ten- and twenty-dollar bills to see the
bragging nigger . . . How do *I* know who the greatest fighter was?

> **Muhammad Ali,** to a *Los Angeles Times* reporter in
> 1977, setting the record straight about his most im-
> modest statement.

14 We stink. We're an expansion team. Look, how consistent can we
be? It's hit or miss with us . . . It's bull that a last-place team is
loose. The only time you're loose is when you're in first place.

> Former Toronto catcher **Doug Rader,** assessing the
> 1977 Blue Jays and the myth of playing loose when
> you're out of it.

15 So I go out there and do the routine stuff. I go out early and catch
my hundred grounders and make my hundred throws and then I'm
like the batting practice pitcher. They give me my 20 bucks and
say, 'take a hike.'

> **Fred Stanley,** who thought he was going to be the
> regular shortstop in New York in 1977—until the
> Yanks traded for Bucky Dent.

16 No matter how cruel it is, when a kid comes into the league who looks like a hitter you've got to nail him to the cross or he'll own you the rest of your life. Let the kid get a couple of hits the first time he sees you and he thinks, 'This guy is my pigeon,' and he'll come off the bench swinging and wear you out.

> **Ed Lopat,** nobody's pigeon with either the White Sox or the Yanks, more recently a pitching coach.

If we had the standards of ten years ago, I know I'd be making $60,000. I'm not a superstar. The $100,000 salary was reserved for the superstar. **17**

> New York Met **Ed Kranepool,** who made it to the magic figure by lasting fifteen years with one team.

There's nobody left to trade on strictly performance grounds. You've got guys with long contracts, no contracts or restrictive contracts. What happens now is you go around begging teams to take guys off your hands. **18**

> **Sparky Anderson,** while he was still managing the Cincinnati Reds, on the escalating effects of free agency and arbitration.

We've got the worst in this league, Earl Weaver, Billy Martin, Ralph Houk, Gene Mauch—you name them, they're all maniacs. You can't reason with those guys. You don't try. **19**

> AL umpire **Jim McKean,** on the irascible 1977 crop of managers in the junior circuit.

I'm kind of bitter about people saying I did this to make money. It just isn't so. I was pretty well off as a physician, and I'm pretty poor as a tennis pro. **20**

> Transsexual **Renee Richards,** in 1978. Three years later, Richards hung up her racket, and went back to ophthalmology.

Not playing every day helps some guys stay in the big leagues. No one wants to admit it, but after a while as a backup you get afraid that playing regularly will expose the weaknesses that put you on the bench to begin with. **21**

> Sportscaster **Fran Healy,** who averaged fewer than 150 at-bats over the nine seasons he was a second-string catcher with Kansas City and New York.

What helped me develop my quickness was fear. I think the rougher the opponent, the quicker I am. **22**

> **Sugar Ray Leonard,** just before his second fight with Roberto Duran in 1980.

23   Phil Jackson is one of the most intelligent players I ever saw. He's
so smart, he can commit 12 fouls and only get caught for four.

> New York Knicks coach **Red Holzman's** tribute to
> the cagy Jackson. A New Jersey Net in 1980, Jackson
> played under Holzman throughout most of his career.

24   I myself would like to see more white athletes. I think they are
overlooking a good profession. I don't think it is good for the
league to have all-black teams and 95% white audiences.

> Cleveland Cavaliers owner **Ted Stepien** in 1981, per-
> haps with an eye on the gate.

25   I have come to view football—and all the things that go along with
it—as a form of prostitution. It's selling my body, and a conscious
decision to do so. The question is whether I'm selling my soul
along with it.

> All-pro defense tackle **Alan Page** in 1981, after 14
> years with the Minnesota Vikings and Chicago Bears.

26   When I die, Steinbrenner will relax. He looks at me as the s.o.b.
who made him overpay for [Winfield]. That's fine with me. I got
big shoulders. As for Dave, he's a .280 lifetime hitter who's hitting
.290. He's a line drive hitter, not a home-run hitter. We never
guaranteed Dave Winfield would hit .400 or lead the Yankees to
the promised land.

> **Al Frohman,** Dave Winfield's agent, in the midst of
> the Steinbrenner-Winfield Foundation wrangling in
> midseason of 1982.

27   He had the man on the fringes of death.

> Referee **Larry Hazzard,** explaining why he stopped
> the 1982 Marvin Hagler-Bill "Caveman" Lee middle-
> weight championship fight after 67 seconds, with Lee
> about to go down for the second time.

28   This was without any doubt the biggest victory in our history. We
have rated the big victories in West Virginia football history, and
the triumph at Norman [over Oklahoma] will now be No. 1, replac-
ing the previous No. 1, a 25-0 triumph over Princeton in 1919.
Besides, no one remembers now why that one was so important.

> An exuberant **West Virginia official** after the
> Mountaineers victory over the Sooners early in the
> 1982 season.

29   It isn't easy playing ball and have people calling you a bleep bleeper.

I had to hear it from people on the streets and from opposing players. You put anybody's life under a microscope like that and it can get pretty ugly. You know, cheap talk is good talk in a small town.

> Cincinnati outfielder **Clint Hurdle,** in spring 1982, commenting on the rumor that he was a homosexual. Rumor originated when Hurdle and a friend were arrested during 1981 season on a speeding charge, and their being mistakenly linked with a group of gays being booked on disorderly conduct charges at the same time.

Humor

There have been a number of compilations of sports quotes and most of them are liberally sprinkled with what is labeled "humor." Since most sports figures (and especially athletes) are not supposed to be very articulate, any reasonably droll observation by someone connected with sports has a better-than-even chance of making it into one of these ephemeral collections. *Whether or not it has anything to do with sports.* So what happens is that you read three or four of them, chuckle, sigh, and decide it's time to go shave.

Relevance to sports, therefore, became our first criterion of selection here. We also looked for quotes that might have some lasting value, as opposed to those which might be called gripless quips. Lastly, we looked for those situations out of which humor sprang inadvertently. A ring announcer who informed a fight crowd that the contender was missing wasn't trying to be funny, but you can bet he brought the house down.

What follows are the quotes that we'd like to think Ring Lardner, James Thurber, and Red Smith would find funny if they were reading the sports pages today. And maybe even Jimmy Cannon.

I'll take you and a player to be named later. **1**

> Remark at the outset of a 1969 rhubarb between Montreal and Pittsburgh, by 6-foot-6-inch 265-pound Expo pitcher **Dick Radatz** to 5-foot-6-inch 165-pound Pirate shortstop Freddie Patek.

This team finished last on merit. **2**

> **Branch Rickey,** usually kind to his players, reflecting on the talents of his 1952 Pittsburgh team.

3   Your heart might be in the batter's box, but your ass ain't.
> An **old baseball saying,** about the fear of getting hit by a pitch.

4   Fractured, hell! The damn thing's broken.
> **Dizzy Dean's** response to being informed that his foot was fractured by a batted ball during the 1936 All-Star Game.

5   Look at that guy. Can't hit, can't run, can't catch. Of course, that's why they gave him to us.
> Former New York Mets manager **Casey Stengel,** talking about one of his new players.

6   I won't mention the name of this particular team we were playing, but at half time we came in, pulled off our socks and began putting iodine on the teeth marks in our legs.
> **Red Grange,** remembering a particularly strenuous afternoon of college football.

7   I'll tell you one thing, if we ever play this team again, it'll be on a Friday.
> Illinois coach **Bob Zuppke** at half time, when he saw the dental evidence of first-half play.

8   Don't read Landry's playbook all the way through. Everybody dies at the end.
> Former New York Giant wide receiver **Pete Gent** to a Dallas Cowboy rookie.

9   Stay close through the early innings, and I'll think of something.
> Manager **Charley Dressen's** favorite admonition to his 1950s Dodgers.

10   I'd like to see him do it again.
> **Charley Dressen's** comment after watching Willie Mays make a spectacular catch against his team in the 50s.

11   I'd play the pilot in a war film who dropped his first bomb and it was incomplete. Or more likely, intercepted.
> **Don Meredith,** former Dallas Cowboy quarterback, speculating after the 1970 season on his future in films.

Philadelphia fans would boo a funeral **12**
> Much-traveled pitcher (and playboy) **Bo Belinsky** on
> the City of Brotherly Love.

It was like I was throwing punches at the water and the water kept   **13**
hittin' back. My big aim was to keep from drownin'.
> Heavyweight champion **Joe Frazier** on the perils of
> the 50-meter swim event in ABC-TV's "The
> Superstars" competition.

I guess the first thing I ought to say is that I thank everybody for   **14**
making this day necessary.
> **Yogi Berra,** as he was being inducted into baseball's
> Hall of Fame in 1972, taking off on himself.

He got on first once this year [1974] and asked me whether to   **15**
steal on the second pitch. The only trouble was there was already
someone on second.
> Former Oakland Athletics coach **Irv Noren's** critique
> of one of Charley Finley's great experiments,
> "designated runner" Herb Washington.

I cussed him out in Spanish, and he threw me out in English.   **16**
> New York Yankee outfielder **Lou Piniella,** after
> clashing with fellow Spanish-speaking umpire
> Armando Rodriguez.

I don't think you would ever hear a sports announcer say, 'The   **17**
Washington Redskins have the ball, third down and 9.144 meters
to go.'
> Former Secretary of Commerce **Maurice H. Stans** in
> 1971, when asked what the chances were that the
> sports world would adopt the metric system.

I keep both eyes on my man. The basket hasn't moved on me yet.   **18**
> Basketball star **Julius Erving,** with the Philadelphia
> 76ers in 1977, criticized for keeping one eye on the
> basket and the other on his man.

He keeps both sides in the game.   **19**
> Former Columbia University basketball coach **Jack
> Rohan** about one of his talented but erratic back-
> court men.

Harry [Dalton] offered me a job with the Angel organization, but I   **20**
wasn't paying much attention after he started the conversation off

by firing me.

> **Norm Sherry,** on his prospects in midseason 1977,
> after a brief stint as California Angels manager.

21   When Steve and I die, we are going to buried 60' 6" apart.

> Philadelphia Phil's **Tim McCarver,** who was ace
> pitcher Steve Carlton's favorite batteryman.

22   [Yogi] Berra called me one day. His wife had just had a baby and he said, 'Hey, Piersall, you've got nine kids, how about giving a few tips on changing diapers? . . . ' So I said, 'Yog, you take a diaper and put it in the shape of a baseball diamond. Take the baby's bottom and put it on the pitcher's mound. Take first base and pin it to third. Take home and slide it into second.' He said, 'That's easy. I can do that.' I said, 'Wait a minute, Yogi. One thing about this game, when it starts to rain, there's no postponement.'

> Former Red Sox outfielder **Jimmy Piersall,** on being
> both a ballplayer and a parent.

23   I was catching him in Milwaukee one day. There was a guy on first, and he was stealing. As I took the ball out of my glove, I said, 'Oh hell!' I had grabbed the ball right on the wet spot, and it went sailing into center field.

> Atlanta Braves manager **Joe Torre,** an accurate-armed
> catcher in his day, recalling the hazards of catching
> Lew Burdette, who was known to throw an occasional
> damp one.

24   He talks very well for a guy who's had two fingers in his mouth all his life.

> Former California Angels manager **Gene Mauch,**
> when asked what he thought of ex-pitcher Don Drys-
> dale as a sports announcer.

25   He [Franco Harris] faked me out so bad one time I got a 15-yard penalty for grabbing my own face mask.

> **D.D. Lewis,** Dallas linebacker in 1977, on Franco
> Harris's snaky running pattern.

26   We're the only team in history that could lose nine games in a row and then go into a slump.

> Former Cleveland Cavalier coach **Bill Fitch.**

27   I'm not sure [whether] I'd rather be managing or testing bullet-proof vests.

> Former New York manager **Joe Torre,** when his

harried Mets finally broke a nine-game losing streak
in 1981.

A lifetime contract for a coach means if you're ahead in the third **28**
quarter and moving the ball, they can't fire you.
> University of Arkansas football coach **Lou Holtz,** on
> job security.

Show me a guy who can handle a pitching staff and I'll show you a **29**
guy hitting .210.
> Telecaster **Joe Garagiola,** commenting on the rarity
> of good hitting and fielding catchers.

It wasn't your basic Picasso.   **30**
> **Rick Monday,** summing up an error-ridden 1981
> World Series game.

Ladies and gentlemen, the heavyweight contender Larry Frazier is **31**
missing.
> **Fight-time announcement** at the Playboy Hotel and
> Casino in Atlantic City in March 1982.

I'm the only guy on the team with a perforated page in our press **32**
guide.
> Oakland Athletics pitcher **Brian Kingman,** com-
> menting on the rumor he was going to be traded in
> early 1982.

That was a nasty little weapon he brought with him. All I know is I **33**
had to foul three of them off at one point to knock all the juice out
of the ball.
> St. Louis first baseman **Keith Hernandez** about
> Mike Caldwell, after the Milwaukee pitcher shut out
> Cardinals on three hits in 1982 Series opener.

Skate at your own risk.   **34**
> **Sign** at one end of the Totowa practice rink on first
> day of 1982 training camp for New Jersey Devils,
> following the franchise shift from Colorado to the
> Meadowlands.

I had a dream that I was in purgatory and I ran across Bill **35**
Madlock with the ugliest woman I've ever seen. He explained that
was his penance for all the sins he committed on earth. Then I saw
George Steinbrenner with Bo Derek. I couldn't believe it. George
Steinbrenner with Bo Derek? Until somebody explained. 'You

don't understand. This is Bo Derek's penance.'
> Los Angeles manager **Tommy Lasorda,** at a base-
> ball writers' dinner in early 1982.

Hyperbole

Webster's defines hyperbole as "extravagant exaggeration." Elsewhere in this book we have discussed our dislike for hype, garden-
variety hype, the kind that is so common it often goes undetected
("Murphy hit the ball a country mile"; "The New York Sack Ex-
change"; "Navratilova was serving up aspirins today"). The examples below are not the kind you'd be apt to miss. They are quotes from
athletes and sports figures that overshoot the mark. Some are inadvertently funny or silly or bombastic. Others tip over into a kind of
campiness; they border on self-parody. Someone like Los Angeles,
Tommy Lasorda has even created his own hyperbolic heaven, where
Dodger Blue is the most lambent color. And then there's Don King,
who lives by hyperbole, from his stubby fingers to his electric hair.
And Ron Luciano, who escaped from the plodding umpiring ranks
into the dazzle of electronic journalism by never saying—or doing—
anything straight.

For some in the sports fraternity, then, hyperbole is fun, it's
colorful—and it's bankable.

1   To break training without permission is an act of treason.
> College coach **John W. Heisman** (after whom the
> coveted trophy is named) in his book, *Principles of
> Football,* first published in 1921.

2   Those Bullets rose like Lazarus from the ashes.
> **Television sportscaster** during one of the seven
> games of the 1971 NBA semifinal playoffs between
> the Knicks and the Bullets. After 14 playoff games,
> the exhausted Bullets were swept 4-0 by Milwaukee
> in the finals.

3   We'll win if the Big Dodger in the sky wills it.
> Los Angeles manager **Tommy Lasorda** at the outset
> of the 1977 season.

I will not wither in the face of this salvo after salvo of invective and **4**
vituperation. This tournament is as honest as the day is long, as clean
as a spring afternoon.

> Boxing promoter **Don King,** in defense of the
> scandal-beset ABC-TV "Tournament of Champions."

We gave him an unlimited expense account and he's already **5**
exceeded it.

> Washington Redskins president **Edward Bennett**
> **Williams** about controversial coach George Allen, a
> few weeks after Allen had been hired.

I'm going to leave everything I've got on the field. When I walk out **6**
of that game, I'm going to be dead.

> Cornerback **Beasley Reece** in 1977, after being
> picked up on waivers by the New York Giants from
> Dallas, just in time to play against his former
> teammates.

A sack of the quarterback is just like in war when you sink an air- **7**
craft carrier.

> Former New York Jet defensive lineman **Richard**
> **Neal,** playing his version of World War II.

The first one thought about going in. The second one was a brick **8**
.... The third had legs on it. It just kept walking around until it
fell in.

> Former Philadelphia 76er **Lloyd Free** (before he
> changed his name), describing his winning free throws
> in a late-season game with Cleveland.

My greatest strength is that I have no weaknesses. **9**

> **John McEnroe** in 1979, at 20 years of age.

We set Monday night football back 2,000 years. They beat us in **10**
every phase of the game—passing, running, kicking, special teams
and coaching. They even beat us coming out of the tunnel.

> Tampa Bay coach **John McKay,** after a 23-0 loss to
> the Chicago Bears in 1980.

Wilson has unreal speed. He's a walking double. **11**

> Former Yankee **Reggie Jackson,** looking at Kansas
> City's Willie Wilson, before the 1980 American
> League playoffs.

I used more effort winding up than he did in pitching nine innings. **12**

> Hall of Famer **Burleigh Grimes,** describing
> superstar Grover Cleveland Alexander.

13 Aguirre is a phenomenal player. He has such hands that no mortal
can take the ball away from him.

> LaSalle coach **Dave "Lefty" Ervin,** describing
> DePaul's Mark Aguirre, after DePaul beat LaSalle,
> 69-62 in 1981. Aguirre hit for 35 of Blue Demons'
> points.

14 He is the only fighter who fights three minutes per round.

> **Carlos "Panama" Lewis** on WBA champion Aaron
> Pryor.

15 An artist cannot produce great paintings every day. It is true that
once you see her [Mandlikova] play at that special level, you want
to see it every time you come out to watch her play. But she is not
the type to do it every time. That is the way with artists.

> **Betty Stove,** Hana Mandlikova's coach, interpreting
> Mandlikova's sometimes brilliant, sometimes erratic
> play.

16 The planes at LaGuardia had better not fly too low when I'm at
bat.

> **George Foster,** New York Met slugger, promising
> great things in 1982.

17 The celebration was something like relief. Our biggest problem is
we must finish first, our bosses won't let us finish second-best. If
we do finish second, it's a great disaster, bigger than the depression
of the 30s. Steve Ross [chairman of Warner Communications, which
owns the Cosmos] has not told me this personally, but I know it.

> Interim New York coach **Julio Mazzei,** getting car-
> ried away after the Cosmos had eliminated the San
> Diego Sockers on their way to winning the 1982 Soccer
> Bowl.

18 It's like part of America being stopped. I thought the baseball
strike was bad enough, but this [the football strike] is terrible. Why
doesn't the whole world strike and get it over with?

> Singer **Margaret Whiting,** filling in on TV for NFL
> football on the first Sunday of the 1982 strike, ringing
> the clarion of doom.

19 [This is] the greatest marriage in the history of sports. The man's
[Nelson Skalbania] a genius. I absolutely love the man and so does
Vince [Ferragamo].

> Agent **David Fishof** in 1981, after Vince Ferragamo
> signed a four-year-guaranteed $2.5 million contract

with the Montreal Alouettes. The following year, Skalbania had unloaded the franchise, Ferragamo was back with the Los Angeles Rams, and Fishof was preparing to sue the Canadian "genius" for most of that unpaid $2.5 million.

It's a tough decision, and Gussie Busch, he'll hire 25,000 people **20** with blotters if he has to get this game in . . .

> Telecaster **Joe Garagiola,** after the rains came in the sixth game of the 1982 World Series, with St. Louis leading Milwaukee, 5-0. The Cards won to tie the Series, and finished off the Brewers in the seventh game.

Put-Downs

Athletes consider themselves professionals, and the word, as they use it, has many special connotations. One of them is a continuous striving toward perfection—not necessarily ever achieving it, but making the maximum effort to. Some of the quotes below come from exasperation with teammates and opponents who make less than a total effort; people who don't know how to—or are constitutionally incapable of—exploiting their God-given talents. Not being a complete pro is a cardinal sin to a pro.

Another put-down criterion is connected with idiosyncratic behavior, with what used to be called "flakiness." (It is still called that, but acceptable parameters for a "flake" have expanded considerably since the day Joe Pepitone introduced the personal hair dryer into the Yankee locker room.) Here the rule of thumb seems to be very simple. It's okay to be a little flaky if you're producing and keeping the guys loose, but if the team's going down the tube, forget it, buddy. Save it for the off-season back in Klamath Falls.

And then, of course, there's always the element of pure malice, the black-hearted desire to shred an opponent or teammate.

From unintentional to witty to mean-spirited, here are the put-downs.

In the pressure games, always bet against the Dallas Cowboys, the **1**

San Francisco Giants and Germany.
> **Gamblers' axiom,** suspended temporarily when
> Dallas finally won its first Super Bowl.

2   There isn't enough mustard in the world to cover Reggie Jackson.
> Pitcher **Darold Knowles,** a teammate of Jackson's at
> Oakland, commenting on the famous "hotdog" label
> pinned on Jackson.

3   They didn't give him a cake. They were afraid he'd drop it.
> Former New York Mets manager **Casey Stengel,** at
> a team birthday party for first baseman Marvelous
> Marv Throneberry.

4   I've seen better ice on the roads in Saskatchewan.
> **Emile Francis,** on the condition of the Madison
> Square Garden rink, when he was coaching the New
> York Rangers.

5   Pete Rozelle does not understand the meaning of due process.
Rozelle makes up the rules without consulting the players, hires a
private police force to enforce those rules, determines who should
be investigated and sits and listens to hearsay evidence and un-
supported allegations against players.
      Rozelle then acts as grand jury, prosecutor, judge, jury and
apellate court. Most important, he can destroy a person's career
by simply stating publicly that the player is guilty.
> **Ed Garvey** of the NFL Players Association, in 1974.
> Garvey was incensed because the football com-
> missioner had fined eight San Diego Chargers for
> alleged drug use without a hearing before an impartial
> arbitrator.

6   Did you ever consider hitting it closer to the hole?
> **"Gentle" Ben Hogan,** during a 1975 golf tourna-
> ment, reacting to a fellow player's gripes about his
> own putting.

7   The NHL is not known to be very progressive. Only a few years
ago, they were dragged kicking and screaming into the 20th century. It will take another few years before they get into the second
half.
> Sports attorney **Roy McMurty,** in 1975. McMurty's
> view might have been slightly jaundiced: he was rep-
> resenting a one-eyed hockey player who had been re-
> fused permission to play with the Buffalo Sabres

using a special protective mask.

He throws nickels around like manhole covers.   **8**
> All-pro end **Mike Ditka,** paying tribute in 1976 to
> the fabled parsimony of all-time Chicago Bears owner
> George Halas.

It was unbelievable in Chicago. You felt you had to pitch a shutout   **9**
to tie.
> **Rich Gossage,** then with Pittsburgh, reflecting on his
> former team, the 1976 Chicago White Sox.

In '77 I led the White Sox with 15 wins despite the fact that we   **10**
had Alan Bannister committing 40 errors at short, Jorge Orta, the
only second baseman with a Teflon glove, Eric Soderholm, who
had limited range, at third, and Ralph Garr in left, who could have
played an entire game without his glove and nobody would have
known the difference.
> Former Baltimore Orioles pitcher **Steve Stone,** a Cy
> Young Award winner in 1980, looking back on his dog
> days with the Chicago franchise.

Howard: There's Connie Dobler. He's become perhaps the best-   **11**
          known offensive lineman in professional football. Sup-
          posed to be the dirtiest man in the game, but that may
          be more reputation and press than fact. Yet he revels
          in the notoriety he's been receiving. He was talking to
          Dandy Don Meredith one day and he said, 'Don, before
          I'm done, they'll know me better than you.'
Don: How you do carry on! I've never met him.
> Curious exchange between **Don Meredith** and his
> more verbose colleague, **Howard Cosell,** on "Mon-
> day Night Football" in the fall of 1977.

I wonder if she knows what's going on yet. That's great. She's win-   **12**
ning. Wait'll she learns how to choke.
> Veteran **Billie Jean King's** comment on 14-year-old
> Tracy Austin, after the pigtailed youngster's victory
> over fourth-seeded Sue Barker in the 1977 U.S. Ten-
> nis Open championships.

He [Killebrew] hasn't much range, but anything he can get to, he'll   **13**
drop.
> Red Smith's recollection of Harmon Killebrew's
> Minnesota **teammates' assessment** of his hot-
> corner abilities.

14 Pitchers aren't athletes.

> Former New York Met **Chuck Hiller,** who's played
> second base and coached.

15 He's a guy with no brains who makes up the rules as he goes along.

> **Earl Weaver,** Baltimore Oriole manager in 1978,
> about umpire Marty Springstead, after the latter threw
> him out of a game for the sixth time.

16 I don't care. He's no Marilyn Monroe. Do you think I want to look
at that midget every day?

> **Marty Springstead** about Weaver, after being told
> what the volatile Baltimore manager had said.

17 The man [Bud Collins] is totally ignorant of the game itself. Every
shot played on the court is to him 'a topspin.' The word is used in
every sentence. A blind man can see that this is utter nonsense.
But Collins has really driven this to the hilt: He has invented the
topspin lob! The whole purpose of the lob, passive or aggressive,
is to lift the ball over the opponent's reach. To give this ball a topspin that would reduce its height and serve no purpose what-
soever, even when it hits the ground, is an absurd notion.

> **Dr. Paul Singer** of Summit, N.J., in a letter to *New
> York Times* TV critic John J. O'Connor.

18 I always considered Al [Davis] a charming rogue, but in my business judgment he has become an outlaw.

> **Pete Rozelle's** succinct dismissal of the Raiders'
> owner in a 1981 press conference, shortly after Davis
> and the Los Angeles Memorial Coliseum Commission
> brought a $160-million suit against the NFL for refusal
> to let the Raiders move the Oakland franchise to Los
> Angeles.

19 Enos [Cabell] stands over there at third.

> San Francisco manager **Frank Robinson,** describing
> his third baseman in 1981. Cabell had made 11 errors
> in his first 59 games, and went to Detroit in 1982.

20 Beat me, whip me, make me listen to the Giants.

> **Bumper sticker** seen in Oakland, just over the bridge
> from San Francisco.

21 I dirty three uniforms in a day. He [George Foster] dirties three in
a month.

> **Pete Rose's** reaction to former teammate George

Foster's signing a $2-million-a-year contract with the
New York Mets in 1982.

The Knicks used to be run with dignity by a guy by the name of   **22**
Ned Irish. Now I get the feeling they're being run by a carpetbag-
ging conglomerate.

> Golden State Warriors owner **Franklin Mieuli,** after
> matching the New York club's five-year $4.5 million
> offer sheet to the Warriors' Bernard King, who had
> opted for free agency in 1982. King finally did sign
> with the Knicks.

I told [Peter] Cook in Sydney [Australia] that beards don't fit in   **23**
with my business. I told him I would introduce him to a lot of New
York trainers and that he could earn $400,000 a year if he worked
at it.

He broke his agreement. He arrived with the beard. Sure I
called him a pinhead. Any grown man who will sacrifice $400,000
for a beard is a pinhead.

I had him at the barn and he was always looking in the
mirror, stroking his beard. I think he thought he was Tony Curtis.

> New York horseman **Wayne Murty,** after firing
> bearded Australian jockey Peter Cook.

Cooney is what we called in the old days, a 'game quitter.' This is   **24**
to say that he won't lay down, but he'll take punishment. But he'll
quit as far as winning the fight is concerned. Cooney would not
compete and he felt he wasn't going to win that fight. He wasn't
trying that hard. The fight was close, closer than we originally
thought.

> Former fight manager and boxing maven **Cus
> D'Amato,** after watching the Larry Holmes-Gerry
> Cooney 1982 fight for the third time.

I'm not a member of the union, I don't read any newspapers and I   **25**
don't watch much TV, except for 'Bonanza.' So I don't have the
slightest idea what's going [on about the football strike]. I don't
think most players really do, either. But I will say this: The strike
is the fault of two people—Mr. Garvey and Mr. Donlan. Their personalities and egos have gotten involved in this, and that's a
shame. You would think that two grown men of their caliber
wouldn't be shootin' for the Personality of the Year award. But
they are.

> Houston Oilers star **Earl Campbell,** assigning blame
> for the 1982 football strike—which was costing him
> $20,000 a week.

Sour Grapes

Since only one team can win in a division, a conference, or a league, anywhere from five to ten teams must lose. Everyone has known that, since Pythagoras and the early Greeks. If you lose down at the bottom of the pack, however, it does take a lot of the pressure off you. Nobody expected much from you in the first place. But for those who finish from the middle to second, the pressure is—as the expectations were—greater. Accepting loss, in the circumstance, calls for grace under pressure—a relatively rare commodity in the cauldron of competitive sports.

Of course, the grapes are not all that turns bitter when the margin of defeat or disappointment is narrow. The owner who bought the franchise anticipating unimagined riches and glamour and then discovers no one wants to watch his tatterdemalion team or buy a hot dog in his stadium; the player who's traded to an overrated club and finds that the fans expect him to earn at least part of his embarrassingly large salary; the trainer whose pampered thoroughbred loses a big purse to a horse without blood lines who was a $25,000 claimer in the spring—are all as aggrieved as the coach who loses the Stanley Cup in overtime on the final game of play.

The pain and frustration must be blamed on *somebody*, and that's when rashness, scapegoating, and meanness strike out.

1 Anyone can run where the holes are. A good football player makes his own holes.

> Fullback-halfback **Joe Don Looney,** brilliant at Oklahoma, analyzing his pro career: six years, four teams.

2 The track was a disgrace. It's been bad for 100 years and they're going to leave it bad for the next hundred.

> **LeRoy Jolley,** trainer of Kentucky Derby winner Foolish Pleasure, after the latter lost the 1975 Preakness at Pimlico.

3 New York is all right for guys who want publicity and limelight. I don't need it . . . New York didn't do anything for me. I was there a year and I didn't do any of those commercials or endorsements.

Former Detroit pitcher **Mickey Lolich,** who ended
his baseball career as a New York Met in 1976.

I hit him 20, he hits me one and the crowd goes yeaaaa. I'd hit him   **4**
some shots but he'd hit me the last shot and they'd go yeaaa.
They're thinking, he's the poor guy, he don't have a chance, but
look, he's landing. That's what sways the judges.
>   **George Foreman,** explaining his loss to Jimmy
>   Young from the vantage point of his hospital bed the
>   day after the fight.

There's no team in the world good enough to lose one of 40 games   **5**
at home. I knew we were gonna get it tonight. You get stiffed up
here. They call all the penalties against us until Montreal gets a
nice lead, then they gave Montreal condescending penalties at the
end of the game.
>   Former Boston Bruin coach **Don Cherry,** after a
>   penalty-filled game at the Montreal Forum in the late
>   70s, when the Canadiens were flying high.

I lost $600,000 in 1976 and $1.1 million in 1977. When you lose   **6**
like that, it ceases to be fun. So this is the bleakest day of my life.
>   Departing Oakland A's owner **Charley Finley's** part-
>   ing shot at baseball. Finley didn't seem comforted by
>   the fact he had bought club for $4 million (1960) and
>   sold it for $12.5 million (1977).

You don't need much to replace him [Don Gullett]. Anybody who   **7**
can pitch 115 innings will replace him. He only pitched 114
innings for us.
>   Former Cincinnati manager **Sparky Anderson,**
>   minimizing the loss of Don Gullett, considered one of
>   the best left-handers in baseball, to the Yankees via
>   the free agency route.

If anyone thinks I'm over the hill, it's just pure ignorance. That   **8**
hasn't been Johnny Miller out there. That's been somebody else
with somebody else's swing.
>   **Johnny Miller,** in May 1977, laying his poor play at
>   the door of an imposter.

I just wish when I get vindicated on a charge that the newspapers   **9**
would put a headline on that instead of all this other stuff. You
don't beat babies when they don't have their fingers in the cookie
jar. That's called child abuse.
>   **Don King,** complaining about the bad press he'd

received since his ABC-TV boxing tournament was cancelled because of charges that the stats had been rigged.

10   If the little SOB had batted me second, ahead of Mantle, I would have gotten pitches to hit and I would have made the Hall of Fame. Instead, he batted me eighth, in front of the pitcher, and I never got pitches to hit. That's why I'm not in the Hall of Fame.

> Round-robin manager **Billy Martin,** on how Casey Stengel kept him out of baseball's Pantheon.

11   Garber was pitching like it was the seventh game of the World Series. He had a 16-4 lead. I'm not saying anything about him bearing down. I just said he should challenge somebody. I had one pitch to swing at that was a strike. Most pitchers in baseball just challenge a guy in that situation. He was just trying to in-and-out, up-and-down you.

> **Pete Rose,** beefing about Atlanta reliever Gene Garber, who ended Rose's 44-straight-games hitting streak by striking him out in his last at-bat.

12   What will I remember about this year? I'll remember that it proved to me that baseball is a business. One big industry. You stop producing, and people forget what you've done. You're only as good as your last time at bat.

> Pittsburgh's **Dave Parker,** at the end of the gloomy 1981 season, the year the Pirate fans got on him.

13   Defense does make pitching, but the defense doesn't have to be sensational. If they just make the routine plays, that's all you want. Spectacular plays are overrated.

> New York Mets manager **George Bamberger** in spring training, 1982. Following the trade of Doug Flynn, generally considered the best glove man at second in the league, Bamberger was facing the new season with a rookie combination at second and short.

14   There's a lot more future in hamburgers than in baseball. The fun in it is all gone for me. Baseball isn't baseball anymore. I've been disillusioned by everyone I met. Ballard [Smith] can do anything he wants with the team. Baseball has brought me nothing but aggravation.

> Crusty **Ray Kroc,** who owns both the San Diego Padres and McDonald's. Fined a record $100,000 for remarks interpreted as tampering with players on other teams, Kroc turned over the reins of the Padres to son-in-law Ballard Smith in 1980.

Cliches

Every sport has its own set of cliches, as well as the ones that apply to all sports. It would be difficult to contemplate watching, say, an entire telecast that was free of cliches. There probably would be hundreds of phone calls to the channel, complaining that something was missing.

So cliches have their uses; they are the soiled grout of communication. Their currency is explained in part by how easy they are to use. When Frank Gifford describes a linebacker as "some kind of ballplayer" he has saved himself the trouble of telling you *what* kind. Think of some of the possibilities: splendid, over-the-hill, outstanding, journeyman, premier, first-rate, washed up. Some of these might be considered kind of fruity. Others have been patented by other sportscasters: Phil Rizzuto favors "outstanding," which he breaks up, as though it were two words. That's probably the safest one, though. So you see, the qualifying adjective requires thought, and probably should be checked out with the channel's attorneys first.

Cliches are also comforting for the audience. We've been there before, many times, and know how cozily they fit. Even the most rabid Yankee fan knows Gossage doesn't really throw aspirins over the plate. It's just another way to indicate that his fastball is humming, that his high hard one is rising, that he's throwing smoke.

Cliches are frequently invoked to bail the telecaster out of awkward situations. No one's going to question what he means when he says "Maloney's got his work cut out for him," about a goalie who's just gotten into the game—in time to defend against a power play against the top team in the league on their home ice.

Lastly, cliches mean you never have to say you're sorry. Assuming anyone's listening, any meaning that was there years ago has become so rubbed away by overuse that it is virtually non-existent. So no one can misunderstand what you say, no one gets his feelings hurt—no runs, no hits, no errors.

An effective relief pitcher has to have ice water in his veins. **1**
Mike [Marshall] does.
       Walt Alston, Los Angeles Dodgers manager in 1974.

He's some kind of ballplayer. **2**

Frank Gifford, innumerable times on "Monday Night Football." Unfortunately, Gifford doesn't hold the copyright on this classic.

3 This game goes in cycles. The small forward role was invented because there weren't enough big ones to go around. But a good big man is better than a good little man.

Former Washington Bullets coach **Dick Motta,** commenting on the new trend to big guards, and proving that old cliches never die, they just get recycled.

4 We're just getting ready for tomorrow's game. If we deserve first, we'll get it. If we don't deserve it, we won't.

New York Islanders coach **Al Arbour,** four games before the end of the 1976-77 hockey season. He was right. They didn't get it.

5 If you're going to lose, lose like champions.

Former Boston Celtics' coach **Red Auerbach,** doing his version of Knute Rockne before the sixth game of the 1977 playoffs with the 76ers. The Celtics won, 113-108, and lost like champions in the seventh game.

6 Managing isn't all that difficult. Just score more runs than the other guy.

Ted Turner, Atlanta owner and one-time manager, who retired as a manager with an 0-1 record.

7 This game is gonna be won in the trenches.

Any NFL coach on any given Sunday between August 16th and Super Bowl Sunday.

8 I won't know until I see the films.

Pro football coach on Monday, after a disastrous Sunday.

9 I'm not trying to replace anyone because I can't do what the guys they got rid of did. I can only be me.

Cincinnati Reds rookie outfielder **Paul Householder** in spring training, 1982. George Foster and Ken Griffey are two of the "guys they got rid of."

10 Harvey [Kuenn]'s theory is that it's a game of inches but if the inches go with you, you're gonna win.

Telecaster **Joe Garagiola,** quoting Milwaukee manager Harvey Kuenn, in game 5 of the 1982 World Series.

The game's never over until the last out.   **11**
> **Baseball sportscasters,** about 55 times a season,
> sometimes when the score is 13-2 in the ninth inning.

- These two teams came here today to play football.   **12**
- The name of the game is the quarterback.
- To win, they've [the Eagles] got to get the momentum back on their side.
- The vertical game is the deep game.
- I don't know if miracles that big can fit inside the Super Bowl, but that's all the Eagles have left.
> **Various members of the NBC-TV announcing team,** plotting the progress of the 1981 Super Bowl game.

Rank Optimism

Rank optimism has to do with denying the facts. Or trying to rearrange them into more fortuitous patterns. Or seeing them from another angle, and thereby changing them. Everyone does it at some time in his/her life, and athletes do it a little more often. They are human, they are caught up in severely competitive situations and the temptation is always there to put a little blue sky into what might otherwise be a very threatening overcast.

This is best illustrated by what may be the oldest joke about boxing. The one about the fighter who is taking a terrible beating and returns to his corner round after round to be told by his manager, "He never laid a glove on you, Kid." Peering through battered eyeslits, the Kid finally responds: "Then keep an eye on the ref—*somebody* out there is murdering me."

That is the essence of rank optimism: two parts self-delusion, one part myopia, the formula for whistling your way past the graveyard of moribund hopes.

There has never been any violence in the NHL.
> **Clarence Campbell,** president of the NHL in 1974,   **1**
> after studying a government-sponsored report called
> "Inquiry into Violence in Amateur Hockey," which
> accused the NHL of setting a bad example for
> Canadian youngsters.

2 The funny thing is, except for the teams going under, our league has never been in better shape.

> All-time great **Gordie Howe,** reporting on the state of the World Hockey Association in 1976.

3 He can score seven touchdowns and gain 500 yards and I'll still be pleased—if we score one more point. Dorsett is not going to affect us psychologically.

> Penn State coach **Joe Paterno,** before his team's 1976 season-closer with Pittsburgh. Penn State lost, 24-7, with Dorsett gaining 224 yards. Garnering 11 NCAA records and the Heisman Trophy, Tony must have psyched *somebody.*

4 Jimmy Young is a sparring partner who went 15 rounds with a powder puff. In a way, I resent fighting fellows like this, but what the heck.

> **George Foreman,** before the Young fight, which hastened his early retirement.

5 I am the fastest boxer in the world. I have seen Muhammad Ali on films, I have seen Sugar Ray Robinson on films, I have seen myself on films. They can't compete with me. I've got blindness speed.

> Olympic lightweight champion **Howard Davis,** after his third pro fight. Also fast of lip, Davis promised himself a world lightweight championship in "two-and-a-half to three years."

6 Let's Go Mets!

> Preposterous **battle cry** first heard in the old Polo Grounds on Opening Day, 1966. New York fans had already watched their newest team lose over 400 games in their first four seasons. Despite the forlorn appeal, Mets lost to Pirates, 4-3.

7 We're No. 1.

> **Toronto Blue Jays fans' chant**, in the eighth inning of the first game of the expansion team's first season (1977). Toronto beat Chicago, 9-5, rewarding the fans who had waited 25 years for a major-league franchise.

8 We feel that soccer is the fastest-growing sport. It's unquestionably the sport of the future. That's why we decided to buy the Cosmos.

> **Jay Emmett,** a Warner Communications vice-

president, in 1975. Emmett explained that Warner
had passed up "five basketball, two baseball and
several hockey teams" in deciding that soccer was
going to be the hot sports ticket.

I figure on going for another six years until I'm 40. Then I'll try the   **9**
pro golf circuit. I'm as good right now as any of them.
> Daredevil **Evel Knievel,** mapping out his career
> throughout the 70s and not excluding the possibility
> of winning a U.S. Open.

Me. On instant replay.   **10**
> **Derek Sanderson,** Boston Bruin center in the early
> 70s, when asked to name the greatest hockey player
> he had ever seen.

If I only had a little humility, I would be perfect.   **11**
> Yachtsman **Ted Turner,** suspended Atlanta Braves
> owner, after winning the America's Cup in 1977.

I no longer think of our trade as the Tom Seaver trade. I now   **12**
think of it as the Steve Henderson trade.
> Former New York Mets manager **Joe Torre,** after
> the Mets had dealt off "The Franchise" to Cincinnati.
> Henderson was never accepted by New York fans,
> was dealt to Chicago in 1981.

There is no doubt that soccer will one day challenge football and   **13**
baseball as the No. 1 sport in America.
> NASL commissioner **Phil Woosnam,** keeping his
> fingers crossed in 1982, while soccer attendance con-
> tinued its downward trend.

Suppose I had an MVP year? I'd have been locked into that   **14**
contract.
> **Ron Jackson,** who turned down a $750,000 three-
> year contract with the Detroit Tigers in 1982 (on his
> agent's advice), and wound up in Salt Lake City. He
> caught on with the California Angels, for considerably
> less money.

I don't think any kids on this club are using marijuana or any   **15**
drugs at all. I know no one is using cocaine or heroin and none of
them are on Quaaludes.
> Los Angeles Dodgers team physician **Robert Woods,**
> in 1982.

Understatement

It's no accident that this is perhaps the slimmest category in the book. The expansion of professional leagues, the proliferation of college teams, the introduction of new sports—all the factors that add up to the term "sports explosion"—have created a rising tide of hype about the games, the players, the strategies, and the virtues of spectator sports. It was unavoidable, in the circumstance, that some of this built-in ballyhoo wouldn't rub off on the athlete and others around the playing and packaging of the games.

But now and then some of them resist the pressures of press agentry and drum beating and say something short and sweet, or at least straightforward. In an age of relentless overstatement, these are generally pretty refreshing.

1   It's old.

> **Johnny Unitas,** late in his career, with the San Diego Chargers, explaining why his 40-year-old knee was bothering him.

2   I think it [the Rozelle rule] would turn football into a mercenary sport.

> Former Philadelphia Eagles coach **Mike McCormack,** commenting in 1975 on the proposed repeal of the "Rozelle rule." Under the player option rule, the NFL commissioner was empowered to order a team that signed a free agent to compensate that player's original team.

3   He's not fired. He's just not rehired.

> **Mike Shaw,** publicity director of the Buffalo Braves, explaining the dismissal of coach Jack Ramsay. Available for hire, Ramsay moved on to the Portland Trail Blazers—and won the 1977 NBA title.

4   Sure it [chanting of disaffected fans] bothered me. It was an indication to me that we weren't doing what we should. It was an indication that the fans weren't happy.

> New York Giants' owner **Wellington Mara** at a 1969

press conference, disclosing his reaction to the
"Good-bye Allie" serenade that had become a
stadium lynch chant for disaffected Giant fans.

All I did was bring some people together.   **5**

> **William Shea,** describing his part in the planning
> and construction of Nassau Coliseum in 1971. Some
> of the people he brought together: the NHL, the New
> York Rangers, the NBA, the newly created Islanders,
> the much-traveled New York Nets, and, of course,
> Nassau County.

Aw, why not? I wasn't running well, anyway.   **6**

> Race driver **Whitey Gerken,** who stopped his own
> car at the Indianapolis Fairgrounds in order to pull
> another driver, Jack Bowsher, out of his overturned
> car, in 1970. Gerken was credited with saving the life
> of the unconscious Bowsher.

He hit me on the head with his stick. And he didn't apologize.   **7**

> Former New York Ranger **Rod Gilbert,** explaining
> why he had punched Philadelphia Flyer Bill Lesuk
> during a hard-fought game in 1971.

I should have had a thousand. I relaxed after 900.   **8**

> Yakima (Wash.) basketball player **Ted St. Martin,**
> after setting a new world record for free throws by
> sinking 927 in a row.

We've been waiting thirty years for this, and the pressure was   **9**
beginning to build.

> Kapaa High football coach **Glenn Hayashi,** after his
> 1976 team won its first championship in thirty years
> of interscholastic play on the Hawaiian island of
> Kauai. The league has three teams.

They blitzed. I had to get rid of the ball and he [Ron Jessie]   **10**
wasn't quite as open as I'd have liked him to be.

> Former Los Angeles quarterback **Pat Haden,** in a
> late-season game with Super Bowl-bound Minnesota
> in 1976. Trailing 17-13 with less than three minutes
> to play, Haden's desperation pass to Jessie was inter-
> cepted. Final score: Vikings, 24, Rams, 13.

I'm not all that excited over money.   **11**

> **Dick Allen,** at 35, after signing a one-year

contract with Charley Finley's fading 1977 Oakland A's.
Allen was the last free agent signed that year.

12   We're not perfect. We make mistakes, too. We're only human, and
it appears that we may have made one here.

> **George Steinbrenner,** announcing that the general
> admission upper-stands seats in Yankee Stadium,
> which had been jumped from $1.50 to $4.50, would
> subsequently sell for $2.50.

13   Violence? I don't think of it as violence. I think of it as contact.
And contact is a part of life.

> Pittsburgh Steeler **"Mean Joe" Greene** in 1980, on
> life in the center of the defensive line.

6. SPORTS AS A METAPHOR

Amateur Athletics

Amateur athletics, in some recognizable form, are still evident on the college campus in the forgotten (read, not uniformly televised) sports. Fencing, tennis and lacrosse are examples. And then there are the others, the money-makers. The NCAA TV contracts (now under litigation) for the 1982-85 football seasons with both CBS and ABC total $263.5 million; the rival College Football Association, representing 62 of the big-time schools, has signed with NBC for the same period for $180 million. There are pro leagues that would settle for 5 percent of either figure. Saturday afternoon into evening will thereby have an unprecedented all-networks college football saturation, and even the Love Boat may get blitzed.

Basketball, the second-ranking money-maker, doesn't have such blanket coverage, but has a similar (though more modest) TV financial arrangement.

Very well, apologists argue, but doesn't this enormously profitable university cottage industry also support those other sports that don't inspire such unparalleled generosity from the alumni associations? Well, not quite. A lot of it goes into building more elaborate football stadiums. Money, as they say, goes to money.

The NCAA rules for college athletes are presently being punctured in so many different ways that the debate over amateur vs.

175

professional status has become a worn-out joke. When you bypass or overlook so many restrictions, when you search for and find ways to compensate players for the flimsiest forms of work performed (or worse, the carefully disguised no-show job), you have effectually nullified the proscriptions against turning amateurs into paid athletes.

What has been created, in fact, with longer seasons and more games and year-round practice sessions, is a college-level football league very much like the pros, except that the caliber of play would be about Triple-A (in baseball terms).

The equivalent in college basketball is reflected in the vastly expanded cross-regional tournament play and the new NCAA ruling that prohibits a major basketball team from refusing a tournament bid *no matter where it is sent.* Amateurs, you say? College basketball has become a national game and a lucrative one, largely because of its interlocking tournament structure.

What is being introduced across the sports spectrum, albeit unevenly, are many of the restrictive elements of professional play, geared to conform to TV coverage and stadium revenue, within the phantom framework of do-or-die amateur college athletics.

1	College sports have been developed from games played by boys for pleasure into systematic professionalized athletic contests for the glory and, too often, for the financial profit of the college.
		Statement of the Carnegie Foundation for the Advancement of Teaching, in 1929.

2	I'm very much against this whole thing now, recruitment, scholarships, letters of intent. It's organized for adult men to manipulate 18-year-olds to come to a university and provide it with a winning team, some money and fame . . . . There has to be another way, because the extremes are to break down all sports to intramurals or admit that there is a professional class of athletes in college whose role includes providing vicarious excitement for the rest of the student body.
		New York Knick **Bill Bradley,** who had once decided to attend Duke University as a result of what he later concluded was a "carefully orchestrated recruiting job." Bradley opted for Princeton at the last moment, went on to be a Rhodes scholar, and joined the pros belatedly for a 10-year career.

3	I'd like to see some democracy in athletics. The old concept of the coach as totalitarian ruler just can't make it anymore in amateur athletics. Players seem more aware of themselves as individuals rather than cogs in a machine.

Bobby Ryder, sophomore forward on the 1970
Princeton basketball team. Ryder earned campus
notoriety when he got permission to miss practice in
order to participate in the November 1969 antiwar
mobilization in Washington, D.C.

The money is chicken feed . . . . Cuts had to be made throughout   **4**
N.Y.U. [New York University] and the students and faculty had to
be pacified. You couldn't keep something as highly visible as track
and basketball when you're chopping away at departments that
people now consider more important.

> **Budget director at an Eastern university** com-
> menting on N.Y.U.'s 1971 decision to drop the two
> sports in which it had achieved national prominence
> in recent years.

There are no amateurs anymore. To be good, a skier must literally   **5**
devote from four to six years of his life to the sport. You don't
have time for school or a job, and you must travel the world.
That's hard to do without compensation.

> Skiing champ **Jean-Claude Killy,** in 1972.

The point I'm reaching for in my little crusade is to modernize a   **6**
code that goes back to the Gay 90s . . . . The British aristocracy
had set it up to keep those of a lower social level from competing
against them. But sport is no longer the dilettante thing it once
was, a casual hour-a-day thing. It's an all-out approach that practically demands cheating.

> **John B. Kelly, Jr.,** Association of American Univer-
> sities president, in 1972, charging that the Olympics
> amateur code was more than just obsolete: it was
> leading to wholesale perjury among Olympic athletes.
> (Kelly himself participated in four Olympics.)

The money, it's cool. Why shouldn't we be paid like everyone else   **7**
in our society? I just don't understand the amateur ethic out of
another century.

> Pro high jumper **John Radetich** in 1973, after set-
> ting a world indoor record of 7 feet, 4 and 3/4 inches.
> The money was small—and so were the crowds; the
> pro track circuit closed in 1976.

Nobody ever told me if you practiced swimming that all this would   **8**
ever happen to you . . . . Swimming is too demanding. It's also boring.
You work six or seven hours a day just so you can splash water
faster than anyone else. There's gotta be something more to life.

> **Mark Spitz,** Olympic swimming champion in 1972, two years and countless TV commercials later.

9 I felt obligated to stay and play out my four years because the college gave me a scholarship. But then when I saw my coach leave because a pro team made him an offer with more money, I decided it was every man for himself.

> **Unidentified college basketball player,** who decided in 1975 to play for pay.

10 I really wouldn't feel bad if one of my players left school early for a lot of money. But some of these kids are getting bad advice. Many of them aren't in the superstar category and they won't get that much. The in-between players should stay in school.

> **Unidentified college basketball coach,** in 1975.

11 The thing is that 90 percent of the colleges are abiding by the rules, doing things right. The other 10 percent, they're going to the bowl games.

> **Tony Mason,** University of Cincinnati football coach, in 1975.

12 It's time we let kids grow up naturally. Suppose they don't grow up to be athletic superstars. That isn't so terrible. Let them find their own interests and their own levels. Let them be kids instead of forcing them to play being adults.

> Penn State football coach **Joe Paterno,** whose teams turn up regularly in post-season play and whose disinclination to become a pro mentor is almost legendary.

13 There have been quite a few allegations of what is regarded by many as an arbitrary, somewhat autocratic organization [the NCAA] that deals with the athletes and institutions as though they had minimal rights. There is question as to the adequacy of hearing procedures, whether there is any significant due process involved in methods used by the NCAA in imposing penalties and undertaking its general regulatory functions.

> Rep. **John E. Moss** (D., Calif.), chairman of a Congressional subcommittee investigating the actions of the NCAA, in 1978.

14 If coaches and athletic directors can hold national conventions, so can college presidents. If they want to reaffirm amateurism, then they must restructure the sanctions for illegal aid, recruiting unqualified players and falsifying transcripts. This is the responsibility of college presidents.

Syracuse coach **Frank Maloney** in 1980, after learning that five Pacific 10 Conference schools had been
ruled ineligible for both the league championship and
bowl games because of rules violations.

[College athletic programs are] out of control when the evaluation   **15**
of academic transcripts is subverted by anyone—powerful friends
of the university, coaches, university administrators. It is out of
control when grades for athletes are falsified on a systematic
basis . . . . It is out of control when the recruiting of blue-chip
athletes involves, in some systematic fashion, the top business,
political and corporate leadership of the community and the
state . . . . It is out of control when decisions of the most far-
reaching consequence—for example, enlarging the football
stadium or shifting to a different athletic conference—are made
without regard for the usual processes of internal review and
consultation.

> **Harold Enarson,** president of Ohio State University
> in 1981, looking at the wide range of NCAA violations
> on major American campuses.

. . . Just as other students are paid for on-campus jobs, football   **16**
players, who labor in a hazardous occupation and produce huge
revenue, should be paid.

> State Senator **Ernie Chambers,** who introduced a
> bill (LB 363) in the Nebraska Senate in 1981 that
> would classify college football players as employees of
> the university. Though NCAA regulations forbid
> payments to athletes, Chambers felt his bill would
> simply legitimize the unacknowledged "reim-
> bursements" players generally receive.

To allow injured students who receive athletic scholarships to   **17**
claim workmen's compensation would broaden the scope of the
workmen's compensation law to an unacceptable degree.

> **NCAA statement** asking permission to file a "friend
> of the court" brief in a landmark Indiana court deci-
> sion in 1982. The decision awarded workmen's com-
> pensation to a college football player severely injured
> during practice. NCAA feared the precedent would
> blur the "clear line of demarcation between college
> athletics and professional sports."

More than 2,000 colleges maintain active athletic programs today.   **18**

More than 700 are members of the National Collegiate Athletic Association. Of these 700, only 100 or so are involved in what is termed "big-time college sports"—that is, big-money football and basketball programs. The athletic programs at most colleges are self-supporting and seldom receive money from any outside sources.

Dick Holub, former New York Knick, who teaches English and helps oversee the student athlete academic program at Fairleigh Dickinson.

19 College athletics is truly at the crossroads. Once the atmosphere of a genuine amateur environment is totally destroyed, it will be virtually impossible to re-create it. If there can be substantiation of the recent charges leveled by Coach Digger Phelps of Notre Dame—that many schools across the country are paying star basketball players a rate of $10,000 a season—then the colleges that are in danger of losing academic credibility may also lose athletic credibility. The empty seats that follow some pro basketball teams from city to city may one day be found on college campuses.

Francis J. Lodato, chairman of Manhattan College's athletics committee, in 1982.

20 The contracts for the televising of college football for the 1982-85 seasons are void and of no effect. NCAA has seriously restricted free market forces in the economics of college football television. NCAA was aware of the anti-trust implications of the controls and has attempted to conceal the extent of its anticompetitive activities. These controls make NCAA a classic cartel . . . which has almost absolute control over the supply available to the networks, the advertisers and the viewing public.

Federal Judge Juan Burciaga in his 98-page opinion voiding all NCAA football TV contracts in 1982.

21 The Court does not know and need not determine whether the NCAA administration, in formulating the controls at issue, was motivated by genuine concern for NCAA members, by a lust for power, or by rank and greed. What is clear is that NCAA has violated the antitrust laws . . . .

Ibid.

22 I will not listen to or accept a single open-market bid to televise one of our football games for all the money in the world next week or the rest of this season. I feel morally bound to the NCAA television contract, no matter what was ruled by this judge.

University of Michigan athletic director **Don**

> Canham's reaction to Judge Burciaga's 1982
> decision (see 20, 21 above) voiding NCAA's television
> contracts.

People forget that the judge [Juan Burciaga] not only threw out all **23**
controls and made a shambles of the football scene [by voiding
NCAA contracts], but he took from the NCAA its only real strong
weapon for penalizing those who violate our rules. The only
penalties that count against those who cheat academically or in
recruiting is the penalty that bars a team from television
appearances and bowl games. I think he wiped that out.
> Arkansas University athletic director **Frank Broyles,**
> in defense of NCAA policies.

The court's decision and judgment replaced an organized and car- **24**
efully administered system of controls with an unfettered license
for the colleges to televise games anywhere anytime. Uncontrolled
license amounts to anarchy, and this is what will result in the
televising of college football unless some authority to avoid it is
found or restored.
> NCAA general counsel **George H. Gangwere,** on
> Judge Burciaga's far-reaching decision in *University of
> Oklahoma and University of Georgia vs. NCAA* (see
> 20, 21 above).

The Olympics

"The most important thing in the Olympic Games is not to win but to
take part, just as the most important thing in life is not the triumph
but the struggle."
     These were the words that Baron Pierre de Coubertin used
around the turn of the century to convince world leaders that the
Greek games should be revived. And revived they were, after a series
of Lucullan banquets at which the Baron stressed the grandeur and
spectacle of the Games more than the Greek ideals out of which they
purportedly sprang.
     That they have survived more or less continuously in a world
racked by division of every sort is remarkable. Despite boycotts and
in-fighting, despite the illegal use of drugs and steroids and massive
sports medicine programs, despite the endless and shifting con-

troversy surrounding the very definition of amateurism, the prestige
of the Games seems virtually unaffected. Until recently, cities actually competed for the honor of being chosen as the site of the summer
or winter Games. Then someone noticed that the Games do everything for a municipality but make money. Montreal's windblown
Olympic Village is mute testimony to that. And—for the first time in
history—Los Angeles's bid for the 1984 summer Games was the only
bid, leading to speculation that perhaps the Games had gotten too
big, too unwieldy, too ungovernable.

The International Olympic Committee, perhaps the most
exclusive club in the world, runs the Games, makes the rules, sometimes even rigidly enforces them. There are only 76 members in this
elite club: those from the West tend to be businessmen; those from
the East are generally political functionaries. Politics, of course, is
supposed to have no impact on the Games whatever. But the selection of Berlin for the site of the 1936 Games partly legitimized
Hitler's Germany in the eyes of many, and practically every subse-
quent selection has had political or economic overtones. At least until
the monetary costs of the ever-expanding Games became evident.

Then, in 1972, a new entry was added to the host city balance
sheet. ABC-TV bought the rights for the Munich Games for $12
million. Four years later, Montreal upped the ante to $32 million. By
1980, NBC had to go to the $100-million mark to wrest the Moscow
Games from ABC. Rebounding, ABC outbid NBC, CBS, ESPN, and
Tandem Productions for the rights to televise the 1984 summer
Games in Los Angeles. The price this time: $225 million.

Ironically, while televising of the Games may have made them
economically viable for cities that have had to say no in the past, it has
also created a global stage for world-class athletes. And this has led to
huge security problems. At Montreal, for example, in the light of the
tragic events at Munich in 1972, security costs reached the $100-
million range. A force of 14,000 men, including local and provincial
police and elements of the Canadian Army, were used to screen out
potential terrorists. Even the possibility of attack on the stadium
with portable nuclear weapons was not ruled out. Los Angeles faces
the same set of problems.

The world has come a long way since the periodic truces that
permitted the Games to be played at Olympia and Delphi, and at
Nemea and Isthmia, in the spirit of fair play and athletic excellence.

1   If I had decided to play in the Olympics, I would have had to
maintain my amateur standing. Then if I got hurt, who would have
taken care of me? . . . Basketball is my profession. I have been
looking forward to the pros for 17 years. I think the Olympics are
more for the average players. Going to the Olympics is their last
chance at glory.

Elvin Hayes, an All-American (36.2 points per game) at Houston in 1968, on why he passed up that year's Olympic team.

My first responsibility as a director is to assure the present and **2** future financial security of these boys. I personally have a better conscience than Mr. [Avery] Brundage. I would never occupy myself with sports if someone told me that when the athletes have run their race, they would be offered the place of a *clochard* [bum] in a doorway.

Maurice Martel, president of the French Ski Federation, defending, in 1971, his policy of cash awards to Olympic athletes on the basis of performance.

When the skiers allow their photographs or their names to be used **3** to promote ski products, they become agents of the industries. To let them compete would change the Games to a competition between industrialists, not between sportsmen. If the Olympics are not honest, let them come to an end.

Avery Brundage, International Olympic Committee chairman in 1972, reiterating that group's stand against amateur athletes endorsing equipment.

This is not sport. I appeal to every single sportsman not to come **4** to the Olympic games for political purposes, or, commercial exploitation. If this is not accomplished, then the Olympic movement and all sport is doomed. We shall retreat into barbarism.

Lord Killanin, Brundage's successor, after several 1974 international athletic events were dominated by politics rather than athletes. The same year, however, the IOC broke with precedent, permitting athletes to be allowed time and compensation for official Olympic training.

All minor sports play second fiddle in the United states. Countries **5** like East Germany and Russia are really pushing Olympic sports. We would win every gold medal if we did. The public is only concerned about the Jack Nicklauses, the Arnold Palmers, the Joe Namaths.

Jim Counsilman, U.S. Olympic Men's swimming coach in 1976.

Behind every Olympic gold medal there is an entire collective of **6** doctors, technicians and coaches—just like mission control when an astronaut is sent up into space.

Professor **Kurt Tittel,** at the Montreal summer
Olympic Games in 1976. Tittel is the director of the
sports medicine division at Leipzig's German Sports
Institute. East German athletes won 40 gold, 25
silver, and 25 bronze medals, second only to the
USSR.

7 We're out of date. We shake our old, untended sports trees once
every four years and gather whatever plums fall off. Other nations
cultivate their orchards day by day, pruning, nursing, root-feeding
them and harvesting ever more plums.

Telecaster **Howard K. Smith,** surely the most
quoted member of the President's Commission on
Olympic Sports, in 1977.

8 We believe that the abuses of the amateur status are widespread
and cannot be controlled. Therefore, it would be more honest for
sports and the Olympic movement to face up to this fact and have
completely open Olympics.

Sir Robin Brook, chairman of Britain's Sports
Council, urging an end to the hazy distinction between amateur and professional status before the
1980 Olympics.

9 You see, it's not an easy situation for a coach to be in. We have
two guys here capable of breaking the world decathlon record.
But . . . I think one of them has the better chance, but he can't win
the decathlon without using steroids. It's very unlikely for *any*
athlete to win a medal in a weight event without using them. It's
been that way for several Olympiads, and, sure, it's against
Olympic rules, but . . .

Len Miller, head track coach at the University of
California's Irvine campus, in 1977.

10 . . . I kinda hate the direction I've seen amateur athletics take in
my lifetime. And I've seen a lot of potential Olympians fall by the
wayside because coaches and parents push them too hard too
soon . . . They're taking someone like Linda Frattiane [the 16-
year-old U.S. figure-skating champ] and turning her into Seattle
Slew—a piece of meat trained to perform at maximum potential.
She'll be burned to a cinder after she wins the gold medal. Will
she be happy then?

Ibid.

11 In the last 24 hours, I've had a tough decision to make. When I
met the President, I kind of decided then to put my country first.

Mr. Carter kissed me and told me he fell in love with my skating. I feel I have a job to do for my country.

> **Linda Fratianne,** after deciding she would compete in the world figure skating championship in 1980 before turning pro.

The Olympics is the biggest sports event on earth . . . worth every **12** penny—every single million bucks—you have to spend to get it.

> ABC-TV sports director **Roone Arledge** in 1978, when estimates for televising the 1984 Summer Games in L.A. were set at $66 million.

The 1984 Olympics are a classic situation. They will be the first **13** Summer Games to be played in the United States in modern broadcast history, some 50 years, and most of the events will be televised live. Patriotism and national pride will figure into it, and American industry and advertisers will want to be associated with the Games.

> **Frederick S. Pierce,** president of ABC-TV, in 1979. ABC paid a record $225 million for the TV rights, almost four times the original estimate.

The Amateur Athletic Union regrets that it permitted Mr. Thorpe **14** to compete in amateur contests during the past several years and will do everything in its power to secure the return of prizes and the re-adjustment of points won by him and it will immediately eliminate his records from the books . . . . The American Olympic Committee and the Amateur Athletic Union feel that . . . Mr. Thorpe is deserving of the severest condemnation for concealing the fact that he had professionalized himself by playing baseball.

> **Resolution forwarded to the International Olympic Committee,** which stripped Jim Thorpe of the medals he had won at the 1912 Olympic Games in Stockholm. He had received $2 a day in expense money for playing minor-league baseball. In 1982 Thorpe's amateur status was posthumously restored and his pentathlon and decathlon medals returned by the IOC.

Sports and Politics

People are always a little surprised when they learn that athletes have political opinions, prejudices, and nationalistic feelings and that these attitudes affect their desire to participate in—or boycott—international sporting events. Man is a political animal, even when he is an athletic animal, and we are all affected by political decisions (as witness the ceasarean birth of the New Orleans Saints below (No. 2), with Hale Boggs acting as midwife).

Overall, athletes have a good record in the balance sheet of international fair play. At times, they seem to have a better grasp of world fellowship than their national leaders. Hitler may have behaved badly in the 1936 Olympics in Berlin, but the German athletes' behavior was, from all reports, exemplary.

Sports has always been an arena for the display of ideological differences, however, and today's focal points are the East-West struggle to prove each has the better economic system and can turn out the best athletes (if not the best human beings); and South Africa's apartheid challenge to the emerging Third World countries.

By 1981 the latter had festered to a point where the threat of "blacklisting" athletes who had participated in South African sporting events had produced a list of 165 names of athletes from 16 countries, including Mike Weaver (former WBA heavyweight champ), Guillermo Vilas, Dick Stockton, and Shlomo Glickstein. Once the blacklist was announced by the United Nations Centre Against Apartheid, world-class athletes began scurrying for cover. The idea was to get off the list at all costs. Whether the motivation was ideology or endangered tournament money was never made clear.

The irony here was that while all this was happening (effectively) on the political scene, most black African nations were increasing their trade relations with South Africa. Politics is politics, and economics is economics.

More economics: shortly after, a proposed tour of South Africa by an Irish rugby team led to a warning by Nigeria and other African nations that economic sanctions might be leveled against Irish industries. That Irish industry took this seriously was made evident by the fact that Guinness Breweries subsequently denied annual leave to several of its employees who happened to be rugby players going on the tour.

Politics and sports, you might conclude from all this, seem to mix like gasoline and sugar—sometimes with the same sputtering results.

I honestly feel that it would be best for the country to keep   **1**
baseball going ... these players are a definite recreational asset to
at least 20 million of their fellow citizens.

> **President Franklin D. Roosevelt** in a letter to
> baseball commissioner Kenesaw Mountain Landis in
> 1942, urging him to keep the national pastime going
> as a morale factor throughout World War II.

—Well, Pete, it looks good.   **2**
—Great, Hale, that's great.
—Just for the record, Pete, I assume we can say the franchise for
New Orleans is firm.
—Well, it looks good, of course, Hale, but you know it still has to
be approved by the owners. I can't make any promises on my own.
—Well, Pete, why don't you just go back and check with the
owners. I'll hold things up here until you get back.
—[Pause] That's all right. You can count on their approval.

> Conversation as reported in the *Los Angeles Times*
> between the NFL's **Pete Rozelle** and **Rep. Hale
> Boggs** (D., Louisiana) an hour before the House was
> to consider antitrust exemption rider permitting
> merger of the NFL and the AFL in 1966. The bill was
> passed; Rozelle got his merger; New Orleans got NFL
> franchise, and has been host of five money-producing
> Super Bowls.

Ali-eee! Ali-eee! There I'll be, wearing a sheet and whispering   **3**
Ali-eee. I'll be the ghost that haunts boxing, and people will say,
'Ali is the real champ, and everyone else is a fake.'

> **Muhammad Ali,** after being stripped of his title in
> 1968 because of his refusal to report for the draft.

I don't know about the plane. Suppose the Russians ... did some-   **4**
thing to the motor or something. I mean, people don't realize how
important chess is to their image. They'd really like to get rid of
me now.

> **Bobby Fischer,** after 19 straight international tour-
> nament wins, explaining why he'd hired a private
> plane for a brief 1972 vacation.

Walton wanted to speak his mind on politics, and he can. We put   **5**
that into his contract. A basketball player doesn't give up his
religious and political rights; this is especially true with some of
the players who are followers of Islam. I have had to put into their
contracts their right not to salute the flag if they don't wish.

> **Sam Gilbert,** who has represented a number of

UCLA athletes in negotiating their pro contracts.

6 Sports and politics do mix. Behind the scenes, the two are as inextricably interwoven as any two issues can be. I'm sure politics are involved when teams get franchises or when cities build stadiums. It is unrealistic to say you shouldn't bring politics into sports.

> **Arthur Ashe,** who has personally made South Africa's apartheid policies an international issue, and who was finally granted a visa to visit that country in 1973.

7 The government defense is that people abroad are just talking rubbish about South Africa. They haven't been here. How can they criticize? Ashe criticized for years, but he was regarded as just a bleating liberal from another part of the world. Now he has come and seen Soweto . . . . He has the feel, the smell, the knowledge that you can get only by visiting . . . . You don't hurt the government—as you might suppose—by staying away.

> **David Thebehali,** Soweto counselman, after Ashe's visit.

8 I start with the assumption that the Communists are right in saying that a nation's sports strength is a direct reflection of the viability of its political system. I want to see the U.S. do well in international sports to prove the strength of our system . . . with a format that fits *within* the American system. If the free enterprise system works at all, it should work with sports, too. If private industry is supposedly the answer to problems in other sections of our society and economy, why should we have to turn to the government when it comes to amateur sports?

> Manhattan investment banker **F. Warren Hellman,** president of the U.S. Ski Educational Foundation, which organizes the funding that allows American ski teams to compete internationally.

9 What can be more un-American than baseball uniforms made in another country? . . . Could you justify it if the American flags flown at the ball parks throughout the country were made in another country?

> **Harold Wolfe,** executive secretary of the National Association of Uniform Manufacturers, on learning that the 1977 Pittsburgh Pirates uniforms were made in Japan.

10 If Americans could just see what happens when we play in other

countries, they would never cheer for anyone but an American.
Foreign fans are so anti-American and so pro their own guy they
even make the linesmen cheat in their favor. Just go to Rumania,
Spain or South America and see for yourself. It's unbelievable.
            Billie Jean King, in 1978.

It is humanity that counts more than competition.   **11**
            Filbert Bayi, Tanzanian world-record holder at
            1,500 meters, in announcing that he would not run in
            the 1978 Commonwealth Games if New Zealanders
            were competing. New Zealand was under boycott
            because its rugby team had toured South Africa.

To take from our sportsmen and our sporting bodies the right to   **12**
make their own final decision on whom they would play against, or
with whom they would play, would be to take from them a
freedom which they have always had and which is just one of the
many freedoms which the citizens of a civilized country should
enjoy.
            New Zealand prime minister **Robert D. Muldoon,**
            explaining why his government had decided not to
            refuse visas to South Africa's all-white Springbok
            rugby team in 1981, as other Commonwealth nations
            had done.

Personally, I'd be upset if I show up at meets in Europe and can't   **13**
run against Miruts Yifter [Ethiopian Olympic champion]. I find it
very disturbing that sportsmen can't compete for love of sport. All
these major corporations are wheeling and dealing with South
Africa. Why are we used? We become political weapons, and we
end up suffering.
            Ireland's **Eamonn Coghlan,** who holds the indoor
            record for the mile, talking about threats of boycotts
            and blacklists by anti-apartheid groups, in 1981.

Let me ask you this: Is there hypocrisy in the Soviet system? If   **14**
there is, maybe there is here. The point is, we have to have some
sort of a system whereby our athletes can continue to train on an
equal level with the people of the Eastern bloc. The way that
sports has progressed in this day and age you can't expect someone to live by the amateur ideal as it was conceived in the 19th
century.
            Spokesman **Peter Cava** of the Athletics Congress
            (TAC), the governing body for track and field in the
            United States, just before the 1982 New York City
            Marathon.

15 • Please stop torturing me.
     • Please deliver my body to my family.

Two entries from a mock Spanish-English phrase booklet issued by the British National Union of Journalists in 1978 for members attending the World Cup games in Argentina, where the military junta had proven itself even more violent than the soccer fans.

Race

When the then-Brooklyn Dodgers brought Jackie Robinson up from Montreal in 1947, thus breaking baseball's long-held color barrier, they started a process of integration that has changed the face of sports and the nation. Integration, of course, has come a long way since Robinson broke in. To one degree or another, the black presence is felt in every major American sport except hockey, and at least economically and psychologically this has been a leading factor in the patchquilt racial revolution of our time.

The influx of blacks, plus the growing number of Latin players, has led, among other things, to a level of harmony on the sports scene unmatched in any other arena of American life. In a country in which polarization of the races is still a fact of daily life, you'd hardly know it on the playing fields. In this sense, sports may be said to be showing the way.

There are, of course, dissonances. Tennis, golf, and hockey, to name three, have remained virtually lily-white, the first two for what might be called class reasons, the third for geographic and climatological reasons. (There are other major sports where the explanation is not so ready to hand.) But even within such major sports as football and baseball where acceptance is an established fact, there are surprising pockets of racial distinction. The black quarterback is a rare figure ghosting across the sports pages: the black linebacker has only appeared in the last few years. In baseball, there have been black pitchers and catchers—a few outstanding ones. But the ordinary ones, the simply competent ones, the John Roseboros and Dock Ellises, are seldom found on teams that might have an all-black starting outfield. Here's a quick test: there are 26 major league franchises. Name *one* black shortstop for each league.

The unpalatable truth is that these are considered "head"

positions. What it comes down to is segregation on a positional level,
a last vestige of the pre-Robinson mentality. In the 36 years since the
color-line was broken, there have been three black managers—and
relatively few coaches.

This category is like a box filled with paradoxes. It is a rotating
kaleidoscope that's not always easy to read. There are gains and
defeats, advances and retreats in this crucially important—and
complex—aspect of the sports scene: relations between the races.

You get me Lew Alcindor and I'll integrate my school.   **1**
> **Remark attributed to a high-powered Southern
> basketball coach** in the late 1960s.

His worthy opponent, the new sensational pugilistic product—   **2**
although colored, he stands out in the same class with Jack
Johnson and Sam Langford—the idol of his people, none other
than Joe Louis!
> Ring announcer **Joe Humphries,** introducing Louis
> for his 1935 rematch with Max Baer, from whom he
> had won the championship. Louis retained the title.

Everyone crowded around the radio the nights Joe fought. You'd   **3**
have to turn the radio up loud so the people outside could hear it
through the window. Joe was the new Jack Johnson. He was so
important for us.
> Sixty-year-old truck driver **George Woody** at Joe
> Louis's funeral, recalling the Brown Bomber's impact
> on the black community in Lynchburg, Va., in the
> 1930s and 40s.

I don't understand—I never have understood—why Branch Rickey   **4**
took the full credit for breaking the color line with Jackie Robinson.
If I hadn't approved the contract transfer from Montreal, the
Dodgers' farm, to Brooklyn, Robinson couldn't have played. No
chance.

In January 1947 in a meeting in the Waldorf-Astoria Hotel
in New York, the major league owners had voted 15-1 against it.

For 24 years Judge Landis, the former commissioner, had
not let blacks into the majors. Suppose Landis had been commissioner in 1947 and Rickey had asked Landis to approve the
transfer, what do you think Landis would have said?
> **A.B. "Happy" Chandler,** looking back on his most
> momentous decision as commissioner of baseball.

If you do this you are through, and I don't care if it wrecks the   **5**
league for 10 years. You cannot do this, because this is America.

National League president **Ford Frick's** message to
the St. Louis Cardinals players who were talking
about a strike to protest Jackie Robinson's presence
on the 1947 Dodgers.

6 I ain't got no quarrel with those Vietcong. They never called me
'nigger.'

Muhammad Ali, when he refused to enter the armed
services in 1966 on the grounds he was a conscien-
tious objector. Ali was stripped of his championship
title, fined $10,000 and got a five-year prison sentence.
The sentence was never served; the Supreme Court
overturned Ali's conviction in 1970.

7 This *must* be a big event for Atlanta. I hear the Regency Hotel is
full up with colored people.

Muhammad Ali, before the high-rolling Jimmy
Quarry fight in 1970.

8 A black athlete must try to get the best of everything . . . The
challenge of basketball intrigues me. But I don't think the game
will have much to hold me. I wouldn't mind being mayor of New
York, though.

Columbia University guard **Heyward Dotson,** in
1970. A Rhodes scholar, Dotson practices law today.

9 The only change is that baseball has turned Paige from a second-
class citizen into a second-class immortal.

Satchel Paige, after being named to the Hall of
Fame's new wing for old-time Negro players.

10 This man [Jackie Robinson] turned a stumbling block into a
stepping stone.

Rev. Jesse Jackson, in his eulogy of Jackie
Robinson in 1972.

11 I have always said it's more important who's going to be the first
black sports editor of the *New York Times* than the first black
baseball manager.

Basketball's **Bill Russell,** player, coach, broadcaster,
TV commercial actor, in 1973.

12 We're going to have to face the problem of minority ownership.
Forty percent of the players in the League are black. Yet we have
almost no blacks in front-office positions. We will have to consider
that seriously when we determine our expansion plans. It could, in

effect, wind up as discrimination in reverse.
> NFL commissioner **Pete Rozelle,** in 1973.

I think I've gotten twice as much publicity as I deserve because **13**
I'm the Great White Hope in a game dominated by blacks.
> UCLA's All-Everything center, **Bill Walton,** in the
> spring of 1973.

A lot of people ask me, 'Do you get jealous of guys like [Dave] **14**
DeBusschere and [Jerry] Lucas? You're supposed to be the star of
the team, but they're doing all the commercials.' But I'm a very
understanding person. They're white and the product that they're
selling—Vitalis—goes mainly to white people. I understand the
media and what they're trying to do.
> Former New York Knick **Walt Frazier,** in 1973.

Wrestling probably has more racism than other sports. It's a Mid- **15**
western white sport with few minorities participating.
> Wrestler **John Logan,** undefeated for three years at
> Wesleyan University. Logan and other black wrestlers
> accused referees and officials of prejudice in selecting
> U.S. amateur teams.

If a Latin player is sick, they say it is all in his head. **16**
> Pittsburgh's **Roberto Clemente** in early 1973, re-
> sponding to charges that he was a malingerer. He'd
> only played in 102 games in 1972, due to injuries, but
> still managed to hit .312—five points below his 18-
> year career average.

Why should I have read about a man playing a game that I **17**
couldn't get into at the time?
> **Hank Aaron,** explaining in 1973 why he knew so little
> about the legendary Ruth.

Once the remarks about race in baseball were meant to hurt and **18**
ridicule. Now there's a different kind of humor, open and
intelligent, recognizing black and white but not putting anyone
down seriously. I'm happy I've been around to see the change.
> **Larry Doby,** one of the first black players, and a
> Cleveland coach in 1974.

The only thing in this country that blacks really dominate, except **19**
for poverty, is basketball. And they're letting white guys screw it
up.
> Former Marquette basketball coach **Al McGuire,**

noting the influx of players' agents into college
basketball.

20   I have become convinced that we blacks spend too much time on
the playing field and too little in the libraries . . . . While we are 60
percent of the National Basketball Association, we are less than 4
percent of the doctors and lawyers. While we are about 35 percent
of major-league baseball, we are less than 2 percent of the
engineers.

> **Arthur Ashe, in** 1977.

21   Play two blacks at home, three on the road and five when you are
behind.

> **Unidentified basketball coach's adage,** unearthed
> in 1977 in connection with the New York Mets'
> alleged limited use of black players.

22   Finally, Jack [Robinson] had a big impact on me personally. We
had many conversations about things, and I'd ask: 'Do you think
blacks and whites will ever get along smoothly?' And he'd say:
'Yes, it'll work, give it some time.' I used to say to him later, 'You
know, I didn't particularly go out of my way just to be nice to you.'
And Jack would say, 'Pee Wee, maybe that's what I appreciated
most—that you didn't.'

> Former Dodger shortstop **Pee Wee Reese,** recalling
> in 1977 some of his more intimate moments with the
> man who broke baseball's color line.

23   Once the color line was broken for managers, I thought it would be
a slow but steady opening up. But baseball has gone backwards.
It's like they said to themselves, 'Okay, we've had our black
manager. The heat is off. Back to business as usual.'

    And I think a lot of teams have black coaches only as win-
dow dressing. No team has a black third-base coach. They must
figure that blacks are a little too slow to accurately relay signs
from the manager to the batter and don't have sufficient judgment
to make go-no-go decisions for runners trying to score.

> **Frank Robinson,** who managed the Cleveland
> Indians (1975-77), coached for Baltimore and now
> manages the San Francisco Giants, assessing big-
> league managerial and coaching prospects for blacks
> in 1980.

24   There's no need for a white athlete to have another dimension,
unless you're a Steve Garvey or a Bill Bradley. A Goose Gossage
or a Conrad Dobler—all the fan cares about is what he does on

the field. But there's a need by fans for the black athlete to be multi-dimensional because he's the most-watched personage in America. I'll bet that seven out of 10 black faces you see on television are athletes. The black athlete carries the image of the black community. He carries the cross, in a way, until blacks make inroads in other dimensions.

> **Arthur Ashe,** on the black athlete's special role in American society.

Women and Sports

If the role of women in sports were symbolized by representation in a slow-pitch softball game, one woman would play and she would be the catcher. Except for outstanding individuals in golf and tennis, women have certainly gotten short shrift. All this is changing now, due to the elevation of consciousness, new female and male self-concepts, and the mixed blessings of Title IX. Congress passed Title IX in 1972 as an amendment to the 1964 Civil Rights Act. It forbids discrimination against women in the allotting of federal monies for athletic facilities at every level of education. But the changes are new, relatively untested, and in the case of Title IX, embattled.

There are three intermeshing factors governing whether (and how soon) women will realize something like equal status on the sports scene: expansion of and extensive participation in intercollegiate athletics, the creation and nurturing of women's professional leagues, and serious media coverage of both.

The most progress has been made in the first, which of course is the seeding ground. Despite the internecine warfare between the NCAA and the Association of Intercollegiate American Women in the last decade (1971-81), the number of colleges offering women athletic scholarships has increased tenfold (from 60 to 635), the number of female collegiate athletes has doubled (from 50,000 to 120,000), and the AIAW has created 40 national women's championships.

The NCAA has played a peculiar double role in all this. On the one hand they have finally opened the organization to women, pulled a few onto its governing boards, welcomed women as partners—well, junior partners. On the other hand they have tried to usurp some of those potentially lucrative national championships and, more important, still have a lawsuit pending that challenges the application of Title IX to intercollegiate athletics.

In this same decade, the allotment of college athletic budgets for women's sports has zoomed from an average of 1 percent to around 17 percent. While this is remarkable, the same proclivity to pour it all into one or two sports has emerged as happened earlier with men's sports. To ensure that federal funds will keep flowing and increase, it will be necessary to resist becoming a one-sport school and broaden the spectrum of women's sports, in the spirit of Title IX. Some of the same evils have shown up on the women's recruiting level as the men's, and caught up in the struggle for equal status, there has been a tendency to sweep recruiting irregularities under the rug. Once again, ethics has become an overlooked casualty in a power struggle.

The creation, resuscitation, and promotion of women's professional leagues will prove to be difficult enterprises, full of contingencies and questions. There is a parallel in soccer, where presumably 7 million American schoolboys (and girls) are presently kicking the ball around enthusiastically while the newest American team sport is foundering. The game (as a sports enterprise) will simply have to mark time until these kids grow up to be the North American players of the future and the new fans who will fill the stadiums. When the number of women athletes emerging from the colleges is so great that they cannot be ignored, something similar may happen.

Saying all this does not solve the problems of regional biases, competing for stadium space against male athletes, changing women's attitudes about watching other women play professional sports, changing the conception of sports as an intrinsically masculine domain, and most important, getting the media to break ground and adopt a more even-handed approach in its coverage of the sports scene. One more opportunity for cable to play an innovative role.

There have been great strides forward in the last decade to be sure, but attitudinally we all still have a long way to go, baby.

1 From the moment that the starting gate opens until my horse hits the wire, I'm a man competing against men. But by the time I get to the winner's circle to have my picture taken, I'm reaching for my false eyelashes and I'm all girl. After scratching my way from the Oklahoma bushes to the big time and busting my ass and being on the critical list three times, I don't have to put on any acts to prove I'm tough. All I have to do is win.

> Jockey **Mary Bacon,** described in *Newsweek* in 1974 as a "petite package of reset broken bones, fierce courage and rough-talking self-confidence."

Who needs it? You muck a few stables, gallop 10 or 12 horses, and **2**
if that doesn't put color in your cheeks, nothing will.
>Jockey **Diane Crump,** back in 1969, when she was
>asked by a reporter if she ever wore makeup.

I'm not money-hungry, but I cared about the $100,000 figure   **3**
because it was a milestone for women. We're finally appreciated
as athletes.
>**Billie Jean King,** the first female athlete to reach
>the $100,000 mark in any sport in a given year (1971).

It doesn't do girls any good to be stuck around together all the   **4**
time. They become desexed, a terrible thing. It's easy to get
caught up, not caring how you look, and lose the good points of
one's sex. I'd rather win half as much money and enjoy myself
completely.
>**Virginia Wade,** on the 1972 tennis trails, on the sub-
>ject of femininity and slamming the ball.

If someone says it's not feminine, I say screw it.   **5**
>**Rosemary Casals,** with another view.

For kids under 12, baseball should be fun for everybody, and it   **6**
shouldn't matter if girls play. But I'm afraid that some people
have emphasized serious competition so much that they've taken
all the fun out of the game.
>Former major-league pitcher and manager **Dallas
>Green,** looking at the Little Leagues.

Girls aren't hot dogs like some of the men. We play a fundamental   **7**
game and don't emphasize statistics.
>U.S. 1974 women's lacrosse team member **Leigh
>Buck,** on why she doesn't bother keeping records.

Equality? They ought to play the women's final on opening day.   **8**
Everybody knows who's going to be in it.
>**Jimmy Connors,** at the U.S. Open in 1976, on the
>issue of equal prize money for women.

It's so much better now that women athletes are starting to be   **9**
accepted. But people think that things start at the grass-roots
level, and I say that's not true. I think things start at the top, when
interest, motivation and a role model are created in a sport. That's
when the acceptance begins.
>**Billie Jean King** (Wimbledon champion, co-founder
>of the Women's Professional Softball League, and

founder of the Women's Sports Foundation), who starts
things at the top.

10   The point is—and this is necessary to understand the difference
between male and female athletes—that in the arena, men take for
granted the fact that they are males and concentrate on being
athletes. Women never forget that they are females.

> Former track star **Dick Lacey,** now coach of the New
> Rochelle High School girls' track team.

11   Any woman can pass or fail that [sex-chromosome] test on any of
several different occasions. There were women who are playing
now who were required to take it a second time because they
failed it. I'm being required to take it again because I passed it. I'll
be asked to take it until I fail it and that's the only one they'll use.

> Transsexual **Renee Richards,** responding to a 1977
> ruling of the Women's Tennis Association making it
> necessary for her to undergo another sex-chromosome
> test.

12   She wore a tennis dress and eye make-up, but she had a deep
voice and wasn't what you'd call feminine. I was thinking, is it a
man or a woman? I was psyched out.

> Twenty-year old **Robin Harris,** describing her
> opponent (Renee Richards) in the 1976 La Jolla finals.

13   We're going to get the best women's basketball team that money
can buy . . . within the rules, of course.

> **Rev. Oral Roberts,** when asked about Oral Roberts
> University's plans for women's sports.

14   How do you measure what women have paid in their quest for
equality? When Title IX [1972 legislation barring sex discrimination in scholastic athletics] came along we had to take the whole
bag, and that started the dilemma. Men were getting blazers, so
we wanted them, too. Women are no different than men when it
comes to handling power. When we get it, the same negatives will
apply.

> Former Queens (N.Y.) College faculty member and
> AIAW spokesperson **Cal Papatsos.**

15   I didn't hear anybody [women's athletics directors] mention her
budget when we were talking about providing tutors for athletes. I
didn't hear anybody mention her budget when we were voting to
give scholarships. But now that we're asking a school to provide
other sports besides basketball, all I hear is how budgets won't
allow them.

> **Karol Kahrs,** assistant director of women's athletics
> at the University of Illinois, at the 1978 AIAW
> convention.

Girls historically have not received the same attention as   **16**
boys ... in scholastic athletic programs .... The court
must ... see if there is a way to help ... [But] ... the reach of Title
IX [barring sex discrimination in education] extends only to those
education programs or activities which receive direct Federal
financial assistance.

> Federal Judge **Charles W. Joiner,** in a 1981
> Michigan sex-discrimination case involving high
> school athletic allotments. While paying homage to
> the U.S. government's "equal opportunity" stance,
> the judge's decision reinforced the NCAA's position
> on Title IX, which specifies that federal education
> funds should be equally allotted for men's and
> women's athletic facilities.

I'm telling you that people out there care about women's sports,   **17**
but everywhere we go it's the same story. In one city the new
USFL team kept us out of the papers. In Dallas Tony Dorsett did
something and that kept us out. In Houston it was Moses Malone.
Know what one writer in Houston told us? If one of us shoots the
other two, then it's a story.

> Diver **Jennifer Chandler,** a gold-medal winner at
> the Montreal Olympics, who was touring the country
> with two other former Olympians, Wyomia Tyus and
> Nancy Thies Marshall, in 1982.

When I was first running marathons, we were sailing on a flat   **18**
earth. We were afraid we'd get big legs, grow mustaches, not get
boyfriends, not be able to have babies. Women thought that something would happen to them, that they'd break down or turn into
men, something shadowy, when they were only limited by their
own society's sense of limitations.

> **Katherine Switzer,** the first woman to run (illegally)
> in the Boston Marathon in 1967, when women were
> barred. Switzer has run the 26-mile race seven times
> since.

I've never seen women as strong, as well developed. They have a   **19**
long, lean, confident look. They arrive here outgoing, confident,
with a good self-image. It's beginning in their hometowns, where
athletic scholarships have become status symbols. They're not
hiding in their rooms with people saying, 'Oh, those phys-ed

majors.' They're like male athletes. They're revered.
                    Donna Lopiano, University of Texas director of
                    women's athletics, in 1982.

7. FOR THE RECORD

Hall of Fame Quotations (And Candidates)

"It ain't nothin' till I call it." So said Bill Klem, sharp-tongued (and quotable) umpire to a batter unhappy with his hesitancy in making a call. This, we feel, has been a metaphor for the quote in the world of sports. It ain't nowhere. For a century and a half athletes have been saying exasperating unto brilliant things, and only a small scattering of these witticisms have ever been written down.

And so we are creating a long-overdue Hall of Fame for the *bon mot*, a collection of quotes that have both lightened and enlightened the arena of sports. And since men go on speaking, and what they say often makes fine sense, there must needs be a Hall of Fame Candidates category, those quotes that are seasoning in the cellars of the mind.

And so to speak, here are the Hall of Famers—and the Candidates.

1   I hit 'em where they ain't.

> **"Wee Willie" Keeler,** the diminutive place hitter
> with a lofty career (1892-1910) average of .343.

2   Gentlemen. It's the old story. I fought once too often.

> **John L. Sullivan,** after losing his heavyweight title
> to "Gentleman Jim" Corbett on Sept. 7, 1892, just
> short of his 34th birthday.

3   All horse players die broke.

> **The most famous anonymous quote** on the sport of
> kings.

4   Say it ain't so, Joe.

> **Small boy** to "Shoeless Joe" Jackson, after news of
> the Chicago "Black Sox" scandal broke in 1919.

5   A champion is one who gets up when he can't.

> **Jack Dempsey,** summing up the fight game.

6   You've got to be a football hero to get along with the beautiful
girls.

> **Song lyric** of yesteryear, from the song "You've Got
> to Be a Football Hero."

7   Honey, I forgot to duck.

> **Jack Dempsey,** explaining to his wife how he came
> to lose the heavyweight championship to Gene
> Tunney in 1926.

8   Sometime, Rock, when the team's up against it, when things are
going wrong and the breaks are beating the boys, tell them to go in
there with all they've got and win just one for the Gipper. I don't
know where I'll be then, Rock, but I'll know about it and I'll be
happy.

> What quarterback **George Gipp,** dying of a viral
> throat infection, is supposed to have whispered to
> Notre Dame coach Knute Rockne. Biding his time,
> Rockne finally told the boys at halftime during a
> scoreless Army-Notre Dame game in 1928, and the
> boys went back out and "won one for the Gipper."

9   Oh yeah? Well, I had a better year than he had.

> **Babe Ruth,** in 1930, when it was pointed out to him
> that not even President Herbert Hoover was making
> the $80,000 the Bambino was asking for as his new
> salary.

Don't look back, somebody might be gaining on you.   **10**
> **Satchel Paige's** unique philosophy summed up in one
> immortal sentence.

We wuz robbed!   **11**
> Max Schmeling's manager, **Joe Jacobs,** after Jack
> Sharkey was awarded the heavyweight title in a close
> 15-rounder in 1932.

I should have stood in bed.   **12**
> Fight manager **Joe Jacobs,** at a World Series game
> in Detroit on a snappy October day in 1934. Jacobs
> got out of a sickbed to attend the game, then bet on
> the wrong team.

He has muscles in his hair.   **13**
> **Lefty Gomez's** description of Jimmy Foxx back in
> the 30s, when he was the strongest hitter Gomez had
> to face.

Clean living and a fast outfield.   **14**
> **Lefty Gomez,** explaining why he had such a great
> Series record as a pitcher.

Good field. No hit.   **15**
> Telegram **Mike Gonzalez** sent to John McGraw after
> scouting a minor-league prospect for the New York
> Giants manager. This laconic expression became
> baseball shorthand for describing most infielders.

Don't send out your laundry.   **16**
> **Old baseball adage** heard every spring around cut-
> down time.

Is Brooklyn still in the league?   **17**
> Giants manager **Bill Terry,** two days before the end
> of the disastrous 1934 season.

You can't steal first.   **18**
> **Skeptical manager of an opposing National
> League club,** on hearing how fast Eddie Mayo was.

Stick it in his ear.   **19**
> **Baseball manager's cry** to pitcher hesitant to use
> brush-back pitch. Generally (and perhaps unfairly)
> attributed to Leo "the Lip" Durocher, in the stormy

days when he was Brooklyn's highly quotable
manager.

20   You can't die on the race track, because you're always waiting for
the good one that runs tomorrow.
> **Veteran horse player's maxim.**

21   Lou just told me he felt it would be best for the club if he took
himself out of the lineup.
> New York Yankee manager **Joe McCarthy,** after Lou
> Gehrig decided to bench himself in April 1939, after
> having played a record 2,130 consecutive games.

22   If you can't beat 'em in the alley, you can't beat 'em on the ice.
> What Toronto Maple Leaf owner **Conn Smythe** used
> to tell his players in the bad old days.

23   I'll moider da bum.
> **"Two-Ton Tony" Galento,** before his 1939 fight
> with Joe Louis. Galento did deck the Brown Bomber
> in both the 2nd and 3rd rounds, but a stout-hearted
> Louis rallied to win by a TKO in Round 4 of a sen-
> sational brawl.

24   He can run, but he can't hide.
> Heavyweight champ **Joe Louis,** predicting the out-
> come of his first fight with quick-moving Billy Conn.
> Ahead on points after 13 rounds, Conn got overconfi-
> dent and Louis caught him.

25   Gentlemen, start your engines!
> Traditional command uttered by **Tony Hulman Jr.,**
> president of the Indianapolis Speedway, in starting
> the annual Indy 500.

26   He can't run, he can't hit, and he can't throw, but if there's a way
to beat the other team, he'll find it.
> **Branch Rickey,** on the elusive talents of Eddie
> Stanky.

27   Nice guys finish last.
> Brooklyn Dodger manager **Leo "The Lip"
> Durocher**.

28   Take two and hit to right, kid.
> **Anonymous manager** of a second-division team.

- The bases are f.o.b.—full of Brooklyns.   **29**
- It's brewing up into a real rhubarb.
- [Erskine's] in the catbird seat now.
- [Walker] parks under the can of corn and takes it easily.
> Dodger announcer **Red Barber,** bringing his
> Southernisms— and a few Detroitisms—to Brooklyn
> baseball broadcasts in the uproarious 40s.

- The ball is going . . . going . . . gone!   **30**
- How about that!
> **Mel Allen's** inimitable enthusiastic style back
> in the 40s and 50s when he was the "voice of the
> Yankees."

The Giants is dead.   **31**
> Dodger manager **Charley Dressen,** circa 1949.

The Giants win the pennant! The Giants win the pennant! I do not **32**
believe it! I do not believe it! They're going crazy!
> Giants announcer **Russ Hodges,** on the occasion of
> Bobby Thomson's historic home run against the
> Dodgers in the 1951 playoffs. An astonished Hodges
> never actually called the play because he was so
> caught up in the delirium.

I couldn'ta done it without my players.   **33**
> **Perfesser Stengel,** while managing the Yanks to a
> cycle of pennants.

Oh, them bases on balls!   **34**
> Harrassed Chicago Cubs manager **Frankie Frisch,**
> circa 1950, watching one of his pitchers burrow into
> deeper and deeper trouble.

Nobody roots for Goliath.   **35**
> **Wilt Chamberlain,** back in the 60s, looking down on
> a world full of Davids.

I am the greatest.   **36**
> **Cassius Clay** in 1964, before the Liston fight,
> borrowing the phrase from wrestler Gorgeous George.

Float like a butterfly, sting like a bee.   **37**
> **Cassius Clay,** before, after, and probably during his
> 1964 Liston fight. His corner man, Drew (Bundini)
> Brown, is generally credited with having coined this
> bit of ring poetry.

38   It's not over until it's over.

> Canny observation by **Yogi Berra** about individual
> games, pennant races, Series games, etc.

39   Winning is not the most important thing: it's everything.

> Green Bay's **Vince Lombardi.**

40   You gotta believe!

> Ace reliever **Tug McGraw,** as the Mets closed in on
> a surprise divisional title in 1969.

41   We are fam-a-lee!

> Pittsburgh Pirates **rallying cry** in 1979, when they
> went all the way under the spiritual tutelage of Willie
> (Pops) Stargell.

42   Holy cow!

> Yankee telecaster **Phil Rizzuto** in almost any critical
> or bewildering situation.

43   Just shake hands and I'm warm.

> **Old football players' saying,** recalled at the end of
> the 1982 strike by an NFL Players Association rep
> when asked if the players were in shape to resume
> play in mid-November after an eight-week layoff.

Hall of Fame
(Candidates)

1   If I'd known Paul was going to pitch a no-hitter, I'd have pitched
one too.

> **Dizzy Dean,** after his brother Paul had held the
> Dodgers hitless in the second game of a 1934 St.
> Louis-Brooklyn doubleheader. Diz had pitched a 3-
> hitter in the opener.

There you is and there you is going to stay.   **2**
> **Satchel Paige,** after walking the lead-off batter in a
> game against the Yankees. Page bore down and
> struck out the next three batters.

Fuck Babe Ruth!   **3**
> **Japanese battle cry** during World War II.

You gotta be a man to play baseball for a living but you gotta have   **4**
a lot of little boy in you, too.
> **Roy Campanella,** former Dodger catcher and future
> Hall of Famer, in 1957.

Every Sunday you have the pleasure of dying.   **5**
> The late **Carroll Rosenbloom,** who owned the
> Baltimore Colts and later the Los Angeles Rams.

A ball player's got to be kept hungry to become a big-leaguer.   **6**
That's why no boy from a rich family ever made the big leagues.
> Former New York Yankee great **Joe DiMaggio,** in
> 1961.

I always turn to the sports section first. The sports section records   **7**
people's accomplishments; the front page nothing but man's
failures.
> **Earl Warren,** former Chief Justice of the U.S.
> Supreme Court, in 1968.

Bench me or keep me.   **8**
> **Chico Salmon,** utility catcher with the Cleveland
> Indians and Baltimore Orioles (1964-72), was sup-
> posedly the first bench-rider to utter these immortal
> words. In his nine years in the majors, Salmon
> averaged 73 games per season.

We're No. One!   **9**
> **Battle cry of New York Met fans** in 1969, the year
> of the "miracle."

This is no $6.50 fight. For $6.50, they can stand outside and hear   **10**
the yelling.
> **Seattle ticket broker,** responding to criticism on the
> high price of tickets to the 1971 Ali-Frazier cham-
> pionship fight.

11   A well-paid slave, but nonethless a slave.

> Outfielder **Curt Flood's** assessment of his status as a
> $90,000-a-year player in the process of being traded
> from St. Louis to Philadelphia. Flood brought suit a-
> gainst baseball's reserve clause and lost; but he laid
> the groundwork for others to follow and win.

12   I won't play for less than a million dollars. I'd rather go to work in
a factory.

> Providence College star center **Marvin Barnes,** in 1974.

13   He made two mistakes. The first was a slider that didn't slide. The
second was a curve that didn't curve.

> **Richie Zisk,** then a Pittsburgh Pirate, after hitting
> two home runs in a 1974 game against Houston's
> Claude Osteen.

14   When you're the champion, there's always some upstart gunning
to shoot you down.

> Tennessee truck driver **Grover Collins** in 1975, after
> being crowned champion in the world's first annual
> butterbean-eating contest.

15   If this interpretation [which nullified the reserve clause] prevails,
baseball's reserve system will be eliminated by a stroke of the pen.

> Former baseball commissioner **Bowie Kuhn** in late
> 1975, following arbitrator Peter Seitz's ruling that led
> to the death of the reserve clause. The owners ex-
> tracted their vengeance against Seitz (he was sum-
> marily fired), but the decision stood.

16   This team, it all flows from me. I've got to keep it going. I'm the
straw that stirs the drink.

> **Reggie Jackson,** new to the Yankees in 1977, es-
> tablishing his star status in spring training.

17   Let's face it, everyone knows the name of the game is 'get the
quarterback.'

> **Joe Namath,** after a particularly bruising exhibition
> game in 1978.

18   The fourth quarter belongs to us.

> Denver coach **Red Miller,** in January 1978. The
> Broncos had outscored the opposition 87-24 in the

final period throughout the season on their way to the
Super Bowl.

Everybody says a tie is like kissing your sister. I guess it's better   **19**
than kissing your brother.

> Arkansas coach **Lou Holtz,** after the Razorbacks and
> UCLA played to a 10-10 tie in the 1978 Fiesta Bowl.

The two of them deserve each other. One's a born liar, the other's   **20**
convicted.

> **Billy Martin,** Yankee manager in 1978, describing
> Reggie Jackson (then with New York) and George
> Steinbrenner to the press. Forced to resign, Martin
> was replaced in midseason by Bob Lemon.

Time for me to go fishing.   **21**

> **Ralph Houk,** in retiring as manager of the Detroit
> Tigers in 1978, at age 59. Two years later Houk had
> had his fill of piscatorial delights. He decided to come
> back and manage the Boston Red Sox.

When I was a kid, I wanted to play baseball and join the circus.   **22**
With the Yankees, I've been able to do both.

> Third baseman **Graig Nettles,** after Steinbrenner
> expressed displeasure with the team's 1980 post-
> season play.

My three best punches were the chokehold, the rabbit punch and   **23**
the head butt.

> Ex-fighter **Chuck Wepner,** generally assumed to be
> the model for the hero of *Rocky*. The occasion was
> Wepner's being honored by Madison Square Garden
> in 1980 for his "15 years as a true gentleman of
> boxing."

Ninety feet between bases is perhaps as close as man has ever   **24**
gotten to perfection.

> The late **Red Smith,** on a "Sixty Minutes" telecast in
> March 1981.

The Press

One of the arguments almost impossible to settle—not unlike picking an all-time All-Star team in any sport—is whether today's sportswriters are as good as the sports scribes of yesteryear. The lyricism of a Grantland Rice, the pungency of a Ring Lardner, the critical acumen of a Stanley Woodward are seen as perfect models by many old enough to remember their work and those who have subsequently read it. Defenders of the contemporary breed would argue that they are better because they are more sophisticated, less parochial than their predecessors and less complacent about the teams they cover. And their objectivity is assured if they work for the more responsible newspapers that do not allow their reporters to become part of a team's paid-for entourage.

This having been said, it can scarcely escape notice that the nation's sports pages still do not attract—or keep—the best writing talent. Presumably this situation has improved during the sports-minded 1970s and 80s, though just how much is moot. In 1969 the late Leonard Schecter laid down a harsh indictment (in *The Jocks*) of the boys in the press box: "What it [sports writing] needs to be is entertaining, incisive, informative, revealing and intelligent enough to appeal to an adult brain. Instead, what we get, mostly, are stories and columns written by lazy men who are typing, not writing; filling space with cliches and inconsequential blatherings that are often illiterate to boot." What particularly riled Schecter (and others) was the growing proliferation of the nonstory—the warmed-over pap that fills up the early editions of newspapers. The dictum of course is that whether there is or isn't any news, the show of journalism must go on.

And go on it does—as it also does, even more slavishly, in the electronic medium. Lacking the traditions of the print media as guidelines, it didn't take TV coverage long to get to its current distancing methodology. Watching sports events on TV in the early days, one got the feeling that no decision was ever made as to what to tell the fans about what they were seeing. Before this dilemma ever got resolved, the emphasis had shifted to personality telecasters, interviews, color—an entire entertainment package designed to shape the game to conform to the hopes and expectations of the fan and the projections (often inaccurate) of the telecasters.

And of course it is antithetical to the nature of the medium for telecasters to admit that the game is dull. They'll tell you that the President's been shot leaving the stadium—but never that the play on the field is listless. The Game of the Week has to be transmitted as the Game of the Decade. It's in the contract: advertisers simply don't sponsor dull games.

While the press—and especially television—helped to create the sports explosion of the last decade, it has not always seen—or met—its responsibility to preserve the integrity of sports. Where does one draw the line between coverage and exploitation? Between reportage and drumbeating? These quotes reveal the multifaceted relationship between the recorders and interpreters of the sports event and the event itself.

The fact that the Cardinals were paid $4,321.96 each for quitting **1** like poltroons to the Yankees . . .

> Sportswriter **Buck O'Neill,** covering the 1943 World Series, in an era when sportswriters were less amiable.

I think the public today is ready to accept a new view of sports. **2** Grantland Rice described Notre Dame's backfield as the Four Horsemen of the Apocalypse. Hell, today they look to me like nothing more than four guys who are probably flunking algebra.

> *Los Angeles Times* sports columnist **Jim Murray** in the late 1960s.

The new young breed of writers are looking for social significance. **3** They dwell too much on whether a player is getting along with a manager or how happy he is at home. They ought to be writing for the gossip columns, not the baseball fans.

> Veteran baseball executive **Paul Richards,** in 1969, then vice-president of the Atlanta Braves.

It's like listening to a description of one continuous mistake. **4**

> **Gene Shue,** in 1971 the coach of basketball's Baltimore Bullets, on hockey broadcasts.

If you guys hadn't started writing about the WHA it never would **5** have existed.

> Former NHL president **Clarence Campbell** in 1972, on the power of the press.

A sports editor or the managing editor of a big daily paper should **6** see that his sports reporters are as businesslike as a good cop on a beat. You'll hear a reporter maintain that he can't get personality material unless he is well acquainted with them. Good cops and good reporters have a pretty fair record of getting information from people they've never met before.

> The *Sporting News'* **C.C. Johnson Spink,** in 1972. Spink believes that sports reporters should periodically be reassigned in the interest of less partisanship and more straightforward journalism.

7   I never defend myself [against press criticism]. The best thing is to say nothing.

> Former New York Knick **Walt Frazier** in 1973.

8   That's the way newsmen are. They are either down on you or they love you. If they don't like you, they're hostile no matter what you say or do. If they love you and they don't think you're behaving just right they're crushed. They turn hostile. How do you win?

> Olympic swimming champ **Mark Spitz,** in 1972. By 1974, he was out of the mainstream of public life.

9   I know your story will make me look like a horse's rear, not a lawyer and an educated man. And your colleagues will agree, because writers are germs who stick together . . . . There hasn't been a good line written about me in five years. I have given America humor and truth, and all I have read about myself is lies.

> **Howard Cosell,** to *TV Guide's* Mel Durslag in a 1975 interview.

10   What can they see? The amount of information they can assimilate with their own eyes and their limited knowledge of the game gives them a dangerous perspective.

> Los Angeles Rams defensive lineman **Merlin Olsen** (who holds a Ph.D.), assessing sportswriters in 1976, his last year in pro ball.

11   The announcers would babble and let their faces hang out. They wouldn't attend events or talk to people. More than anyone else who walked off the street into this business, Howard Cosell is a journalist. He knows people and gets on the phone to find out things. I try to do that all the time. I don't believe that just because you have a network affiliation that you can just show up at an event and get the story.

> **Brent Musburger,** former newspaperman and anchorman on CBS-TV's "NFL Today," on the TV sports fraternity.

12   I'm not the kind of announcer who tells the viewers which players

like strawberry ice cream. I try to explain why one team is ahead
of another and what the team has to do to catch up. My role is to
get viewers to think about what is happening, instead of just
watching the game.

> NBC-TV basketball analyst **Billy Packer,** former
> All-Star guard and assistant coach at Wake Forest.

... most guys who write about sports are just little overweight   **13**
creeps who never touched a basketball in their lives. These guys   13
couldn't make a foul shot, yet they have the right to write anything
about us.

> **"Pistol Pete" Maravich,** when he was still making
> jump shots.

We'd have 30 seconds of respectful silence and then continue with   **14**
enthusiasm.

> Linebacker **George Atkinson** of the 1977 Oakland
> Raiders, when asked what the players reaction would
> be if the press box blew up.

Women were let into the Yankee locker room last night. Chaos did   **15**
not ensue and the morals of the nation survived.

> Attorney **Robert Joffe** in 1978, representing *Sports
> Illustrated* writer Melissa Ludtke, who had sued
> organized baseball for barring women from the
> postgame locker room during the 1977 Series. A
> federal court agreed that the action was
> discriminatory.

Most women in this business don't cover games. Ninety percent of   **16**
us don't—not a good balance. The standard idea of a woman
sportswriter's story is doing Steve Garvey's wife or writing a
feature about Nancy Lopez. The men on the beat are always
aware of that. This is why locker-room access is the heart of it all.
Access is the key to covering games, and you aren't a
sportswriter—you haven't paid your dues—unless you cover
games.

> *Washington Post* sportswriter **Betty Cuniberti,** inter-
> viewed by Roger Angell in the *New Yorker* on the
> locker-room controversy.

The idea of a girl romping through a clubhouse filled with naked   **17**
athletes is not going to be good for the game. I am also very concerned that the baseball establishment is going to use the arrival
of women as an excuse to cut off the clubhouse altogether. Professional athletes make so much money now that they only just
tolerate the press, and Bowie [Kuhn] thinks that we only come

into the clubhouse to agitate the players and to snoop . . . . Ever since television began covering the game, the clubhouse has been the writer's beat. The players and the general managers and the Commissioner are agreed on one thing—we are the enemy.

> *New York Post* columnist **Maury Allen,** in the same interview.

Best Predictions

Everyone loves to predict things in some familiar area, and we are all pleased when we turn out to be right. There is the thrill of having read the signs aright and called the shot, as well as the sense of control over a haphazard destiny. In this respect, athletes and other sports figures are no different than the rest of us. They go out on the limb of conjecture regularly, and sometimes they are Olympian in their prophecies.

If the essence of sports is the striving for excellence, as we have said elsewhere in this book, then it must have parameters. If excellence has an end-point—or at least a direction—it also has a beginning. To be able to detect that beginning—that is, to predict early on or in a given circumstance that someone or some team will perform well—gives one a sense of having a sound grasp of the elements needed for winning in that sport. It makes one feel knowledgeable, always a nice feeling.

The quotes below are the ones that turned their speakers into instant gurus—or at least mavens. For the flip side of the coin, see "Worst Predictions" below.

1 And we're going to win Sunday—I'll guarantee it.

> Former Jet quarterback **Joe Namath,** before the 1969 Super Bowl. Broadway Joe proved as accurate in his prophecy as in his passing, despite the fact that Jimmy the Greek had made the Colts 18-point favorites.

2 There's no question that Alcindor eventually will dominate the game. He has the height and the moves, and when he fills out he'll have the strength. He'll put on about 20 more pounds and it won't affect his speed at all.

New York Knicks general manager **Eddie Donovan,**
evaluating Lew Alcindor, then a 20-year-old junior
with UCLA, in 1968.

[O.J.] Simpson will be getting more than any rookie has been paid   **3**
since the merger, and Buffalo will be getting what it feels is an
outstanding football player who one day may take a place among
the great running backs of this game.
> Buffalo Bills owner **Ralph C. Wilson,** announcing the
> signing of the Heisman Trophy winner after the USC
> star's holdout.

We urged that a realistic schedule be drawn up that would not tax   **4**
the players as it does now. But it begins to appear that they will
do just the opposite and make a bad situation worse by sticking to
the 162 games, plus a playoff, plus the World Series.
> **Marvin Miller,** executive director of the baseball
> union, anticipating both the lengthened season and
> extended post-season play in 1968.

Once I get back in the groove, I'll be all right . . . the big one—   **5**
Ruth's record—is still ahead. And if I stay healthy, I think I can
make it.
> **Henry Aaron,** after tying Willie Mays in June 1972
> for second on the all-time home run list.

The owners can't pass this Hunter thing [the signing of "Catfish"   **6**
Hunter to a multimillion dollar free-agent contract] off as a unique
situation. They've opened the floodgates. I'm hearing from a lot of
my clients.
> Attorney-agent **Bob Woolf,** after the Yankees signed
> free agent Jim "Catfish" Hunter. The floodgates are
> still open.

There's only one way I'm gonna lose. That's if they carry me out.   **7**
> **George Foreman,** before his exhausting fight with
> Jimmy Young, which got him hospitalized.

Night thoroughbred racing will be very big. The idea is to present   **8**
entertainment to the most people available. No one has to feel he
is cheating by going to the races at night.
> The Meadowlands' **Sonny Werblin,** calling the shot
> on flat racing at night, which had never been
> attempted in the New York area before 1977. An ins-
> tant success, the Meadowlands lured bettors from
> both the New York and Philadelphia areas.

9   Bit of a prima donna all right. But she [Martina Navratilova] has the strength and ability to overpower all the other sheilas [women], including Chris [Evert] .... I think she'll learn to love the hard work she needs—once she sees where it can put her. Right out front.

> Australian tennis coach **Roy Emerson,** looking at Martina in 1977.

10   Everybody is saying that we're a cinch to win, and that means that everybody will be pointing for us. But I can promise you one thing. We won't be one of those even-money favorites that staggers home sixth.

> **George Steinbrenner,** in winter of 1976. Yanks had won the pennant in 1976, repeated in 1977, then went on to win Series as well.

11   This new baseball is like a golf ball. I think there are going to be a lot more dents put into the wall at Fenway Park this year.

> Former Boston Red Sox manager **Don Zimmer,** before the start of the very lively 1977 season.

12   It's going to be tough making this team.

> Twenty-two-year-old **Ted Cox,** after getting hits in his first six at-bats with Boston in September 1977. Cox was dead on. He didn't break into the heavy-hitting Red Sox lineup; traded to California the following year, he didn't make the Angels either.

13   I've got my new shower shoes, my T-shirts, a couple of dozen bats. I'm ready. I hope I can add that one dimension to get this club into the World Series.

> **Pete Rose** in early 1979, after signing with Philadelphia as a free agent. Shower shoes and all, Rose and the Phils got there a year later, winning it all.

14   This is the deepest team we've had since I've been here. We've got more people who can do the job, and the responsibility has been spread around. But you never know. I don't think George [Steinbrenner] is ever going to assemble a team as good as the one we had in 1978. We had chemistry then. We refused to lose. Now we've got a lot of big names. But if big names don't have big years, what good does it do to have big names?

> Veteran outfielder **Lou Piniella** in spring 1982, sensing that the Yankees were only formidable on paper. The team played .500 ball all season, and was never in contention.

Worst Predictions

And then there are the predictions that fall on their faces. They may have seemed well thought out at the time, logical, even unavoidable, and then suddenly they were howlers. How could someone with so much savvy get caught off base that way?

The common thread that struck us about most of these misbegotten predictions was their emphatic and flat-out quality—as though the speaker were trying to convince himself as much as his audience. Moral: beware of the unqualified, underscored statement. Perhaps it's overkill.

Not all of the quotes below have this common denominator, of course. A few are just wishful thinking that got derailed. Ali, for example, was so hypnotized by his own hype that he was unwilling to believe he could lose even a *computerized* fight.

And so, in the overgrown orchard of Predictions, here are the lemons.

That kid can't play baseball. He can't pull the ball. **1**
> **Tommy Holmes,** manager of the Braves' Triple-A team, on Hank Aaron in 1952.

If I lose, it's got to be science fiction. **2**
> **Muhammad Ali,** after watching himself lose the 1970 computerized fight with Rocky Marciano. One million fans paid $5 each to see the make-believe bout.

If Dick Williams goes to the Yankees or any other team, I'd love to **3** go with him. But Mr. Finley has told me that I'll die in his green and gold.
> **Reggie Jackson,** with Oakland during the 1973 World Series, wrong on both counts.

He'll never be more than a 13-14 game winner. He's a momma's **4** boy.
> Top-ranked pitching coach **Johnny Sain,** a great pitcher in his day, about Tommy John, with the Chicago White Sox in the early 70s.

5   We plan absent ownership. I'll stick to building ships.
> **George Steinbrenner** in 1973, the year his group
> bought the New York Yankees from CBS.

6   I don't want to play in Philadelphia, it's as simple as that. I signed
with the Knicks because of personal preference and a matter of
economics.
> **George McGinnis,** before NBA commissioner Larry
> O'Brien ended the All Pro forward's brief Knick
> tenure. McGinnis played with Philadelphia after all.

7   We want the whole world to know this time we're going to win the
Super Bowl.
> **Fran Tarkenton,** Minnesota's veteran quarterback,
> in late 1976. The Vikings had lost in three previous
> Super Bowl bids, and despite Tarkenton's assurances,
> made it four straight against Oakland, losing 32-14.

8   We've come to the mountain and Muhammad must fall.
> **Blackboard slogan** in Earnie Shavers's training camp
> before the Ali-Shavers fight in 1977. Muhammad did
> not fall.

9   By the early 1980's, I think we'll be outdrawing both the Giants
and the Jets in season attendance. That's separately, not both
football teams combined.
> **Clive Toye,** former president of the New York Cos-
> mos, in early 1977.

10   Bobick is a very durable fighter.
> **Ken Norton,** at the weigh-in before his one-round
> fight with Duane Bobick.

11   Doc Ellis is not going anywhere.
> Yankee owner **George Steinbrenner,** a week before
> Ellis left for Oakland.

12   This won't happen again next year. We'll have a very peaceful, calm
season. All of this will be straightened out.
> Yankees owner **George Steinbrenner,** looking for-
> ward to 1978. It wasn't.

13   Sparky [Lyle] will absolutely not be traded and he's been so informed . . . I know this is my first public statement as executive vice
president of the Yankees, so I'm staking my credibility.
> **Al Rosen,** on assuming his new job with the volatile

New York club in early 1978. Lyle was traded to
Texas at season's end. Rosen didn't last much longer
under Steinbrenner.

[Dan] Driessen is going to be a great player. And I mean great, not **14**
good. You take every player in the game and break down their
abilities—speed, power, defense, average—and I'll bet he rates in
the top five.

> **Sparky Anderson,** Cincinnati's manager in 1978,
> going overboard over Dan Driessen, after the Reds
> traded Tony Perez. Driessen proved an adequate
> replacement, but never hit with Perez's power—let
> alone achieved greatness.

Take the San Diego Chargers. It was alleged [in 1973] that **15**
amphetamines and barbiturates were given out like jelly beans,
and team officials were aware of this. This doesn't happen in basketball, and I don't think it ever did. In the NBA, everyone han-
dles the ball, and if your coordination was impaired it would be
obvious.

> **Jack Joyce,** the NBA's director of Security since
> 1972, in 1979. The following year the *Los Angeles
> Times* reported that 40 to 75 percent of NBA players
> were using cocaine.

This time, Leonard will kiss the floor of the ring because he talks **16**
too much.

> **Roberto Duran,** before his second fight with Sugar
> Ray Leonard in 1980. He lost.

No man was great enough to come back three times. I will do it a **17**
fourth time because it's there.

> **Muhammad Ali,** at 39, just before his 1981
> comeback bid to win the heavyweight championship
> one more time. He fought Canadian champ Trevor
> Berbick—and lost a 10-round decision.

Bob Lemon is going to be our manager all year. You can bet on it. **18**
I don't care if we come in last. I swear on my heart he'll be the
manager all season.

> **George Steinbrenner,** the owner of the New York
> Yankees in 1982. Lemon was fired in April, 14 games
> into the season.

Departures

Athletes, even the immortals, ultimately die. Or retire. When they pass from the scene many silly and extravagant things are said or written about them. Apocryphal anecdotes about them are revived, anecdotes are invented to promote their images or present them as supermen. But occasionally another player or a sports figure will capture something more—as Yogi Berra did in just five words about Jackie Robinson. These quotes are funny or evocative or endearingly absurd in their carefully framed sports metaphors. And sometimes, as in Art Hill's account of the day Gehrig didn't play, they are quite moving. They are the memorable farewells.

1   He was a hard out.
>   **Yogi Berra,** speaking of the late Jackie Robinson.

2   ... the words, 'Dahlgren, first base,' stunned the crowd into a moment of unplanned silence, which was followed by the unprecedented sound of several thousand people sighing in unison. Then Gehrig trudged painfully up to the plate, carrying the lineup card without his name on it. It was one of the most moving moments in sports history, high drama of the sort you cannot make up.
>   **Art Hill's** account of the day Lou Gehrig, terminally ill, didn't play, in Hill's evocative book, *I Don't Care If I Never Come Back.*

3   Naw, I didn't die last night. I wasn't even out of the house.
>   Former featherweight champ **Willie Pep,** commenting on the report of his death the previous night.

4   He [Leonard Shecter] was like a tough policeman on the beat. He thought there were too many 'house men' who refused to confront the Establishment. He was never afraid to confront the Establishment, even if it meant alienating people.
>   A **former colleague** of sportswriter Leonard Shecter, whose first book, *The Jocks,* was subtitled "An Iconoclastic View of Sports in America."

5   Start counting 10 over him. He'll get up.

Author **Wilson Mizner,** when he heard that fighter
Stanley Ketchel (known as the Michigan Assassin)
had been shot to death.

Danny Murtaugh won the admiration of the whole civilized world.   **6**
Now, all stand up as he dashes across the home plate of life.
        The **Rev. Francis P. O'Reilly,** eulogizing the former
        player and Pittsburgh Pirate manager.

The Lord has taken him to his place of rest. Let us hope it is a   **7**
place where he will see nothing but great defensemen and that the
ice will always be smooth.
        The **Rev. John Casey,** chaplain of the Philadelphia
        Flyers, officiating at the funeral of former player and
        assistant coach Barry Ashbee, who died at 37 of
        leukemia.

I think that's the thing I'm most proud of, coming back from the   **8**
adversity of those injuries. I never played as well as I would have
liked to have played, but I played for 13 seasons when my doctor
thought I would play for four. And I played despite a lot of
adversity.
        Joe Namath in 1978, retiring after 13 years with
        great quarterback stats.

I sat down in Chicago with him Tuesday night. Thinking back on it   **9**
now, it was almost as if he was giving his own eulogy. Near the end
of the conversation, he looked at me and said, 'I just want the fans
to remember me the way I was—stretching a single into a double.'
        New York Yankee telecaster **Frank Messer,** recalling
        his last conversation with Thurman Munson a few
        days before the catcher's tragic death.

Joe [Louis] was lacking in grandeur except when he entered the   **10**
ring.
        Boxing writer **Barney Nagler,** on an ESPN tribute
        to Joe Louis in 1981.

Sources

Part I

Playing the Game

1. *Sports Illustrated,* Sept. 16, 1974.
2. *Life,* Oct. 13, 1967.
3. *Sports Illustrated,* March 3, 1975.
4. *Sports Illustrated,* Sept. 6, 1976.
5. *New York Times,* May 15, 1977.
6. *Sports Illustrated,* May 9, 1977.
7. *Ibid.*
8. *New York Times,* Sept. 20, 1977.
9. *Ibid.*
10. *New York Times,* Feb. 13, 1978.
11. *New York Times,* Dec. 18, 1978.
12. *New York Times,* July 9, 1979.
13. *New York Times,* April 18, 1980.
14. *New York Daily News,* May 23, 1980.
15. *New York Times,* Feb. 29, 1980.
16. *New York Daily News,* Jan. 20, 1980.
17. *New York Daily News,* Sept. 21, 1980.
18. *Football Digest,* October 1980.
19. *Playboy,* August 1981.
20. *New York Times,* May 10, 1981.
21. *New York Times,* March 8, 1982.
22. *New York Times Magazine,* May 16, 1982.
23. *New York Daily News,* March 8, 1982.
24. *New York Daily News,* March 14, 1982.
25. *New York Times,* April 11, 1982.
26. *Sunday News Magazine,* June 27, 1982.

Coaching and Managing

1. The famous Lombardi building-block dictum.
2. *New York Times,* Feb. 24, 1977.
3. *New York Times,* March 20, 1977.
4. *West Coast Review of Books,* Sept. 1977.
5. *New York Post,* March 24, 1982.
6. *West Coast Review of Books,* Sept. 1977.
7. *Sports Illustrated,* March 1, 1971.
8. *Sports Illustrated,* Nov. 13, 1972.
9. *Sports Illustrated,* April 9, 1973.
10. *Sports Illustrated,* May 20, 1974.

11. *Sports Illustrated,* July 21, 1975.
12. *New York Times,* Oct. 21, 1975.
13. *International Herald Tribune,* Aug. 18, 1980.
14. *Sports Illustrated,* July 12, 1976.
15. *Sports Illustrated,* March 15, 1976.
16. *New York Times,* July 11, 1976.
17. *New York Times,* April 10, 1977.
18. *New York Post,* March 29, 1977.
19. *New York Times,* June 26, 1977.
20. *New York Post,* May 18, 1977.
21. *New York Times,* Sept. 26, 1977.
22. *Newsweek,* Nov. 28, 1977.
23. *New York Times,* Sept. 9, 1977.
24. *New York Times,* Jan. 17, 1978.
25. *New York Times,* Nov. 26, 1978.
26. *New York Times,* Dec. 31, 1978.
27. *New York Times,* Feb. 2, 1978.
28. *Sport Magazine,* Aug. 1981.
29. *New York Times,* Jan. 5, 1979.
30. *New York Times,* March 5, 1980.
31. *New York Times,* Feb. 2, 1981.
32. *Ibid.*
33. *New York Times,* Feb. 8, 1981.
34. *New York Daily News,* May 16, 1982.
35. *Ibid.*
36. *New York Daily News,* March 5, 1982.
37. *New York Times,* June 13, 1982.
38. *New York Times,* Aug. 6, 1982.
39. *Ibid.*

Officiating

1. *West Coast Review of Books,* Sept. 1977.
2. *New York Times,* Dec. 12, 1978.
3. WPIX telecast, June 23, 1982.
4. *Newsweek,* Sept. 1, 1975.
5. *New York Times Magazine,* Jan. 25, 1976.
6. *New York Times,* March 28, 1982.
7. *New York Times,* Dec. 15, 1977.
8. *Sports Illustrated,* June 9, 1969.
9. *Sports Illustrated,* Dec. 6, 1971.
10. *Newsweek,* Dec. 22, 1975.

11. *New York Times,* Aug. 8, 1976.
12. *Sports Illustrated,* March 7, 1977.
13. *Sports Illustrated,* May 27, 1974.
14. *New York Times,* Nov. 11, 1980.
15. *New York Times Magazine,* Sept. 16, 1979.
16. *New York Times,* Oct. 27, 1982.
17. *New York Times,* June 3, 1981.
18. *New York Daily News,* July 9, 1982.
19. *Sports Illustrated,* June 13, 1977.
20. *Sports Illustrated,* July 29, 1974.

Injuries

1. *Sports Illustrated,* Dec. 1, 1969.
2. *Sports Illustrated,* July 27, 1970.
3. *New York Times,* Oct. 18, 1975.
4. *New York Times,* Dec. 2, 1976.
5. *New York Daily News,* April 16, 1982.
6. *New York Times,* Sept. 16, 1977.
7. *Sports Illustrated,* Jan. 17, 1977.
8. *Sport Magazine,* March 1977.
9. *New York Daily News,* March 18, 1979.
10. *New York Times,* April 9, 1978.
11. *New York Times,* Feb. 27, 1980.
12. *New York Daily News,* Dec. 27, 1981.
13. *New York Daily News,* March 14, 1982.
14. *New York Times Magazine,* June 15, 1980.

Violence

1. *Rolling Stone,* May 3, 1979.
2. *Sports Illustrated,* Sept. 21, 1970.
3. *Sports Illustrated,* March 8, 1976.
4. *Sports Illustrated,* Nov. 13, 1972.
5. *New York Times,* Oct. 27, 1982.
6. *Sports Illustrated,* Jan. 6, 1975.
7. *New York Times,* Oct. 17, 1976.
8. *Sports Illustrated,* March 1, 1976.
9. *New York Post,* Dec. 13, 1977.
10. *New York Post,* Mar. 1, 1977.
11. *New York Times,* Feb. 18, 1979.
12. *Sports Illustrated,* Sept. 4, 1978.
13. *New York Times,* May 9, 1977.
14. *New York Times,* Sept. 22, 1977.
15. *Sunday News Magazine,* May 28, 1978.
16. *New York Times,* March 9, 1979.
17. *New York Times,* July 23, 1979.
18. *New York Daily News,* Sept. 19, 1981.
19. *Ibid.*
20. *New York Times,* Oct. 5, 1980.
21. *New York Times,* Nov. 1, 1980.
22. *New York Post,* Feb. 25, 1980.
23. *New York Post,* Sept. 24, 1981.
24. *Football Digest,* October 1980.
25. *Sport Magazine,* Aug. 1980.
26. *New York Daily News,* May 16, 1982.

Rookies

1. *Sports Illustrated,* May 27, 1974.
2. *New York Post,* Oct. 22, 1978.
3. *New York Times,* March 18, 1979.
4. *New York Times,* Aug. 1, 1978.
5. *New York Times,* July 4, 1976.
6. *New York Times,* Oct. 17, 1976.
7. *New York Times,* Sept. 25, 1977.
8. *New York Times,* Nov. 14, 1976.
9. *Sports Illustrated,* Jan. 3, 1977.
10. *Sports Illustrated,* April 4, 1977.
11. *New York Post,* Sept. 29, 1981.
12. ABC telecast, *"Monday Night Football,"* Sept. 20, 1982.
13. *New York Times,* Sept. 5, 1981.
14. Famous baseball saying.

Sports Arenas

1. *New York Times,* Jan. 30, 1981.
2. *Look Magazine,* Oct. 5, 1971.
3. *Ibid.*
4. *Sports Illustrated,* June 18, 1973.
5. *Sports Illustrated,* Feb. 25, 1974.
6. *New York Times,* May 26, 1980.
7. *New York Post,* Oct. 17, 1978.
8. *Sports Illustrated,* May 19, 1975.
9. *Sports Illustrated,* July 22, 1975.
10. *Ibid.*
11. *Ibid.*
12. *Sports Illustrated,* March 15, 1976.
13. *Ibid.*
14. *New York Times,* March 28, 1982.
15. *Village Voice,* April 26, 1976.

Part II

Psychology of the Game

1. *Life Magazine,* Oct. 13, 1967.
2. *Ibid.*
3. *New York Times,* July 9, 1979.
4. *New York Times,* Nov. 9, 1978.
5. *New York Times,* March 3, 1977.
6. *Newsweek,* June 3, 1974.
7. *Sports Illustrated,* Feb. 3, 1975.
8. *Sports Illustrated,* Sept. 15, 1975.
9. *Sports Illustrated,* Feb. 17, 1975.
10. *Sports Illustrated,* March 28, 1977.
11. *New York Times,* Jan. 23, 1977.
12. *New York Post,* March 28, 1977.
13. *New York Post,* March 30, 1977.
14. *New York Post,* July 11, 1977.
15. *New York Times Book Review,* July 31, 1977.
16. *New York Post,* Sept. 22, 1977.
17. *Newsweek,* May 2, 1977.

18. *New York Times,* July 6, 1977.
19. *New York Post,* May 14, 1977.
20. *Ibid.*
21. *New York Post,* March 28, 1977.
22. *Sports Illustrated,* May 15, 1978.
23. *New York Times,* Jan. 30, 1978.
24. *New York Times,* Oct. 26, 1980.
25. *Football Digest,* Oct. 1980.
26. *New York Times,* May 23, 1981.
27. *New York Daily News,* Sept. 30, 1982.
28. *New York Daily News,* Oct. 12, 1982.

Rivalry

1. *New York Post,* Oct. 6, 1982.
2. *New York Times Magazine,* Sept. 16, 1979.
3. *New York Times Book Review,* July 3, 1977.
4. *Sports Illustrated,* Feb. 2, 1976.
5. *Sports Illustrated,* July 15, 1974.
6. *Newsweek,* Jan. 26, 1976.
7. *New York Post,* Jan. 22, 1977.
8. *Basketball Digest,* April 1977.
9. *New York Daily News,* July 10, 1977.
10. *New York Times,* March 18, 1977.
11. *New York Times,* April 1, 1977.
12. WPIX telecast, Sept. 25, 1977.
13. *New York Times,* April 10, 1977
14. *New York Post,* Oct. 8, 1977.
15. *New York Times,* July 9, 1979.
16. *New York Times Magazine,* Sept. 7, 1980.
17. *New York Daily News,* Aug. 25, 1982.
18. *New York Times,* Oct. 17, 1982.
19. *New York Times,* March 8, 1982.
20. *New York Times Magazine,* June 20, 1982.
21. *New York Post,* March 25, 1982.
22. *New York Daily News,* April 4, 1982.
23. *New York Times,* Oct. 31, 1982.

Pressure

1. *Sports Illustrated,* April. 27, 1970.
2. *Sports Illustrated,* July 17, 1972.
3. *Sports Illustrated,* July 24, 1972.
4. *Sports Illustrated,* Aug. 13, 1973.
5. *New York Post,* Jan. 26, 1977.
6. *New York Times,* Oct. 17, 1975.
7. *Sports Illustrated,* Feb. 16, 1976.
8. *New York Times,* Aug. 15, 1976.
9. *New York Times,* May 7, 1976.
10. *New York Daily News,* Oct. 9, 1977.
11. *Penthouse,* Sept. 1978.
12. *New York Times,* Feb. 2, 1979.
13. *New York Times,* Jan. 9, 1980.
14. *New York Times,* March 22, 1982.
15. *International Herald Tribune,* Aug. 20, 1980.
16. *New York Daily News,* Nov. 10, 1980.

17. *New York Daily News,* Sept. 8, 1982.
18. *New York Times,* April 18, 1982.
19. *Ibid.*
20. *New York Times Magazine,* June 20, 1982.
21. *New York Times,* May 30, 1982.
22. *New York Times,* Sept. 13, 1982.
23. *New York Daily News,* Sept. 13, 1981.

Winning

1. *Sports Illustrated,* Jan. 29, 1973.
2. *New York Daily News,* July 4, 1982.
3. *Sports Illustrated,* Feb. 16, 1970.
4. *New York Times,* April 18, 1982.
5. *Sports Illustrated,* Nov. 24, 1974.
6. *New York Post,* March 28, 1977.
7. *Newsweek,* July 11, 1977.
8. *New York Times,* Sept. 13, 1977.
9. *New York Times,* Dec. 29, 1977.
10. *New York Times,* April 24, 1977.
11. *New York Times,* Oct. 9, 1977.
12. *New York Times,* Sept. 26, 1977
13. *New York Post,* Jan. 24, 1977.
14. *New York Times,* Dec. 31, 1978.
15. *New York Times,* July 23, 1978.
16. *Sunday News Magazine,* June 27, 1982.
17. *New York Daily News,* May 23, 1982.
18. *New York Post,* Oct. 4, 1982.
19. *New York Times,* Oct. 27, 1982.

Losing

1. *New York Daily News,* April 23, 1981.
2. *New York Times,* July 15, 1978.
3. *New York Daily News,* Feb. 26, 1982.
4. *New York Daily News,* March 28, 1979.
5. *New York Times Magazine,* Sept. 16, 1979.
6. *Sports Illustrated,* May 22, 1972.
7. *New York Times,* May 30, 1976.
8. *New York Times,* Aug. 15, 1976.
9. *New York Post,* May 6, 1977.
10. *New York Times,* Feb. 23, 1977.
11. *New York Times,* Jan. 24, 1977.
12. *New York Times,* March 13, 1977.
13. *New York Post,* Dec. 13, 1977.
14. *Sports Illustrated,* May 9, 1977.
15. *New York Times,* Nov. 30, 1977.
16. *New York Times,* Jan. 6, 1978.
17. *New York Times,* June 4, 1980.
18. *Newsweek,* Nov. 10, 1980.
19. *New York Daily News,* April 23, 1980.
20. *Sport Magazine,* Aug. 1981.
21. *New York Times,* Aug. 16, 1982.
22. *New York Daily News,* Aug. 22, 1982.
23. *New York Magazine,* Sept. 28, 1981.
24. *New York Daily News,* May 21, 1982.
25. *New York Daily News,* Nov. 7, 1982.

Glory of the Game

1. *New York Times Magazine,* Sept. 16, 1979.
2. *New York Times,* May 27, 1979.
3. *Ibid.*
4. *New York Times,* Aug. 23, 1981.
5. *Sports Illustrated,* Dec. 4, 1972.
6. *Sports Illustrated,* July 17,1972.
7. *Sports Illustrated,* Jan. 8, 1979.
8. *Ibid.*
9. *Sports Illustrated,* June 3, 1974.
10. *New York Times,* May 13, 1977.
11. *New York Daily News,* April 10, 1977.
12. *New York Daily News,* July 25, 1979.
13. *New York Daily News,* Nov. 14, 1980.
14. *New York Times,* July 21, 1980.
15. *New York Daily News,* Nov. 7, 1982.

Real Pros

1. *Saturday Evening Post,* Dec. 16, 1967.
2. *New York Times,* July 24, 1978.
3. *Sports Illustrated,* March 11, 1968.
4. *Sports Illustrated,* May 11, 1970.
5. *Sports Illustrated,* Jan. 14, 1974.
6. *New York Times,* Jan. 23, 1977.
7. *New York Times,* Feb. 13, 1977.
8. *New York Times,* Sept. 23, 1977.
9. *New York Times,* Aug. 21, 1977.
10. *New York Times,* June 12, 1977.
11. *New York Post,* Feb. 18, 1977.
12. *New York Times,* May 11, 1978.
13. *New York Times,* March 16, 1980.
14. *New York Times,* June 1, 1980.

Part III

Play for Pay

1. *Sports Illustrated,* May 13, 1972.
2. *New York Times,* May 30, 1976.
3. *Sports Illustrated,* April 26, 1976.
4. *Sports Illustrated,* July 28, 1969.
5. *Sports Illustrated,* May 12, 1975.
6. *Sports Illustrated,* Oct. 28, 1974.
7. *New York Times,* Jan. 20, 1977.
8. *Sports Illustrated,* May 6, 1974.
9. *New York Post,* March 30, 1977.
10. *New York Times,* Feb. 13, 1977.
11. *New York Post,* March 17, 1977.
12. *New York Times,* May 15, 1977.
13. *New York Post,* March 28, 1977.
14. *New York Times,* Feb. 20, 1977.
15. *Newsweek,* Aug. 15, 1977.
16. *New York Times,* Sept. 20, 1977.
17. *New York Post,* Nov. 5, 1978.
18. *Newsweek,* Dec. 18, 1978.
19. *New York Times,* Aug. 16, 1981.
20. *New York Daily News,* Feb. 13, 1981.

21. *New York Daily News,* March 22, 1982.
22. *New York Daily News,* March 28, 1982.
23. *New York Times,* March 28, 1982.
24. *New York Times,* June 6, 1982.
25. *New York Times,* Aug. 6, 1982.
26. *New York Daily News,* March 9, 1982.

Free Agency

1. *Sports Illustrated,* April 26, 1976.
2. *New York Times,* Feb. 19, 1974.
3. *New York Times,* March 17, 1974.
4. *New York Post,* March 7, 1977.
5. *Sports Illustrated,* June 28, 1976.
6. *Sports Illustrated,* Aug. 15, 1977.
7. *New Times,* June 10, 1977.
8. *New York Times,* Jan. 8, 1977.
9. *New York Times,* Jan. 26, 1977.
10. *Sports Illustrated,* March 21, 1977.
11. *New Times,* June 10, 1977.
12. *Ibid.*
13. *The Trib,* Feb. 9, 1978.
14. *Sunday News Magazine,* May 22, 1977.
15. *New York Times,* Dec. 31, 1978.
16. *New York Times,* Aug. 16, 1981.
17. *New York Times,* Jan. 23, 1981.
18. *New York Daily News,* March 22, 1982.
19. *New York Daily News,* April 25, 1982.
20. *Ibid.*
21. *New York Times,* Oct. 26, 1982.

Unions

1. *Sports Illustrated,* Aug. 3, 1970.
2. *Sports Illustrated,* Aug. 10, 1970.
3. *Sports Illustrated,* April 17, 1972.
4. *New York Times,* May 8, 1974.
5. *New York Times,* July 15, 1974.
6. *Penthouse,* May 1977.
7. *Sports Illustrated,* March 7, 1977.
8. *New York Daily News,* April 24, 1981.
9. *New York Times,* July 25, 1982.
10. *New York Daily News,* July 12, 1982.
11. *New York Times,* Sept. 26, 1982.
12. *New York Times,* Sept. 27, 1982.
13. *New York Times,* Sept. 26, 1982.

Sports As A Business

1. *New York Times,* Sept. 22, 1977.
2. *New York Times,* Sept. 30, 1975.
3. *Sports Illustrated,* Feb. 1, 1971.
4. *Sports Illustrated,* Feb. 25, 1974.
5. *Sports Illustrated,* May 12, 1975.
6. *New York Times,* Feb. 13, 1976.
7. *New York Times,* Dec. 7, 1976.
8. *New Times,* Dec. 9, 1977.
9. *Sports Illustrated,* July 26, 1976.

10. *New Times,* Dec. 9, 1977.
11. *Sports Illustrated,* April 15, 1977.
12. *New York Times,* Dec. 9, 1977.
13. *New York Times,* July 23, 1977.
14. *Newsweek,* April 3, 1978.
15. *New York Times Magazine,* Sept. 16, 1979.
16. *TV Guide,* Nov. 8, 1980.
17. *Ibid.*
18. *Ibid.*
19. *New York Times,* Aug. 30, 1980.
20. *Oui Magazine,* October 1981.
21. *Esquire,* June 1982.
22. *New York Times,* Jan. 25, 1981.
23. *New York Times,* Aug. 16, 1981.
24. *New York Times,* April 18, 1982.
25. *Business Week,* April 5, 1982.
26. *Esquire,* June 1982.
27. *New York Daily News,* May 23, 1982.
28. *Esquire,* June 1982.
29. *New York Daily News,* March 24, 1982.

Owners

1. *New York Times Magazine,* Sept. 30, 1979.
2. *Sports Illustrated,* July 13, 1970.
3. *Sports Illustrated,* Aug. 3, 1970.
4. *Sports Illustrated,* April 7, 1972.
5. *New York Times,* Sept. 1, 1974.
6. *New York Times,* July 21, 1974.
7. *Sports Illustrated,* Nov. 4, 1974.
8. *Sports Illustrated,* April 26, 1976.
9. *New York Times,* June 14, 1977.
10. *New York Times,* July 6, 1977.
11. *New York Times,* May 7, 1978.
12. *New York Times,* April 17, 1977.
13. *The Trib,* Feb. 9, 1978.
14. *Saturday Review,* July 22, 1978.
15. *New York Post,* Nov. 4, 1978.
16. *New York Times,* Sept. 24, 1979.
17. *New York Times,* March 20, 1979.
18. *New York Post,* Oct. 31, 1980.
19. *New York Times,* Sept. 20, 1981.
20. *New York Daily News,* April 12, 1982.
21. *New York Daily News,* July 11, 1982.
22. *New York Times,* June 27, 1982.
23. *New York Times,* Sept. 26, 1982.
24. *Ibid.*
25. *New York Daily News,* Oct. 26, 1982.

Sports and TV

1. *Sports Illustrated,* April 7, 1975.
2. *New York Times,* Jan. 17, 1971.
3. *TV Guide,* June 24, 1967.
4. *Sports Illustrated,* Oct. 11, 1971.
5. *Sports Illustrated,* May 12, 1975.
6. *Sports Illustrated,* July 8, 1974.

7. *New York Times,* May 21, 1976.
8. *New York Times,* Nov. 3, 1976.
9. *New York Times,* June 29, 1975.
10. *New York Times,* Feb. 6, 1977.
11. *Newsweek,* May 23, 1977.
12. *New York Times,* Dec. 8, 1977.
13. *New York Times,* June 7, 1978.
14. *Village Voice,* Sept. 25, 1978.
15. *Bostonian Magazine,* August 1978.
16. *Ibid.*
17. *New York Post,* Nov. 26, 1978.
18. *New York Daily News,* June 10, 1979.
19. *Sports Illustrated,* Feb. 19, 1979.
20. *New York Times,* April 19, 1981.

The Fans

1. *Sports Illustrated,* Oct. 15, 1973.
2. *Sports Illustrated,* Oct. 22, 1973.
3. *New York Times,* July 10, 1977.
4. *New York Times,* Sept. 7, 1977.
5. *West Coast Review of Books,* Sept. 1977.
6. *New York Times,* Sept. 28, 1977.
7. *Ibid.*
8. *New York Post,* Oct. 10, 1978.
9. *New York Post,* Nov. 15, 1977.
10. *Atlas World Press Review,* October 1978.
11. *New York Times,* Jan. 20, 1979.
12. *Ibid.*
13. *The Sporting News,* Feb. 23, 1980.
14. *New York Daily News,* May 1, 1981.
15. *New York Daily News,* Aug. 23, 1981.
16. *New York Times,* June 16, 1981.
17. *New York Times,* Sept. 28, 1981.
18. *New York Daily News,* April 29, 1982.
19. *New York Daily News,* Sept. 20, 1982.
20. *New York Times,* Sept. 26, 1982.
21. *New York Times,* Sept. 27, 1982.

Gambling

1. *Sports Illustrated,* Oct. 5, 1970.
2. *New York Times,* Jan. 22, 1975.
3. *Ibid.*
4. *Ibid.*
5. *New York Daily News,* Sept. 26, 1982.
6. *New York Times,* March 12, 1977.
7. *New York Times,* Sept. 12, 1981.
8. *Ibid.*
9. *New York Times,* Oct. 18, 1981.
10. *New York Daily News,* Sept. 26, 1982.
11. *Ibid.*

Recruiting

1. *Sports Illustrated,* Sept. 16, 1968.
2. *Sports Illustrated,* July 5, 1971.
3. *Sports Illustrated,* May 31, 1976.

4. *Sports Illustrated,* Nov. 4, 1974.
5. *Sports Illustrated,* Feb. 10, 1975.
6. *New York Times,* Jan. 26, 1976.
7. *Sports Illustrated,* Feb. 7, 1977.
8. *Ibid.*
9. *Sports Illustrated,* March 10, 1978.
10. *Ibid.*
11. *New York Times,* March 25, 1979.
12. *Ibid.*
13. *Ibid.*
14. *New York Times,* April 22, 1981.
15. *New York Times,* March 22, 1982.
16. *Ibid.*
17. *New York Times,* March 21, 1982.

Future Shock

1. *Sports Illustrated,* Dec. 7, 1970.
2. *Sports Illustrated,* June 10, 1974.
3. *Sport Magazine,* March 1977.
4. *New York Times,* Feb. 6, 1977.
5. *New York Times,* April 17, 1977.
6. *New York Daily News,* Sept. 4, 1977.
7. *New York Times Magazine,* Aug. 7, 1977.
8. *Sport Magazine,* April 1981.
9. *New York Times,* May 22, 1978.
10. *New York Times,* July 25, 1978.
11. *Esquire,* Nov. 7, 1978.
12. *New York Times,* March 21, 1979.
13. *New York Times,* June 29, 1980.
14. *New York Times,* July 9, 1980.
15. *New York Daily News,* Sept. 19, 1980.
16. *New York Times,* Sept. 27, 1979.
17. *New York Daily News,* Sept. 26, 1982.
18. *New York Times,* March 8, 1982.
19. *Sports Illustrated,* Oct. 13, 1975.

Part IV

Image

1. *Sports Illustrated,* March 6, 1972.
2. *TV Guide,* Oct. 1, 1975.
3. *New York Times Magazine,* Sept. 28, 1975.
4. *Sports Illustrated,* Dec. 8, 1975.
5. *New York Times,* June 20, 1977.
6. *New York Times Magazine,* April 10, 1977.
7. *Sports Illustrated,* May 2, 1977.
8. *Sports Illustrated,* June 19, 1972.
9. *New York Times,* April 14, 1977.
10. *New York Magazine,* April 11, 1977.
11. *New York Post,* March 28, 1977.
12. *New York Times,* July 21, 1977.
13. *New York Times,* April 24, 1977.
14. *Ibid.*
15. *New York Times,* July 13, 1977.

16. *New York Times,* June 26, 1978.
17. *New York Daily News,* May 7, 1978.
18. *New York Post,* Feb. 11, 1978.
19. *New York Post,* Jan. 20, 1979.
20. *New York Times,* April 15, 1979.
21. *Sunday News Magazine,* Oct. 5, 1980.
22. *New York Times,* June 29, 1980.
23. *New York Times,* May 22, 1981.
24. *New York Times,* March 17, 1982.
25. *New York Daily News,* March 19, 1982.
26. *New York Daily News,* Sept. 8, 1982.
27. *New York Post,* March 2, 1982.
28. *New York Daily News,* Oct. 10, 1982.
29. *New York Times,* June 20, 1982.
30. *New York Daily News,* June 27, 1982.
31. *New York Daily News,* April 18, 1982.
32. *New York Daily News,* May 9, 1982.
33. *New York Times,* March 8, 1982.
34. *New York Times,* Oct. 27, 1982.

Celebrity

1. *Sports Illustrated,* March 30, 1970.
2. *Sports Illustrated,* Nov. 2, 1970.
3. *Sports Illustrated,* May 31, 1971.
4. *Sports Illustrated,* Sept. 20, 1971.
5. *Sports Illustrated,* Nov. 8, 1971.
6. *Sports Illustrated,* Nov. 11, 1974.
7. *Sports Illustrated,* Nov. 19, 1973.
8. *Sports Illustrated,* Feb. 18, 1974.
9. *New York Times,* July 25, 1974.
10. *Sports Illustrated,* May 3, 1976.
11. *New York Times,* April 12, 1977.
12. *New York Times,* July 31, 1977.
13. *Sports Illustrated,* Jan. 7, 1977.
14. *New York Times,* March 13, 1977.
15. Axthelm, Pete. *The Kid.* 1978.
16. *New York Times,* Jan. 9, 1977.
17. Famous baseball saying.
18. *New York Times,* April 13, 1977.
19. *New York Times,* June 26, 1977.
20. *New York Times,* Oct. 13, 1977.
21. *Newsweek,* Oct. 23, 1978.
22. *New York Daily News,* July 16, 1978.
23. *New York Times,* March 4, 1980.
24. *New York Times,* Oct. 26, 1982.
25. *New York Daily News,* Sept. 3, 1982.
26. *New York Times,* Oct. 26, 1982.

Superstars

1. *Life Magazine,* Oct. 13, 1967.
2. *Sports Illustrated,* Feb. 24, 1969.
3. *Sports Illustrated,* May 10, 1971.
4. *New York Times,* May 10, 1977.
5. *Sports Illustrated,* Aug. 31, 1970.
6. *New York Times,* May 18, 1975.
7. *Sports Illustrated,* May 10, 1971.
8. *Sports Illustrated,* July 31, 1972.

9. *Sports Illustrated*, Sept. 10, 1973.
10. *Sports Illustrated*, July 22, 1974.
11. *Sports Illustrated*, June 2, 1975.
12. *Sports Illustrated*, June 21, 1976.
13. *Newsweek*, July 11, 1977.
14. *Sports Illustrated*, May 9, 1977.
15. *New York Daily News*, Feb. 25, 1979.
16. *New York Times*, Jan. 30, 1979.
17. *New York Times*, Nov. 5, 1979.
18. *New York Times*, July 4, 1980.
19. *New York Daily News*, Jan. 24, 1982.
20. *Esquire*, April 1982.
21. *New York Daily News*, Nov. 7, 1982.
22. *New York Times*, Oct. 17, 1982.

Dreams Come True

1. *New York Times*, Dec. 10, 1977.
2. *Sports Illustrated*, March 17, 1975.
3. *New York Times*, Sept. 12, 1976.
4. *Sunday News Magazine*, July 18, 1976.
5. *New York Daily News*, July 10, 1977.
6. *New York Times*, Feb. 20, 1977.
7. *New York Times*, March 10, 1977.
8. *New York Times*, Nov. 30, 1977.
9. *New York Post*, April 9, 1977.
10. *New York Times*, Sept. 18, 1977.
11. *New York Times*, Aug. 30, 1977.
12. *News World*, Aug. 27, 1978.
13. *New York Daily News*, July 18, 1980.
14. *New York Times*, Oct. 14, 1980.
15. *New York Daily News*, June 27, 1982.
16. *New York Times*, Sept. 27, 1982.

Dreams of Glory

1. *Sports Illustrated*, Aug. 26, 1974.
2. *Life Magazine*, Oct. 13, 1967.
3. *New York Post*, Jan. 29, 1977.
4. *Sports Illustrated*, April 28, 1975.
5. *New York Times*, April 16, 1977.
6. *New York Times*, May 19, 1977.
7. *New York Times*, June 8, 1979.
8. *New York Times*, Oct. 23, 1975.
9. *New York Times*, June 29, 1980.

Scandals and Other Embarrassments

1. *New York Times*, Sept. 4, 1977.
2. *New York Times*, Nov. 15, 1977.
3. *New York Times*, April 20, 1980.
4. *New York Times*, Dec. 31, 1978.
5. *New York Times*, Dec. 27, 1980.
6. *New York Post*, Feb. 26, 1980.
7. *Sports Illustrated*, Feb. 16, 1981.
8. *New York Daily News*, May 4, 1982.
9. *New York Times*, March 17, 1982.
10. *New York Daily News*, Nov. 7, 1982.

11. *New York Times*, Oct. 31, 1982.
12. *New York Daily News*, June 6, 1982.
13. *Ibid.*

Drugs and Alcohol

1. *New York Times*, July 23, 1979.
2. *Playboy*, February 1978.
3. *Ibid.*
4. *New York Daily News*, March 18, 1979.
5. *New York Times*, July 23, 1979.
6. *New York Post*, May 16, 1978.
7. *New York Times*, June 21, 1981.
8. *New York Daily News*, Feb. 13, 1981.
9. *New York Daily News*, March 14, 1982.
10. *New York Daily News*, Feb. 3, 1982.
11. *New York Daily News*, July 6, 1982.
12. *New York Daily News*, July 16, 1982.
13. *New York Times*, Oct. 26, 1982.
14. *New York Daily News*, March 28, 1982.
15. *Sports Illustrated*, June 14, 1982.

Part V

Candor

1. *Sports Illustrated*, Feb. 6, 1970.
2. *Sports Illustrated*, June 15, 1970.
3. *Sports Illustrated*, July 20, 1970.
4. *Sports Illustrated*, June 7, 1971.
5. *Sports Illustrated*, April 17, 1972.
6. *Sports Illustrated*, June 26, 1972.
7. *Sports Illustrated*, Sept. 1, 1975.
8. *New York Times*, Jan. 31, 1976.
9. *New York Times*, Oct. 17, 1976.
10. *Sports Illustrated*, Feb. 28, 1977.
11. *New York Times*, Oct. 10, 1976.
12. *New York Times*, Oct. 17, 1976.
13. *Sunday News Magazine*, Sept. 28, 1980.
14. *New York Post*, Sept. 22, 1977.
15. *Newsday*, July 3, 1977.
16. *New York Times*, March 18, 1977.
17. *New York Post*, March 24, 1977.
18. *New York Times*, Dec. 11, 1977.
19. *New York Times*, March 4, 1977.
20. *Newsweek*, Oct. 23, 1978.
21. *International Herald Tribune*, Aug. 18, 1980.
22. *New York Times*, June 17, 1980.
23. *New York Times*, March 3, 1980.
24. *New York Daily News*, Feb. 1, 1981.
25. *New York Times*, Aug. 2, 1981.
26. *New York Daily News*, July 2, 1982.
27. *New York Times*, March 8, 1982.
28. *New York Times*, Sept. 13, 1982.
29. *New York Daily News*, March 28, 1982.

Humor

1. *Sports Illustrated,* Aug. 11, 1969.
2. *New York Times,* Feb. 20, 1977.
3. *Sports Illustrated,* June 2, 1975.
4. *New York Times,* Oct. 9, 1979.
5. *New York Daily News,* April 23, 1981.
6. *Sunday News Magazine,* Jan. 6, 1980.
7. *Ibid.*
8. *Newsweek,* Jan. 22, 1979.
9. Hickok, Ralph. *Who Was Who in American Sports.* 1971.
10. *New York Daily News,* May 28, 1978.
11. *Sports Illustrated,* Jan. 11, 1971.
12. *Sports Illustrated,* Nov. 13, 1972.
13. *Sports Illustrated,* March 5, 1973.
14. *New York Times,* Aug. 8, 1972.
15. *Sports Illustrated,* July 15, 1974.
16. *Sports Illustrated,* Sept. 1, 1975.
17. *Sports Illustrated,* Aug. 9, 1971.
18. *Sports Illustrated,* March 14, 1977.
19. *New York Post,* Oct. 16, 1978.
20. *New York Times,* July 17, 1977.
21. *Sports Illustrated,* June 6, 1977.
22. *Sports Illustrated,* Feb. 28, 1977.
23. *New York Times,* June 25, 1979.
24. *Ibid.*
25. *New York Times,* Jan. 17, 1979.
26. *New York Times,* April 8, 1980.
27. *New York Times,* May 21, 1981.
28. *New York Times,* Dec. 17, 1978.
29. *International Herald Tribune,* Aug. 18, 1980.
30. *New York Daily News,* Oct. 25, 1981.
31. *New York Times,* March 21, 1982.
32. *New York Daily News,* March 14, 1982.
33. *New York Daily News,* Oct. 14, 1982.
34. *New York Times,* Sept. 13, 1982.
35. *New York Daily News,* Feb. 7, 1982.

Hyperbole

1. *New York Times,* Dec. 8, 1977.
2. *Sports Illustrated,* April 26, 1971.
3. Famous baseball saying.
4. *Village Voice,* March 28, 1977.
5. *New York Daily News,* March 7, 1982.
6. *New York Times,* Sept. 22, 1977.
7. *New York Times,* Sept. 8, 1977.
8. *New York Post,* Feb. 21, 1977.
9. *New York Times,* June 20, 1979.
10. *New York Daily News,* Oct. 8, 1980.
11. *New York Times,* Oct. 6, 1980.
12. *New York Times Book Review,* July 31, 1977.
13. *New York Times,* Jan. 25, 1981.
14. *New York Times,* March 21, 1982.
15. *New York Daily News,* Sept. 11, 1982.
16. *Sunday News Magazine,* April 4, 1982.

17. *New York Daily News,* Sept. 10, 1982.
18. *New York Times,* Sept. 26, 1982.
19. *New York Daily News,* Nov. 7, 1982.
20. NBC telecast, Oct. 19, 1982.

Put-downs

1. *Sports Illustrated,* June 21, 1971.
2. *Sports Illustrated,* Jan. 24, 1977.
3. *New York Daily News,* April 23, 1981.
4. *Sports Illustrated,* March 6, 1972.
5. *New York Times,* May 1, 1974.
6. *Sports Illustrated,* Feb. 3, 1975.
7. *New York Times,* June 22, 1975.
8. *Sports Illustrated,* Nov. 1, 1976.
9. *New York Times,* March 27, 1977.
10. *New York Daily News,* March 7, 1982.
11. *New York Times,* Nov. 22, 1977.
12. *New York Times,* Sept. 5, 1977.
13. *New York Times,* Jan. 11, 1978.
14. *New York Post,* Oct. 8, 1977.
15. *New York Times,* July 7, 1978.
16. *Ibid.*
17. *New York Times,* July 29, 1979.
18. *New York Times,* Jan. 25, 1981.
19. *Sport Magazine,* August 1981.
20. *Ibid.*
21. *New York Post,* March 10, 1982.
22. *New York Daily News,* Oct. 14, 1982.
23. *New York Post,* May 20, 1982.
24. *New York Daily News,* July 4, 1982.
25. *New York Daily News,* Oct. 8, 1982.

Sour Grapes

1. *Sports Illustrated,* Dec. 7, 1970.
2. *Sports Illustrated,* June 2, 1975.
3. *New York Times,* Dec. 12, 1976.
4. *New York Post,* March 18, 1977.
5. *New York Post,* May 11, 1977.
6. *New York Times,* Dec. 15, 1977.
7. *New York Post,* March 17, 1977.
8. *New York Times,* May 8, 1977.
9. *New York Times,* May 15, 1977.
10. *New York Post,* May 28, 1978.
11. *New York Times,* Aug. 6, 1978.
12. *New York Times,* Sept. 10, 1981.
13. *New York Daily News,* March 15, 1982.
14. *New York Times,* Aug. 25, 1979.

Cliches

1. *Sports Illustrated,* Aug. 12, 1974.
2. *New York Times,* Nov. 2, 1975.
3. *Basketball Digest,* April 1977.
4. *New York Times,* April 2, 1977.
5. *New York Post,* April 30, 1977.
6. *New York Times,* May 13, 1977.
7. Famous football telecaster's saying.

8. *New York Times*, Oct. 14, 1976.
9. *New York Daily News*, March 28, 1982.
10. NBC telecast, Oct. 17, 1982.
11. Famous baseball telecaster's saying.
12. *New York Times*, Feb. 1, 1981.

Rank Optimism

1. *Toronto Globe & Mail*, Aug. 23, 1974.
2. *New York Times*, July 4, 1976.
3. *Sports Illustrated*, Dec. 6, 1976.
4. *New York Post*, Feb. 16, 1977.
5. *New York Times*, May 12, 1977.
6. *New Times*, July 8, 1977.
7. *New York Post*, April 8, 1977.
8. *New York Times*, July 27, 1975.
9. *Sports Illustrated*, Feb. 28, 1972.
10. *Sports Illustrated*, April 20, 1970.
11. *New York Times*, Sept. 19, 1977.
12. *New York Times*, Sept. 4, 1977.
13. *New York Times*, May 23, 1982.
14. *New York Daily News*, April 18, 1982.
15. *New York Daily News*, July 4, 1982.

Understatement

1. *Sports Illustrated*, Aug. 6, 1973.
2. *Sports Illustrated*, Jan. 6, 1975.
3. *Sports Illustrated*, May 17, 1976.
4. *New York Times*, Sept. 13, 1969.
5. *New York Times*, April 28, 1977.
6. *Sports Illustrated*, Aug. 3, 1970.
7. *Sports Illustrated*, March 8, 1971.
8. *Sports Illustrated*, Nov. 4, 1974.
9. *Sports Illustrated*, Nov. 22, 1976.
10. *New York Times*, Dec. 27, 1976.
11. *New York Times*, March 11, 1977.
12. *New York Times*, May 4, 1977.
13. *New York Times Magazine*, Nov. 30, 1980.

Part VI

Amateur Athletics

1. *New York Times*, Jan. 19, 1980.
2. *New York Times*, Jan. 17, 1970.
3. *New York Times*, Jan. 18, 1970.
4. *New York Times*, April 24, 1971.
5. *Sports Illustrated*, Feb. 14, 1972.
6. *New York Times*, June 11, 1972.
7. *New York Times*, April 8, 1973.
8. *New York Post*, Aug. 25, 1974.
9. *New York Times*, May 10, 1975.
10. *Ibid.*
11. *Sports Illustrated*, Oct. 27, 1975.
12. *Mainliner*, April 1976.
13. *New York Times*, Feb. 26, 1978.
14. *New York Times*, Aug. 31, 1980.

15. *New York Times*, March 21, 1982.
16. *New York Times*, Feb. 22, 1981.
17. *New York Daily News*, Sept. 19, 1982.
18. *New York Times*, April 11, 1982.
19. *Ibid.*
20. *New York Daily News*, Sept. 19, 1982.
21. *New York Times*, Sept. 26, 1982.
22. *New York Times*, Sept. 19, 1982.
23. *Ibid.*
24. *New York Times*, Sept. 26, 1982.

The Olympics

1. *New York Times*, Aug. 16, 1968.
2. *Sports Illustrated*, Jan. 11, 1971.
3. *Sports Illustrated*, Feb. 7, 1972.
4. *New York Times*, Oct. 22, 1974.
5. *New York Times*, July 11, 1976.
6. *New York Times*, Dec. 22, 1976.
7. *Sports Illustrated*, Jan. 31, 1977.
8. *New York Times*, April 15, 1977.
9. *Penthouse*, September 1978.
10. *Ibid.*
11. *New York Times*, Feb. 29, 1980.
12. *Oui Magazine*, May 1978.
13. *New York Times*, Oct. 18, 1979.
14. *New York Times*, Oct. 17, 1982.

Sports and Politics

1. *New York Times Book Review*, June 15, 1980.
2. *New York Times*, April 18, 1982.
3. *Sports Illustrated*, March 18, 1971.
4. *Sports Illustrated*, July 31, 1972.
5. *New York Times*, July 25, 1974.
6. *New York Times*, Oct. 6, 1974.
7. *Ibid.*
8. *Sports Illustrated*, Feb. 7, 1977.
9. *New York Times*, March 6, 1977.
10. *New York Times*, March 27, 1978.
11. *New York Times*, May 17, 1977.
12. *New York Times*, Aug. 9, 1981.
13. *New York Times*, April 26, 1981.
14. *New York Daily News*, Oct. 24, 1982.
15. *Newsweek*, June 26, 1978.

Race

1. *New York Times*, Jan. 25, 1968.
2. *Sports Illustrated*, May 12, 1980.
3. *New York Times*, April 22, 1981.
4. *New York Times*, March 14, 1982.
5. *New York Times*, April 11, 1978.
6. *National Enquirer*, March 25, 1980.
7. *Sports Illustrated*, Nov. 9, 1970.
8. *Sports Illustrated*, Jan. 19, 1970.
9. *Sports Illustrated*, Feb. 22, 1971.
10. *Sports Illustrated*, Nov. 6, 1972.

11. *Sports Illustrated,* March 12, 1973.
12. *The Progressive,* June 1973.
13. *Sports Illustrated,* April 9, 1973.
14. *New York Times,* March 30, 1973.
15. *New York Times,* April 8, 1973.
16. *Sports Illustrated,* Jan. 15, 1973.
17. *Sports Illustrated,* Aug. 13, 1973.
18. *Sports Illustrated,* July 15, 1974.
19. *Sports Illustrated,* Dec. 2, 1974.
20. *New York Times,* Feb. 6, 1977.
21. *New York Post,* May 11, 1977.
22. *New York Times,* July 17, 1977.
23. *Sport Magazine,* March 1980.
24. *New York Times,* Oct. 26, 1982.

Women and Sports

1. *Newsweek,* June 3, 1974.
2. *Sports Illustrated,* April 4, 1969.
3. *Sports Illustrated,* June 26, 1972.
4. *Ibid.*
5. *Ibid.*
6. *Sports Illustrated,* April 1, 1974.
7. *Sports Illustrated,* July 1, 1974.
8. *New York Times,* Sept. 14, 1976.
9. *New York Times,* Dec. 19, 1976.
10. *New York Times,* Dec. 18, 1977.
11. *New York Times,* April 14, 1977.
12. *Sports Illustrated,* Aug. 23, 1976.
13. *Sports Illustrated,* March 20, 1978.
14. *Ibid.*
15. *Ibid.*
16. *Newsweek,* March 16, 1981.
17. *New York Daily News,* Oct. 10, 1982.
18. *New York Times,* Oct. 29, 1982.
19. *Ibid.*

Part VII

Hall of Fame

1. Famous baseball saying.
2. *New York Times,* Aug. 4, 1978.
3. Famous race track saying.
4. *Los Angeles Times,* Oct. 7, 1979.
5. Source unknown.
6. *Signature Magazine,* October 1971.
7. *New York Times,* April 1, 1981.
8. *New York Times,* Jan. 21, 1981.
9. *Sports Illustrated,* Aug. 13, 1973.
10. *Sunday News Magazine,* April 6, 1980.
11. *New York Times,* April 1, 1981.
12. *Ibid.*
13. *New York Times,* Nov. 9, 1980.
14. Source unknown.
15. *New York Times,* Aug. 9, 1982.
16. Famous baseball saying.
17. Famous baseball saying.
18. Source unknown.

19. *Newsweek,* Nov. 3, 1980.
20. *Sports Illustrated,* June 7, 1971.
21. *New York Times,* Oct. 23, 1980.
22. *Penthouse,* March 1979.
23. *Sunday News Magazine,* May 18, 1980.
24. *New York Post,* Nov. 9, 1982.
25. *New York Times,* Oct. 29, 1977.
26. *New York Times,* June 23, 1977.
27. *New York Times,* Oct. 27, 1982.
28. Famous baseball saying.
29. *New York Times,* Jan. 19, 1975.
30. *Ibid.*
31. Famous baseball saying.
32. *New York Times,* Jan. 19, 1975.
33. *Sports Illustrated,* Oct. 13, 1975.
34. Source unknown.
35. *New York Times,* Nov. 17, 1978.
36. *Sports Illustrated,* Dec. 20, 1976.
37. *New York Times,* Oct. 3, 1980.
38. Source unknown.
39. *Sunday News Magazine,* Sept. 7, 1980.
40. *New Yorker,* Nov. 24, 1980.
41. *Newsweek,* Nov. 3, 1980.
42. Famous baseball saying.
43. WINS radio newscast, Nov. 17, 1982.

Hall of Fame (Candidates)

1. *New York Times,* March 18, 1981.
2. *Wall Street Journal,* Oct. 23, 1978.
3. *Oui Magazine,* Sept. 1977.
4. *New York Times,* April 12, 1957.
5. *New York Times,* April 5, 1979.
6. *New York Times,* April 30, 1961.
7. *Sports Illustrated,* July 22, 1968.
8. *International Herald Tribune,* Aug. 18, 1980.
9. Famous baseball saying.
10. *Sports Illustrated,* March 8, 1971.
11. *New York Times,* Jan. 5, 1970.
12. *Sports Illustrated,* Dec. 2, 1974.
13. *Sports Illustrated,* July 22, 1974.
14. *Sports Illustrated,* May 12, 1975.
15. *New York Times,* Dec. 24, 1975.
16. *New York Times,* Feb. 8, 1979.
17. *News World,* Sept. 3, 1978.
18. *New York Times,* Jan. 2, 1978.
19. *New York Times,* Dec. 26, 1978.
20. *Newsweek,* Aug. 7, 1978.
21. *Times Herald Record,* Sept 23, 1978.
22. *New York Daily News,* Nov. 21, 1980.
23. *New York Times,* Nov. 23, 1979.
24. CBS telecast, "Sixty Minutes," March 15, 1981.

The Press

1. *New York Times,* July 23, 1980.
2. *Newsweek,* July 1, 1968.

3. *Sports Illustrated,* April 14, 1969.
4. *Sports Illustrated,* Sept. 6, 1971.
5. *New York Times,* May 28, 1972.
6. *Cavalier Magazine,* May 1972.
7. *New York Times,* Dec. 5, 1973.
8. *San Francisco Sunday Examiner &
   Chronicle,* Aug. 25, 1974.
9. *TV Guide,* Oct. 1, 1975.
10. *New York Times,* Oct. 17, 1976.
11. *Sports Illustrated,* Nov. 15, 1976.
12. *Sports Illustrated,* Jan. 31, 1977.
13. *New York Post,* March 23, 1977.
14. *New York Post,* Jan. 28, 1977.
15. *New York Daily News,* Sept. 28, 1978.
16. *New Yorker,* April 9, 1979.
17. *Ibid.*

2. *New York Times,* July 4, 1980.
3. *Sports Illustrated,* April 26, 1971.
4. *New York Times,* Jan. 20, 1974.
5. *New York Times,* Sept. 2, 1979.
6. *New York Times,* Dec. 7, 1976.
7. *New York Times,* May 17, 1977.
8. *New York Times,* Jan. 25, 1978.
9. *New York Times,* Dec. 30, 1979.
10. *New York Daily News,* April 19, 1981.

Best Predictions

1. *New York Times,* Jan. 16, 1971.
2. *New York Times,* Jan. 28, 1968.
3. *New York Times,* Aug. 10, 1969.
4. *New York Times,* July 9, 1968.
5. *Sports Illustrated,* June 18, 1972.
6. *Sports Illustrated,* Jan. 13, 1975.
7. *New York Post,* March 11, 1977.
8. *New York Post,* April 29, 1977.
9. *New York Times Magazine,* June 19,
   1977.
10. *Sports Illustrated,* Dec. 13, 1976.
11. *New York Times,* March 17, 1977.
12. *New York Times,* Sept. 20, 1977.
13. *New York Times,* March 1, 1979.
14. *New York Daily News,* March 11, 1982.

Worst Predictions

1. *New York Times,* April 24, 1977.
2. *Sports Illustrated,* Feb. 2, 1970.
3. *Sports Illustrated,* Oct. 29, 1973.
4. *Playboy,* August 1981.
5. *New York Times,* Jan. 3, 1973.
6. *New York Times,* June 8, 1975.
7. *New York Times,* Dec. 27, 1976.
8. *New York Times,* Aug. 19, 1977.
9. *New York Times,* Feb. 17, 1977.
10. *New York Times,* May 11, 1977.
11. *New York Times,* April 28, 1977.
12. *New York Post,* Oct. 18, 1977.
13. *New York Post,* Jan. 26, 1978.
14. *New York Times,* April 9, 1978.
15. *New York Post,* Jan. 9, 1979.
16. *New York Times,* Nov. 24, 1980.
17. *New York Daily News,* Sept. 2, 1981.
18. *New York Daily News,* April 4, 1982.

Departures

1. *New York Times,* Oct. 25, 1972.

INDEX